NICHOLAS BIDDLE
IN GREECE

NICHOLAS BIDDLE
IN GREECE
The Journals and Letters of 1806

Edited by R. A. McNeal

THE PENNSYLVANIA STATE UNIVERSITY PRESS

University Park, Pennsylvania

Library of Congress Cataloging-in-Publication Data

Biddle, Nicholas, 1786–1844.
    Nicholas Biddle in Greece : the journals and letters of 1806 /
edited by R. A. McNeal.
        p.   cm.
    Includes bibliographical references and index.
    ISBN 0-271-00914-4
    1. Greece—Description and travel—1453–1820.   I. McNeal, Richard
A. II. Title.
DF721.B53   1993
949.5'05—dc20
                                                                92-35459
                                                                        CIP

Published by The Pennsylvania State University Press,
Barbara Building, Suite C, University Park, PA 16802-1003

Frontispiece: Portrait of Nicholas Biddle, watercolor by J. B. Longacre. Courtesy of the
National Portrait Gallery, Smithsonian Institution

It is the policy of The Pennsylvania State University Press to use acid-free paper for the
first printing of all clothbound books. Publications on uncoated stock satisfy the mini-
mum requirements of American National Standard for Information Sciences—Perma-
nence of Paper for Printed Library Materials, ANSI Z39.48–1984.

Contents

Acknowledgments

My thanks are due first to Mr. and Mrs. Nicholas Biddle, Jr., of Penn Valley, Pennsylvania, who gave me access to the first of Nicholas Biddle's Greek journals, who have granted permission for its publication, and who graciously allowed me, for two long days, to turn their living room into a recording studio.

Jean Preston, Curator of Manuscripts at Princeton University, answered several of my queries about the two letters in the Firestone Library. These two letters are published with the permission of Princeton University Library.

Roger Kennedy, former Director of the National Museum of American History in Washington, D.C., very kindly provided a transcript of Biddle's second Greek journal, which he had made for himself several years ago by Pamela Scott for a project of his own. Having access to the original autograph, I was able to correct and supplement this transcript in many places. But the mere fact of its existence saved me weeks of labor.

Linda Stanley, of the Historical Society of Pennsylvania, and James Biddle, President of the Andalusia Foundation, made available to me the resources of their respective bailiwicks. The first Greek journal is published with the permission of the Historical Society.

For specialized help with certain parts of this project I am indebted to Judith Binder of the American School of Classical Studies in Athens, to Christopher McKee, Rosenthal Professor and Librarian, Grinnell College, to C. W. J. Eliot, Professor and President, University of Prince Edward Island, to Glen Bowersock of the Institute for Advanced Studies in Princeton, to Father Nicholas Palis of the Greek Orthodox Church of the Annunciation in Lancaster, Pennsylvania, and to several colleagues at Franklin and Marshall College: Angela Jeannet and Lisa Gasbarrone (Department of

French and Italian), Antonio Callari (Department of Economics), and Ira Gurchow (Department of English).

To my colleagues in the Classics Department at Franklin and Marshall College, who now know more about Nicholas Biddle than I suspect they ever wanted to know, I owe a special debt of gratitude for their patience and their never-failing good humor. To Enid Hirsch go my thanks for her help in typing the transcription of the first journal.

And finally there is Sally, whose love and support I can never adequately repay. The two maps I also owe to her.

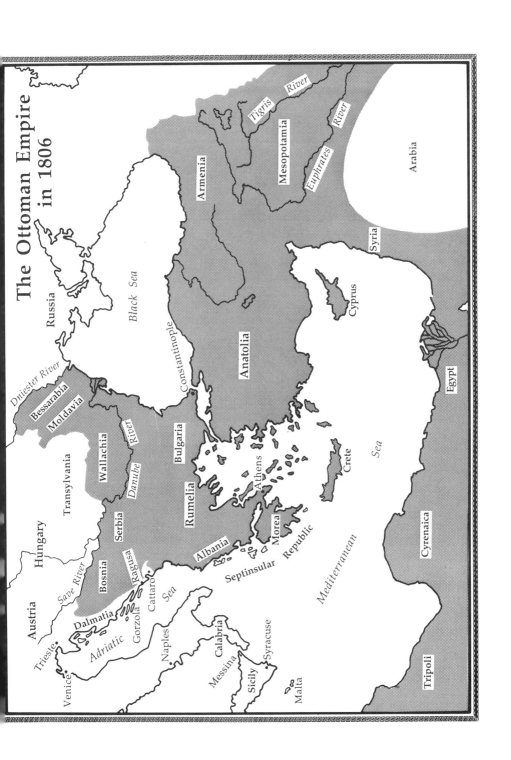

The Ottoman Empire in 1806

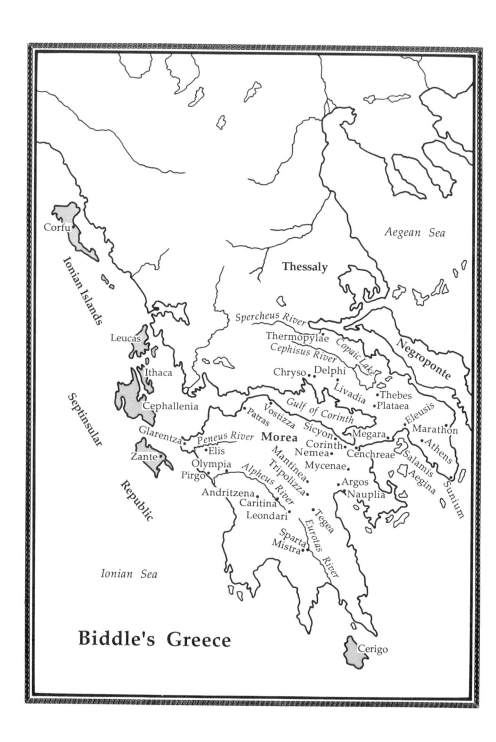

Corfu

Aegean Sea

Ionian Islands

Thessaly

Spercheus River

Leucas

Thermopylae *Copaic Lake*
Cephisus River

Negroponte

Ithaca

Chryso Delphi
Livadia
Thebes
Plataea

Cephallenia

Gulf of Corinth

Vostizza Sicyon
Patras
Eleusis
Marathon

Septinsular

Glarentza
Peneus River **Morea**
Megara
Athens

Corinth
Nemea Cenchreae
Salamis
Sunium

Zante
Elis
Mantinea Mycenae
Aegina

Olympia *Alpheus River* Tripolizza
Pirgo

Republic

Andritzena
Caritina
Argos
Nauplia

Leondari
Tegea

Sparta *Eurotas River*
Mistra

Ionian Sea

Biddle's Greece

Cerigo

Introduction

I. Nicholas Biddle at Home and Abroad

When Nicholas Biddle arrived in Greece in the spring of 1806, he was only the second American to go there, and he would be the first to leave behind an account of what he saw. This account, a journal in two parts together with four surviving letters, is a precious document that deserves to be better known. Born in 1786, just after the United States had gained independence from Britain, Biddle saw the new nation through its formative years and was himself one of the major players in American politics before his death in 1844. Why did he go to Greece? And what kind of account did he write? Answering these questions will help to add substance to Biddle's own intellectual biography and will also clarify the relationship between British and American travel writing in the age of Napoleon.

What emerges from an examination of this journal and its associated letters is the prominence of certain classical ideals. As a product of the Age of Reason, Biddle was very much a neoclassical man, whose education and career were shaped by a vision of antiquity. His debt to the Greco-Roman past is evident not only in his participation in the Grand Tour, the primary objects of which were France, Italy, and later Greece, but also in the journal itself, which, because of the conventions it follows, owes much to classical theory and precedent. Perhaps it would not be too much to say that Biddle's journal is a kind of neoclassical *Bildungsroman*, revealing both why travel to the Mediterranean, and especially travel to Greece, was thought useful and even necessary for a young man, and what effects this journey could have upon the traveler.

The offspring of one of the most prominent families in Philadelphia, which had prospered in the trade with the West Indies, Biddle enrolled in the University of Pennsylvania at the age of ten. But his parents, fearing that, at the age of thirteen, he was too young to graduate, sent him to Princeton, then the College of New Jersey. Arriving there in 1799, he entered a society that would have a profound effect on his life thereafter. John Witherspoon, president of the College from 1768 to 1794 and a member of the Continental Congress and a signer of the Declaration of Independence, believed that the liberal arts should serve the useful purpose of educating the leaders of the new republic. In accordance with this belief, he enlarged the curriculum beyond the customary Latin and Greek to include history, mathematics, natural science, English composition, grammar, and public speaking. Witherspoon's son-in-law and successor, Samuel Stanhope Smith, continued this policy. Thus Biddle came away from his education with a high sense of moral purpose. In these circumstances it is not strange that in his Greek journals and letters he speaks often of his duty to help guide the destiny of his country. This kind of talk, which may now appear naive and pompous, was not just youthful idealism. Like many of his contemporaries, Biddle was genuinely serious about public service.[1]

Apart from his sense of moral purpose, Biddle got something else from his sojourn at Princeton. Always fond of words, and a good linguist, he plunged at once into the social life of the college, which consisted largely of the activities of two rival debating societies, the Cliosophic and the Whig. Since his roommate, Arthur Fitzhugh of Virginia, was a leader of the Cliosophic Society, Biddle was quickly elected to this body and became its president in 1800. Some of his youthful papers and speeches are still preserved, and they show that Biddle early on became what he remained all his life—a Federalist committed to a strong central government and an enemy of Jeffersonian Republicanism, which he considered little better than an invitation to anarchy. In time his partisan views softened; and eventually Biddle even admired Jefferson, but his commitment to Federalist ideas lasted too long for his political good. His early interest in oratory arose precisely because he thought that this was a practical device for influencing others. Oratory was the means by which he thought he could exercise his sense of moral duty. At his graduation at the age of fifteen in September 1801, Biddle was duly awarded the honor of being class valedictorian, an honor he shared with his close friend Edward Watts.

When Biddle came home to Philadelphia to read law in the same office

---

1. For Biddle's early years, cf. especially Thomas P. Govan, "Nicholas Biddle at Princeton," *Princeton University Library Chronicle* 9 (1948): 49–61; Govan was also the author of the still-standard biography: *Nicholas Biddle, Nationalist and Banker, 1786–1844* (Chicago, 1959), which concentrates on Biddle's later years and on the fortunes of the U.S. Bank.

in which his eldest brother, William, was practicing, he returned not only to a thriving center of commerce, but to the city that had been the political capital of the United States from 1790 to 1800 and was still its cultural capital, a role it would continue to play well into the nineteenth century. So many eminent men of diverse learning could be found there that this period in its history has been called "the Philadelphia Enlightenment."[2] Many of them met in an informal institution called the Tuesday Club, which was a forum for the discussion of science, philosophy, and literature. Biddle became a member of this group; and it was here that he met, among many other names, Joseph Dennie, editor of the *Port Folio*, the country's leading literary journal. Meanwhile he read voraciously and acquired a substantial library of his own.

Biddle was soon to have an experience that would enlarge his horizons considerably and set him even farther apart from most Americans of his own age. General John Armstrong, a family friend of the Biddles' who had been appointed minister plenipotentiary to France, a job he was to hold from 1804 to 1810, suggested that young Nicholas accompany him to Paris as an unpaid secretary on his staff. Biddle's parents agreed—reluctantly, because of their son's youth—and provided the necessary funds.

The way in which Biddle prepared for this trip says a good deal about his character. Earnest and ambitious, he wanted to make his mark in the world; and to do so he needed peoples' attention and respect. This craving for recognition, a feature of his character that would mark his whole life, showed itself at this point in his acquisition of titles. Not only did he get an honorary M.A. from Princeton, but he had himself made a colonel in the state militia of New Jersey; and, through the influence of his kinsman General James Wilkinson, he obtained a brevet captaincy in the U.S. Artillery. The latter was an honorary rank, but the former carried with it the right to design a suitable uniform. Biddle was very proud of his buttons, as we learn from his reception by officers of the U.S. Navy on Malta. (This attention to sartorial splendor was another trait of Biddle the banker.) Since he was going to travel at least in part in diplomatic circles, he armed himself with letters of introduction from people like the financier Stephen Girard and Aaron Burr, a friend of Biddle's father and Jefferson's vice-president. As if titles and letters of introduction were not enough to ensure his acceptance in the right quarters, he regularly assumed a gravity of de-

2. Cf. Roger G. Kennedy, *Architecture, Men, Women, and Money* (New York, 1985), where this phrase occurs several times.

meanor beyond his years and, if asked his age, added several years to the true figure. He apparently felt most comfortable with people older than he was and sought out their company. Just as he was closest in affection to his eldest brother, William, so he avoided his own contemporaries as traveling companions. He says that he avoided them because he did not find them intellectually stimulating. We can well believe him. What mattered to Biddle were the opinions of his intellectual equals; and at this time in his life, those equals were almost certainly bound to be his elders.

Once ensconced in Paris, Biddle found himself with plenty of free time.[3] His official duties involved mainly the adjudication of American claims against France arising from the American government's recent purchase of the Louisiana Territory. This experience involved large sums of money and complex financial problems, training that would later be of immense value in Biddle's career in banking.

Having previously traveled in the vicinity of Paris, Biddle embarked, in the summer of 1805, on an extensive tour of eastern France and Switzerland. In November he left for the south of France and Italy. Going via Poitiers, Toulouse, Bordeaux, Montpellier, Nimes, Avignon, Marseilles, Nice, Genoa, and Florence, he reached Rome, where he was in February and March 1806. Sailing from Naples on March 25, he went to Messina in Sicily, then to Malta, whence he took ship for Zante and Greece. His Greek journey took place in May, June, and July. From Zante, he traveled to Patras, Vostizza, Delphi, Livadia, Thermopylai, Thebes, and Athens, where he remained for two weeks. With the approach of summer he made a tour of the Peloponnesos and exited Greece via the Ionian islands of Corfu and Ithaca. After a long and tedious voyage up the Adriatic, he reached Trieste in late July. He had contemplated a trip to Constantinople and to the Greek islands but gave up the idea because he was unsure of being able to get back to France and America any time soon by reliable transportation. He was also hesitant to travel in hot weather when fever was rampant, and he had already seen enough of Greeks and Turks. Further contact with them would not, he thought, be productive of anything but physical discomfort. From Trieste he then returned to Paris by way of Venice, Vienna, and Bavaria. In December 1806 and February 1807, he traveled along the Rhine and in Holland and arrived in England in March 1807. In the fall of 1807 he sailed home.

---

3. For a general view of Biddle's European sojourn, see Anne Felicity Woodhouse, "Nicholas Biddle in Europe, 1804–1807," *The Pennsylvania Magazine of History and Biography* 103 (1979): 3–33.

After his return from Europe Biddle embarked first on a literary life. He gradually took over the running of the *Port Folio* from Joseph Dennie and served as its editor from 1812 to 1814. He himself contributed some pieces to this journal anonymously, and he printed others that accorded with his views. Two such articles were important for their early statement of the relevance of ancient architecture to modern American life. One was written by the architect Benjamin Latrobe, the other by George Tucker of the University of Virginia.[4] More significant, however, was Biddle's selection to be the editor of the journals of Lewis and Clark. Though his name does not appear anywhere in the work, which was published at Philadelphia in 1814, it was Biddle who put the story into an acceptable literary form; and his edition would remain the standard for eighty years.[5]

What Biddle really craved was a life in politics, and he gave up the *Port Folio* to pursue this goal. Though he served two terms in the Pennsylvania legislature (1811–12 and 1814–15), he never was sufficiently popular to gain major political office. He was an opponent of Jefferson and so could hope for no favor from him, and he failed to bolt from the Federalists in time to save his reputation from the crumbling fortunes of that party. But luckily he had a firm friend in James Monroe, who appointed him to the board of the Second United States Bank shortly after this institution had been created to bring order out of the financial chaos that resulted when, after the government failed to recharter the First U.S. Bank, the War of 1812 brought the country to the brink of bankruptcy. As a director of the bank from 1819 and its president from 1823, Biddle presided over a forerunner of the Federal Reserve and gained fame and fortune from his very considerable financial acumen.

Then came Andrew Jackson. Elected in 1828, Jackson distrusted all banks and determined to kill the Second U.S. Bank because he thought it a dangerous monopoly run by a cabal of moneyed aristocrats. All through the 1830s one of the major political issues concerned the place of the U.S. Bank in the life of the nation. Despite Biddle's heroic efforts and perhaps in part because of his own stubbornness and vanity, Jackson finally prevailed;

---

4. Latrobe's article in the *Port Folio*, Series 3 (June 1811), was a printed version of a speech he had given earlier: *Anniversary Oration, Pronounced before the Society of Artists of the United States, by Appointment of the Society, on the Eighth of May, 1811.* This item is most easily accessible in John C. Van Horne et al., *The Papers of Benjamin Henry Latrobe*, vol. 3 (New Haven, 1988), 65–85. George Tucker's article: "On Architecture," *Port Folio*, Series 4 (1814): 559–669.

5. Paul Allen, ed., *History of the Expediton Under the Command of Captains Lewis and Clark* (Philadelphia, 1814).

and the charter of the U.S. Bank was allowed by Congress to lapse in 1836.[6] The institution continued, with Biddle as president, as the U.S. Bank of Pennsylvania; but as a mere state bank without government deposits, it never recovered its former prestige. Biddle stayed on until 1839, when he resigned, still prosperous and respected. In the hands of others who had far less ability, confidence, and daring than Biddle, the bank, already on shaky ground, failed in 1841 in the growing business depression that had been aided by Jackson's hard-money policies. Biddle's own reputation went down with the bank and has never recovered, if only because historians have tended to favor Jackson as a populist hero.[7]

In this brief review of Biddle's education, his travels, and his career, I have touched on a number of themes that can usefully be grouped under the rubric of neoclassicism. The thinkers of the Enlightenment, on both sides of the Atlantic, were alike in their eagerness to mold their ideas and their own conduct in accordance with their view of Greco-Roman antiquity. This is the reason why we can call the movement antiquarian. Since Biddle grew out of this milieu, walking in the shadow of such men as Washington, Jefferson, and Hamilton, it is worthwhile to probe his assumptions in greater detail because there is much about his characteristically eighteenth-century thought that, though it may be superficially familiar, is antipathetic to a modern audience. The problem is that the classical ideal as it was put into practice in the Enlightenment produced a person who may now appear just a little strange.

Like his elders and contemporaries, Biddle thought of virtue in political terms. To talk today about political virtue seems absurd. In our skeptical

6. Like James Monroe and John Quincy Adams, Biddle believed (and, as his Greek journal shows, he so believed as early as age twenty), that party strife was not a fit way to solve a problem, that two gentlemen calmly discoursing with one another should be able to arrive at rational solutions. But since the Bank of the United States was certainly a political creation, Biddle was naive if he expected its problems to be solved by nonpolitical means. What he and his friends meant by politics was, of course, the partisan spirit of the Jacksonian Democrats. Though Biddle's conduct in the affair of the bank's recharter now seems unnecessarily self-righteous, it is worth observing that in this period in America politics were not conducted as an exercise in compromise, but as faithful adherence to republican principles; and tolerance for the other fellow's differing principles was not the order of the day. Hence neither Biddle nor Jackson was inclined to compromise. Each thought that he had the best interests of the country at heart. Cf. Harry L. Watson, *Liberty and Power: The Politics of Jacksonian America* (New York, 1990), 42–72.

7. A brief history of Jackson's war against the bank can be found in Robert Remini, *Andrew Jackson and the Bank War: A Study in the Growth of Presidential Power* (New York, 1967). Remini too rather admires Jackson and has little good to say of Biddle.

or even cynical view of politics as mere haggling for partisan or economic advantage, virtue has no place. Or rather, virtue is something we indulge in private when politics are not at issue. But the combination of high moral purpose and service to the state was one of the outstanding features of Greek and Roman life, or at least of the political thinkers who wrote about that life. Though in actual practice the everyday politics of Athens or Rome were doubtless just as grubby as our own, there was at any rate a pervasive fiction that the citizen should serve the state to the best of his ability. This surrender to public duty, this submersion of individual gain in the glorification of the state, was a leading idea of the Enlightenment, which took as its basic reading the political and historical texts of antiquity. Hence the ancient notion of virtue as something political emerged again on both sides of the Atlantic.

Another side of this insistence on a public morality was a devotion to oratory. Though increasingly literate from the fifth century B.C., ancient society always remained essentially oral: talking, not writing, was the standard means of communication. Even ancient literature was meant to be read aloud. Since the only way to convince an audience was to speak to it, the art of rhetoric flourished and provided the staple fare of education. To speak well was the goal of anyone who expected to make a name for himself in the service of the state.

Even though by the eighteenth century the printing press could spread opinions in written form, the prevalent cult of the antique carried with it a belief in the importance of public speaking. Why is Biddle forever boasting about the glories of oratory and its usefulness for the rising politician? He lived of course at a time when the citizen body, or at least the effective part of it, was still small enough to conduct its business in face-to-face meetings. But to men who were trying to revive the ancient ideal of political virtue the use of the ancient methods of persuasion seemed perfectly appropriate to modern circumstances. Precisely because rhetoric had been an inseparable part of ancient politics and ancient political texts, the neoclassicists of the Enlightenment made a point of trying to ape Demosthenes and Cicero. Sustaining a flood of eloquence, even for hours on end, as Biddle himself became capable of doing, was a common accomplishment.[8]

In the Enlightenment as in antiquity, the politician regarded his own

8. For the importance of Cicero in the life of John Adams, cf. James M. Farrell, "'Syren Tully' and the Young John Adams," *Classical Journal* 87 (1992): 373–90. Farrell has an extensive bibliography on the influence of antiquity in the American Enlightenment.

personal preeminence as vitally important. To be well regarded by others, to have fame, was an integral part of public life. No noble Greek or Roman expected rewards in the afterlife. He displayed his talents in this life so that his contemporaries and even future generations would grant his claim to recognition. This idea goes all the way back to Homer, whose poems were the bedrock of Greek and even Roman education. The pervasive influence of this heroic code (for so it should be called) made of politics in both antiquity and the eighteenth century an arena in which contentiousness was an accepted fact of life. To improve existing society may have been one political goal; but another, and one equally important for the participants, entailed the struggle for individual honor. Since a man's public life was his only important life, his stature as it was perceived by others, or his face—what we would now call his public image—was a matter of much concern.[9]

One of the more colorful results of this belief on the part of America's first politicians in the importance of a public persona is the host of portraits that was one of the legacies of the founding fathers. To memorialize their achievements they repeatedly had themselves painted and sculpted. Such visual artifacts were not only the result of their own large egos (and of course a revival of the Roman practice of portrait sculpture), but were also a kind of teaching device, a way of inculcating the lessons of political virtue by illustration. Everyone can cite numerous examples of a Washington or a Jefferson in paint or stone because these objects have almost attained the status of icons.[10] Biddle too had himself painted and sculpted many times, as if conscious from an early age of the need to craft a public persona. He sat for no less than eighteen paintings, at least three of which were later engraved for a wider distribution, and for five busts.[11] Though he was certainly vain, it was not mere vanity or some amiable eccentricity that led him to commission portraits of himself. It would perhaps not be too much to say that they were all part of his classical program of image management. That he intended to cut a figure consistent with his political prominence was evident even to his contemporaries. Philadelphia's *Sunday Dispatch* for February 9, 1851, said of him:

9. Cf. Douglass Adair, *Fame and the Founding Fathers* (New York, 1974).

10. For the conscious manipulation of a public image in terms of antique precedent, see Garry Wills, *Cincinnatus: George Washington and the Enlightenment* (New York, 1984); John Edie, ed., *Classical Traditions in Early America* (Ann Arbor, 1976); and Harold Talbot Peale, *The Cult of Antiquity and the French Revolutionaries* (Chicago, 1937).

11. Nicholas B. Wainwright, "Nicholas Biddle in Portraiture," *Antiques*, November 1975, 956–64.

Mr. Biddle was a handsome man, and he dressed in a style some would consider foppish, but which became his commanding presence. He was well built and very erect, and he wore his hair—which was parted in the middle over the forehead—in a flowing mass on the back of his neck. We have frequently seen him striding along Chestnut Street, clad in a blue coat with gilt buttons and yellow Nankeen pants, and with hands covered with canary-colored kid gloves—a glossy beaver hat, placed on the back of his stately head, completed the picture.

Biddle on Chestnut Street was more than a match for any aristocratic Roman parading in the Forum in a carefully arranged toga!

If a part of the Enlightenment's cult of the antique was the pursuit of political virtue and personal distinction, another part was a cosmopolitan outlook. The search for an earthly utopia and for universal solutions to local problems led the French philosophers to look beyond the limits of their own country and to take the whole world for their province. This attitude was far more Roman than Greek, inasmuch as the Greeks never, except perhaps in the case of the fifth-century sophists, looked beyond the narrow boundaries of the individual city-state. It remained for the Romans, possessing as they did the whole civilized world, to see their city as coterminous with that world. A revival of this breadth of view was bound to follow the revival of interest in ancient literature, which was for a long time the revival of Roman, and not Greek, literature. Not until the nineteenth century did scholars dig behind the Roman facade to arrive at a non-Romanized view of Greece. Only with the Romantic movement were Cicero and Plutarch ousted from public favor by Plato and Greek drama.

Having seen many members of his own class go back and forth between Europe and America, Biddle refused to be bound by the physical or intellectual limits of his own country, but assumed that the world had much to show him and that travel was the way to learn. Even before he went abroad, he had thought a good deal about the purposes of travel. Emerging from a cultural environment that stressed one's moral duty, he believed that his own development as a responsible citizen had a high priority. He therefore ought to become acquainted with the languages and the learning of others because discussion with and observation of strangers would lead to reflection on morality and incitement to virtue. He said as much in an undergraduate essay entitled "On Overcoming Prejudice."

In accord with this view of travel as a source of moral improvement, Biddle saw himself as a cultural intermediary, a representative of American culture in Europe and a transmitter of European culture to America. Since American travelers were a rare breed, he was something of a curiosity; and, being proud of his country, he promoted it whenever occasion offered both by lending books about it and by praising republican institutions. He had a sharp eye for what he considered the defects of political and social institutions in the Old World, and his journals frequently reflect on the superior condition of life in the United States. One can well imagine his verbal interchanges with foreigners. If he was always as tactless as he was when he talked with the Greek priest aboard the brig *Themistocles*, he may well have appeared bumptious to others. It is a pity that we do not have an assessment of him from the four British travelers whom he met and whom he found so arrogant. In fairness to Biddle, however, he seems to have learned from experiences like these, because he later became well known for his suave handling of people.

But Biddle could also see that Europe had much to give to America, and he tried to convey this heritage to his fellow citizens. When the newly founded Pennsylvania Academy of the Fine Arts wrote him with a request for casts for its new quarters, he went out of his way to do the job superlatively well, going to the French sculptor Houdon for advice and sending the best reproductions he could obtain. From Florence he sent back for publication in the *Port Folio* a letter describing the city. His interest in Europe extended too beyond art and literature. From Malta he sent seeds to Benjamin Smith Barton of Philadelphia, at another time grapevine roots to one of his brothers.

Already as an undergraduate Biddle could take a broad view of social and political problems. He saw the negative effect of local prejudice, as he called it, which could dampen any wish for improvement. This cosmopolitan turn of mind was further reinforced by his trip abroad and would lead straight to his views as a banker. Just as he believed that the United States needed a strong central government, so he became convinced that the country should not retreat into Jeffersonian isolation. Its destiny lay with commerce and manufacturing—with the world across the Atlantic, where these activities were becoming so important. He spent his career trying to promote this view.

Another side of Biddle's cosmopolitanism is less likeable. In their zeal for the revival of the spirit and even the forms of Greek and Roman political institutions, the revolutionaries of the Enlightenment almost always followed a secularizing policy. Human society was, they believed, perfectible; and it was perfectible through human effort. Thus the Christian God became more or less expendable. If the positive side of the political program of the Enlightenment was a new faith in the ability of people to solve their own problems, the negative side was a pronounced anticlericalism. This phenomenon was the result of a return to the humanist bias of Greco-Roman antiquity. In any case, as everyone knows, anticlericalism pervades the thought of the eighteenth century. That is also appears in Biddle's Greek journal should come as no surprise. In fact, one of the most striking features of this journal is its rabid anti-Catholicism. Though nominally a Protestant, Biddle was clearly no more than superficially religious. Like most educated men of his time, he may have observed the outward forms of religious worship for the sake of public appearances; but his true feelings were elsewhere. He had no use for obscurantism or even for religious beliefs and practices that appeared to him to be senseless or demeaning. Catholicism in both its Roman and its Orthodox forms he subjects to a withering scorn. The starkness of his moral judgment may be offensive to modern tastes, but we have to remember that in Biddle's time there were many who saw entrenched religion as the main obstacle to human progress.

Though Biddle's cosmopolitan sympathies were Roman in their origin, his passion for ancient architecture was decidedly Greek and not Roman. In this respect he parted company with the founding fathers and even with such a contemporary architect as Benjamin Latrobe, whose designs were essentially Roman with occasional Greek touches. Biddle was in fact one of the major promoters of a real Greek architectural revival in the U.S. This fact is well known and is the most obvious side of his neoclassicism. Apart from his presidency of the U.S. Bank, Biddle is perhaps best remembered today because of his patronage of architecture. Three buildings still stand in Philadelphia as monuments to his influence: the Second U.S. Bank on Chestnut Street, his own country villa "Andalusia" on the Delaware River, and Founder's Hall of Girard College. So strong was his influence that all the branch offices of the bank were built in the style he approved, and only in this century have banks ceased to look like Greek temples.

But why Greek and not Roman architecture? The answer is simple: Biddle was one of the few people of his generation who actually saw real ancient Greek buildings, or the remains of them, on their home ground. Until the second half of the eighteenth century the Aegean was remote and only barely accessible, and knowledge of ancient architecture tended to be restricted to the Roman version of Greek ideas, whether Roman buildings or Roman architectural treatises. But when Napoleon effectively closed most of Europe, including Italy, to travel for a generation, making Greece one of the few remaining options, and when the ferment of revolutionary ideas brought on the Greek War of Independence and a general wave of philhellenism in Europe and America, Greek architecture came at last to be appreciated for its own merits. But it is still a cause for some surprise that Biddle could promote its utility for America, or that, between 1800 and the outbreak of the Civil War, the so-called Greek Revival could gain such wide popular acceptance. Of what relevance, after all, were the ancient Greeks to modern Americans? The founding fathers, having a thoroughly negative view of Greek political institutions, had gone out of their way to avoid fashioning a revived Greek democracy; and their architecture, classical though it was, was decidedly Roman. Biddle became convinced that true Greek architecture, simple and grand and so different from the baroque fussiness of its Roman incarnation, was a suitable dress for modern republican principles. As American political institutions, though inherited in part from antiquity, had a definitely original style of their own, so they should receive physical and symbolic expression in a new national style of architecture, one derived from the Greek, but not merely an archaeological copy of it. Biddle's trip to Greece saw the genesis of this belief. It is not an accident that he spent almost the whole of his banking career in a building inspired by the Parthenon in Athens or that he was popularly known as "Nick the Greek."[12]

II. The Political Condition of Europe

The French Imperium

To understand the circumstances in which Biddle traveled in the Mediterranean, it is necessary to know something of the political configuration of

12. An excellent assessment of Biddle's architectural Hellenism is Roger G. Kennedy, *Architecture, Men, Women, and Money*, 236–47. Cf. also Kennedy's later book, *Greek Revival America* (New York, 1989), 167–74. This second book makes an interesting case for the idea that after the successful conclusion of the War of 1812, and particularly after about 1825, the United States was virtually refounded by a new generation that wanted to shake off the incubus of the founding fathers and launch the country on the path of a rapid territorial and industrial expansion. The new and robust architecture of the Greek Revival, which broke with the delicate federal style of the founders, accompanied this expansive mood. Paradoxically, despite the Greco-Roman architecture of the Age of Jackson, there was widespread opposition to the study of the classics themselves and a decline in classical

Europe in the late eighteenth and early nineteenth centuries. That politi-
cal scene can be summarized in one word: Napoleon. Biddle arrived in
France in time to see Napoleon crown himself emperor at Notre Dame in
December 1804.[13] Already victorious in Italy and Egypt, Napoleon defeated Austria, Prussia, and Russia in the war of the Third Coalition between
October 1805 and June 1807. His decisive victory over Prussia at Jena
occurred in October 1806, just after Biddle had returned from Greece.
Having embarked on a career of foreign conquest and intervention, a policy
that had already been instituted by the revolutionary republican government in 1792–93, Napoleon upset the normal political situation in Europe. Instead of a balance of power among nation-states, there existed a
highly abnormal French empire; and French revolutionary zeal spread itself
into such normally quiet backwaters of Europe as the Kingdom of Naples,
Dalmatia, the Ionian Islands, and even the Aegean possessions of the Ottoman Empire. From 1792, when the French monarchy was overthrown,
until 1815, a coalition of European monarchies made war against the
French with only two short interruptions, in 1802–3 and 1814–15. Seven-
teen of these twenty-three years were dominated by Napoleon. Biddle's trip
must be placed within the context of this anomalous French imperialism.

At the time of Biddle's passage from Naples to Sicily, Malta, Zante, and
the Morea, the French were in control of all the northern shores of the
Mediterranean that lay outside the Ottoman Empire, and the British controlled the sea itself. Having incorporated northern Italy, together with
Venice, Istria, and Dalmatia by the Treaty of Pressburg (December 25,
1805), a direct result of the battle of Austerlitz (December 2, 1805), in
which he had defeated the Austrians and Russians, Napoleon sent his
armies into the Kingdom of Naples, which had agreed to join the Third
Coalition. In January 1806, the king and queen of Naples fled to Sicily,
their island possession, where they were protected by the British, while the
French army in February occupied the mainland part of the kingdom,
where Napoleon's elder brother Joseph became King of Naples. Nelson's
decisive victory at Trafalgar on October 25, 1805, removed the danger of a
French fleet and made possible the continued British presence in Malta and
in Sicily, a presence that effectively prevented French mastery over the
Mediterranean. Thus two battles and one treaty largely determined the

learning. Cf. Meyer Reinhold, *Classica Americana: The Greek and Roman Heritage in the United States* (Detroit, 1984): 174–203 (chapter VI).

13. For extracts from one of Biddle's French journals that describe the coronation of Napoleon, see Nicholas B. Wainwright, "Glimpses of Napoleon in 1804," *The Pennsylvania Magazine of History and Biography* 102 (1978): 103–8.

political conditions in which Biddle traveled. As a diplomat and a neutral he could go freely between hostile armies, which were everywhere on the march.

After his initial conquest of Venice, Napoleon had taken the Ionian Islands, which had been a Venetian possession for four hundred years. This change of masters was recognized by the Treaty of Campo Formio in 1797. But by then attacking Egypt, Napoleon provoked Turkey to a declaration of war and an alliance with Russia. The combined Turkish and Russian fleets occupied the Ionian Islands in September 1798, expelling the French. In 1800 these islands became a Franco-Russian condominium known as the Septinsular Republic and were recognized as such by France in the Treaty of Amiens in 1802. Though nominally free, they were garrisoned by the Russians, who by their autocratic rule managed to make themselves thoroughly unpopular. By the Treaty of Tilsit in 1807 the Republic was handed back to the French; but the British promptly occupied all the islands except Corfu, which remained in French hands until 1815, when the Treaty of Vienna placed all of them under the protection of the British; and there they remained until their union with Greece in 1864. Biddle passed through the Ionian Islands as their brief period of independence was coming to an end, and his observations on the life and politics of the Septinsular Republic are interesting for this very reason.

The presence of the Russians not only in the Ionian Islands but in the Adriatic is an intriguing sidelight of the Napoleonic Wars. When the Austrians lost Dalmatia and the islands of the Adriatic by the Treaty of Pressburg, the French army seized the area to cut off Austrian support for the British and to extend the Continental·System. The Austrians were supposed by treaty to turn over Cattaro to the French; but they were forestalled by a Russian force under Admiral Siniavin, which had been sent from the Baltic to Cattaro to liberate Dalmatia, to blockade the French, and to aid the Serbians in their uprising against the Turks. The Russians took Cattaro from the Austrians on March 5, 1806, and occupied the islands of Lisa (on March 31) and Curzola (on April 10). Curzola was especially important because it protected the approach to Ragusa, which, though theoretically an independent republic, was being pressured by both the French and the Russians. Blockaded by the Russians from June 14, the town was saved by French reinforcements on July 6. Though the French and Russians signed a treaty in July 1806, Siniavin refused to give up his position and, supported by the czar, continued capturing the Adriatic islands.

By the end of the year, when Ali Pasha of Albania threatened to invade

Corfu and Siniavin had to withdraw most of his forces southward, leaving a garrison at Cattaro, the Russians still controlled the Adriatic. By holding Corfu and Cattaro, the Russians maintained a line of defense along the western border of the Ottoman Empire and effectively checked Napoleon's plans for eastward expansion. The British, by their possession of Sicily and Malta, held the southern line of this defense. Only Albania remained outside it, and both Napoleon and the partners of the Third Coalition tried to court Ali Pasha.

When Napoleon and Czar Alexander came to terms by the Treaty of Tilsit in the summer of 1807, the Russians finally withdrew from the Adriatic and from the Mediterranean. But meanwhile, as a consequence of the Treaty of Pressburg, there had been a growing rift between the Turks on the one hand and the Russians and the English on the other. The memory of Napoleon's conquest of Egypt was growing dim among the Turks; and the traditional influence of the French, in their role as protectors of the Ottoman Empire, was beginning to reassert itself. By February 1806, the Turks were even ready to recognize Napoleon as emperor. As a consequence of Napoleon's victories over Austria, of the Russian occupation of Corfu, and continued naval activity in the Adriatic and support for the Serbians, and not least of Russian military moves on the Dniester, the Turks were growing ever more suspicious of Russian intentions. Hence in August 1806, when the hospodars, or local Greek dynasts, of Moldavia and Wallachia were deposed by the Turks without the consultation, stipulated by treaty, with the Russians, war finally broke out between Turkey and Russia and continued until 1811, when Czar Alexander had to stop it in preparation for Napoleon's attack on Russia.[14]

Thus it was that Biddle, as he was leaving Greece in July bound for Trieste in a Greek boat, met Russians in the Adriatic and became engaged in a minor diplomatic farce, the story of which at the end of his second Greek journal is one of his most charming bits of narrative.

The American War Against Tripoli

Though the United States remained neutral in the Napoleonic Wars, its continuous problems with the Barbary pirates of North Africa resulted in a

14. The complicated diplomatic maneuvers of this period are fully detailed by Paul F. Shupp, *The European Powers and the Near Eastern Question, 1806–1807* (New York, 1931).

war in that quarter and the sending of several successive squadrons of American warships to the Mediterranean. Legally subject to the Ottoman sultan in Constantinople, the virtually independent rulers of Algiers, Tunis, and Tripoli, together with the emperor of Morocco, raised money for themselves by the capture inside and outside the Mediterranean of commercial ships and by the holding for ransom of their crews and passengers, who, until ransom arrived, languished in slavery. The major European powers, rather than suppressing this piracy, as they could easily have done either singly or in combination, paid tribute to the Barbary states to secure immunity, reasoning that the tribute was a minor annoyance in comparison to the advantages that might accrue to their competitors' shipping if the piracy were suppressed entirely. The pirates therefore played one state off against another, gradually raising demands all around and making a practice of attacking the commerce of any state whose payments were insufficient or in arrears.

Almost from the very moment of independence from Great Britain, when the United States lost the protection of the British navy, the Barbary pirates had preyed upon American commerce. But having no navy, the United States was compelled to pay. As demands escalated, American patience grew short; and ships originally built in anticipation of hostilities with the French were dispatched to the Mediterranean to put an end to the problem. War with Tripoli began in 1801, when Jefferson decided on a show of force.

Richard Dale left for the Mediterranean in June with a force of six ships, which included new frigates. Dale returned home in March 1802 and was succeeded by Richard V. Morris, with eight ships. He continued the blockade of Tripoli but was ordered back home in September 1803. His conduct was called in question by some of his own officers, who were hostile to him, on the grounds that he had not kept up a sufficient blockade; and in the end Jefferson summarily dismissed him from the navy, perhaps wrongly.

The next man who was supposed to go out was Thomas Truxtun, a wonderfully efficient officer known for building morale aboard ship. But he was also an egoist; and problems with his superior, the Secretary of the Navy, led him to resign in a huff. Command was therefore given temporarily to John Rodgers, who had served with Morris and who was to hand over command to Edward Preble, who had been appointed commodore of the third squadron and who duly commanded from September 13, 1803, through September 9, 1804, when he in turn was ordered home. It is necessary to note carefully the relationship of command between Rodgers and Preble because it figures prominently in Biddle's account of his own meeting with Rodgers on Malta.

It was in the course of Preble's tenure that there occurred the famous incident involving the frigate *Philadelphia*. Brought too close in shore before Tripoli, the ship stuck on a reef and was captured with all its crew by the Tripolitanians. James Biddle, one of Nicholas's older brothers, was a midshipman on the *Philadelphia* when it was captured on October 31, 1803.[15] The captives, including Captain William Bainbridge, were held for nineteen months before they were ransomed in June 1805. They passed through Malta in July of that year on their way home. Meanwhile, by Preble's order, a daring crew of American sailors led by Stephen Decatur entered Tripoli harbor under cover of night, boarded the *Philadelphia*, and managed to blow it up without the loss of a single man on February 16, 1804, thus depriving the Tripolitanians of a major prize.

Samuel Barron, the next commander, was sent out in the spring of 1804 with fourteen ships to replace Preble, who sailed home in December. Barron did not prosecute the war as actively as Preble had because of the presence of Tobias Lear. Sent out with Preble as consul general to the Barbary states, Lear was charged with finding a diplomatic solution to the whole problem. By appeasing the bashaw of Tripoli and bargaining with him, he was able to end the war on terms in July 1805. On May 22, just before peace was concluded, Barron turned over his command to John Rodgers. Thus Rodgers, who had the largest squadron of all, a total of thirty-one ships, found himself stymied in his plans to end the war by military force and without payment of any tribute. As a man who clearly wanted to make a name for himself, he was embittered by the course of events, as Biddle's journal shows.

Most of the Mediterranean squadron sailed home in July 1806, only three ships being left in the Mediterranean under the command of Hugh Campbell, who himself returned in the summer of 1807. Final peace with the Barbary states came only in 1815–16, though a naval force was kept in the Mediterranean until 1845.

Though Jefferson wanted a show of force in the Mediterranean, he also had to cut the number of large ships as a means of reducing the navy.

15. James Biddle served a long career of forty-eight years in the U.S. navy. He reached the rank of commodore, and his service culminated in the Mexican War on the West Coast. He died in 1848, four years after his brother.

Hence the creation of his famous sixty-foot gunboats, a number of which crossed the Atlantic to join the Mediterranean squadron after Preble's return. Rodgers had sixteen of these gunboats.[16]

The Ottoman Empire

When Biddle set sail from Naples, he thought that he was going to Greece. But in his time there was no such place; or at any rate Greece existed only as a spiritual landscape for western Europeans and perhaps also for certain educated Greeks. The one political reality was the Ottoman Empire, which, since the fourteenth and fifteenth centuries, had absorbed all the European territory of the Greek Byzantine state, the successor of the eastern half of the Roman empire based on Constantinople, and also almost all the various Frankish principalities that had been founded by Europeans in the Aegean in the aftermath of the Fourth Crusade in 1204. In Biddle's time only the Ionian Islands lay outside the area of Turkish rule.

It is odd, and indicative perhaps of the sway of ideas deeply held but never consciously evaluated, that Biddle did not think that he had arrived in Greece until he set foot in the Peloponnesos, or the Morea as it was then called. He had already passed through Naples and Sicily, which, as part of Magna Graecia in antiquity, had been as Greek as any place in the Aegean proper; and he visited Zante, or ancient Zakynthos, not a center of world-historical importance like Athens or Sparta, but nonetheless a part of ancient Greece and destined to be later reunited with the modern nation-state of Greece, which was created after the Greek War of Independence (1821–33). Greece was very much a shifting concept that meant different things to different people. For the Phanariots of Constantinople, the educated Greek speakers of the Turkish capital, who had a big hand in running the affairs of the Ottoman Empire, the center of gravity in the Greek world was

16. A short modern account of the Barbary war that has the merit of referring to the collected primary sources is David F. Long, *Gold Braid and Foreign Relations: Diplomatic Activities of U.S. Naval Officers, 1798–1883* (Annapolis, 1988), 24–32. An old but lengthy treatment is that of Gardner W. Allen, *Our Navy and the Barbary Corsairs* (Hamden, Conn., 1965 [Boston, 1905]). Cf. also Glen Tucker, *Dawn Like Thunder: The Barbary Wars and the Birth of the U.S. Navy* (Indianapolis, 1963); Howard P. Nash, *The Forgotten Wars: The Role of the U.S. Navy in the Quasi-War with France and the Barbary Wars, 1798–1805* (New York, 1968); and *Naval Documents Related to the United States Wars with the Barbary Powers*, 7 vols. (Washington, D.C., U.S. Government Printing Office, 1939–45). There are full biographies of Preble, Rodgers, Decatur, Bainbridge, and others in the various Mediterranean squadrons. See Robin Higham, ed., *A Guide to the Sources of United States Military History* (Hamden, Conn., 1975).

the capital city itself and even the southern Balkans, where lay the principalities of Moldavia and Wallachia, which they themselves ruled—areas that had never been a part of ancient Greece but that had been hellenized to some extent only in medieval times when they adopted Orthodox Christianity. For a European or for an American like Biddle, whose view of Hellas was founded on a classical education, only the lands south of Thermopylai were significant. There was no defined geographical entity, no territorial state, which bore the name of Greece; and at the start of the nineteenth century the many subject nationalities that inhabited the Balkans and the Aegean were not yet recognized as important in any political sense by anyone.

The Ottoman Empire was a vast area stretching, in theory at least, from Algeria in North Africa through Egypt and Palestine to Armenia and Mesopotamia. Its heartland was Anatolia, but its possessions in Europe extended from Bessarabia and Moldavia in southern Russia through Wallachia (the southern part of modern Romania) to Bosnia and Herzegovina and embraced the Adriatic coast from Albania southward. Though they had been the terror of Europe in the sixteenth and seventeenth centuries, the Turks of Biddle's day had fallen on hard times; and their empire was in an advanced state of decay, preserved from complete dissolution only by the greed of the four competing European powers (France, Austria, Russia, and Great Britain), which could never agree how to carve up the spoils.

Even within the empire some parts were virtually independent. The Turks were in many areas a small and arrogant minority whose sole object had become the extraction of tribute from various subject peoples. Egypt, Tripoli, Tunis, and Algiers were ruled by beys or pashas who paid only a nominal allegiance to the sultan. The Crimea had been lost to Russia, which in the late eighteenth century had gained the right of interfering in Ottoman affairs to protect the Christian minorities. Ali Pasha of Ioannina (r. 1778–1822) exercised a quasi-independence in Epiros; and his expansive and predatory policies, abetted by the British, who saw in Ali an ally against Napoleon, made life increasingly hard for everyone on his borders. By 1800 he had built for himself a large empire stretching from northern Albania to the Gulf of Corinth on the south and Thessaly on the east. Serious revolts against the sultan also broke out in Arabia and in Serbia in 1804. As central government failed in the eighteenth century, local notables, for example, the primates of Greece, sprung up everywhere to take charge. They were supposed to be elected under the supervision of local Ottoman governors and were to represent the local inhabitants vis-à-vis the central government, but in practice they were only another level of corruption. Since large areas of the empire were in the control of these notables

(Ali Pasha was only an extreme example of the type), there was a consider-able loss of tax revenues to the sultan. Increasing provincial autonomy was bound to lead to the breakup of the Ottoman Empire, and Serbia and Greece were only the first areas that acquired a taste for independence.

Sultan Selim III (r. 1789–1807), after defeating France in Egypt, tried to reform his administration and army; but his decrees threatened the privi-leges of the Janissaries (a corps of soldiers originally formed by levies of Christian children brought up as Moslems), who grew more and more ob-structive; and in the end they deposed the sultan and then killed him. His empire was not a modern bureaucratic state, even by the standards of Eu-rope in the early nineteenth century; and Selim made no real attempt to change the fundamental character and structure of Ottoman society. Since the Turks were being defeated on land and sea, he tried to introduce West-ern methods of warfare (much as some of his predecessors had done), assum-ing that changes such as these would be enough to save the traditional state. Unfortunately, the failure of the Turks to adapt more thoroughly to their aggressive competitors in the West was the main reason for the ulti-mate demise of the Ottoman Empire. Selim did not believe that a policy of Westernization was necessary. His successors soon learned otherwise.

But to give the Turks their due, we must also understand that as the heirs of a long and distinguished Moslem tradition—and as the successors of the Byzantines—they did not look kindly on what they considered the barbarian West. They, after all, were truly civilized; and there was nothing the West could teach them. For centuries they had been the terror of Eu-rope and had been accustomed to granting favors rather than seeking them. Indeed, until Selim's time, the Ottomans maintained no regular diplomatic corps in any Western capital. Hence arose a policy of isolation and of out-right indifference and even hostility to foreign ways. If the state was suffer-ing setbacks, the solution seemed to be a return to the old ways, not the adoption of new ones. If only the state could be purged of abuses, if only the Turks would remain faithful to the traditions that had made possible the glory days of Suleiman the Magnificent (r. 1520–66), then there would be no reason to adopt foreign customs. This attitude permeated Ottoman society, or at least that small part of it that gave any thought at all to the challenge posed by the West.[17]

17. An excellent analysis of Selim's reforms and the reasons for their failure can be found in Stanford J. Shaw, *Between Old and New: The Ottoman Empire under Selim III, 1789–1807* (Cambridge, Mass., 1971).

The problems faced by the Ottoman Empire were the result not just of incompetent leadership within and of pressure from without, but of the very makeup of the empire itself. Its heterogeneous nature made it liable, in the absence of an active policy of expansion or at least of control, to ultimate fragmentation. This situation is well illustrated by the condition of European Turkey. Since the time of the Romans this area had been forged into an artificial unity and ruled from a distance by outsiders. In the early nineteenth century there were nine major political divisions, or pashaliks, in European Turkey: Belgrade, Bosnia, Scutari, Ioannina, Rumelia, Negropont, Morea, Candia, and Archipelago. The last five of this list comprised most of the territory of ancient Greece, with the exception of the coastal lands of Asia Minor. But within these nine political divisions were six distinct ethnic, or linguistic, groups: Turks, Greeks, Bulgarians, Serbs, Albanians, and Romanians. These groups shared three religions: the Moslem, the Jewish, and the Christian; and the Christians were themselves divided into two hostile camps: Catholic and Orthodox.

These ethnic and religious differences cut across one another in many ways and were further compounded by differences of occupation and status. The case of the Turks themselves shows the complexity of this ethnic omnium gatherum. Though Moslem in religion and in this way divided from the Orthodox Christian Greeks, the Turks in Greece were few in number, except in Macedonia and in some large cities; and most of them spoke Greek because they did not understand Turkish. The more Turks there were in a given place, the greater the admixture of Turkish words that they used. But of course Greek itself was full of Turkish words. A Turk, if he wrote, was therefore quite apt to write in Greek, using more or less a Turkish vocabulary. Speakers of Albanian, a language that originated anciently in Epiros and was not written in Biddle's time, had spread over large parts of Greece. Even rural Attica was thoroughly Albanian. The Albanians had originally been all Orthodox Christians; but many of them became Moslems, if notoriously lax Moslems, to profit from the privileges accorded the conquering religion. Though they also had their own dress, those living in Greece tended to adopt the Greek language and customs of their neighbors and so to assimilate with them. To complicate matters still more, there were the Vlachs, or Wallachians, who spoke Romanian, a Romance language descended from the Latin once spoken in the Roman province of Dacia. The Vlachs, at least the men among them, also spoke and wrote in Greek. Most speakers of Slavic Bulgarian, of whom there were a few in Greece, were also Orthodox Christian, though some were Moslem.

Just as there was no political state other than the Ottoman Empire, so there was no uniform Greek ethnos. Insofar as there were any Greeks in Biddle's day, they existed primarily as a group conscious of its religious and linguistic separation and, among the more educated, of its historical origin. But this group was linked by religion, language, and customs to many other such groups; and there were many gradations between one group and another, so that it is now difficult to define these groups precisely.

It cannot be denied, however, that a certain national sentiment was emerging among the Greeks, especially in the Morea. This part of the Greek world was closest to the West and had had some contact with the ideas of the Renaissance and the French Revolution, both of which had been the catalyst of nationalism in Europe. Intolerant as the Venetians might have been in matters affecting religion and their own methods of rule, their presence over the centuries in various parts of the Morea and their continued occupation of the Ionian Islands helped to increase the self-consciousness of the Greeks and to make them more Western in outlook. Though the Russian invasion of the Peloponnesos in 1770 had ended in disaster, Christianity and trade were protected under the Russian flag; and the Greeks never stopped hoping that one of the great Western powers would deliver them from the Turks. This hope became even more widespread when the ideals of the French Revolution were carried into the Balkans by Napoleon's soldiers. With the spread of learning and business experience among the Greeks, whose language was already widely used for diplomacy and religion in the Turkish empire, the Greeks were more prepared than most of the other ethnic groups for national independence.

The only truly privileged group within the Ottoman Empire were the Turkish Moslems, the descendants of the original conquerors. Everyone else, of whatever religion or ethnic background (including non-Turkish Moslems), comprised a vast herd of cattle (the term applied to them, "rayah," literally meant cattle); and they existed for the benefit of the conquerors, as sheep to be shorn. As inferiors, they were subject to regulations that governed their dress, occupations, and the appearance of their houses; and they were forbidden to carry arms. As long as the tribute and taxes were forthcoming, the subject population was left to its own devices. The basic point of view, or political philosophy, if one can call it that, of the ruling Ottoman class was its own advancement at the expense of the subject population. There was no concern, as there was in western Europe, to protect the individual and give him some way to participate in government.

Official office was considered a means of personal profit—nothing more and nothing less. Hence bribery, corruption, nepotism, and cruelty were the order of the day.

One thing the Turks did not supply was the benefit of government services. The various autonomous subject communities, all with their own laws and methods of education, were outside the purview of the central government. Since the Orthodox Christian population, many of whom spoke Greek, was the largest group, the Turks chose to deal with the Christians as a whole by using the clergy of the Orthodox Church and in particular the Patriarch in Constantinople, who found himself the sultan's point man for internal affairs. It was in this way that the Greeks gradually became accustomed to governing themselves (and others, including Turks, for that matter) within the framework of Turkish despotism.

But it needs to be emphasized that ethnic and religious jealousies kept the subject population from any common sense of purpose or fraternity. Paradoxically, Turkish rule, even over what had been ancient Greece, lasted as long as it did—and might have lasted longer had the western European powers not intervened—precisely because of ethnic and religious diversity. Cultural fragmentation, that is, did not necessarily entail a general demand for freedom from Turkish rule. There were many in the Ottoman Empire, including many Greeks, who were quite happy with the existing state of affairs and who did not want the breakup of the empire into a series of separate nation-states. Those who shared this belief were the heirs of a tradition stretching back over two thousand years.

Biddle's journal makes clear, as do countless others, that the internal condition of the pashaliks of Rumelia and Morea was dismal indeed and apparently characteristic of European Turkey in general. Apart from pockets of prosperity, the population, both Greek and Turk, was declining; and vast areas lay waste for want of people to cultivate them. The Turkish system of extracting resources actively discouraged resourcefulness and industry. Taxes, which tended to be high in proportion to income, could be arbitrarily increased in amount and number; and the whole administrative system was so corrupt that everything could be bought, including justice. Indeed the pashas had to pay yearly for their offices; and they usually borrowed and put a lien on the revenues of their provinces, which they then tried to recoup by letting out the taxes to the highest-bidding tax farmer. The Greek primates, or kodjabashis, a kind of official aristocracy, served as the agents of the Turkish tax farmers. The general insecurity, the repeated ravages of the plague (against which the Turks did nothing to protect themselves), and the deteriorated condition of the roads further suppressed industry. It is hardly surprising that flight from the country or recourse to banditry were common occurrences both for individuals and for groups.

III. The Journals as Literature

In what spirit should we approach these journals and letters, and how should we make some assessment of their literary worth? Some parts of them, for example the bits of narrative in which Biddle describes his own immediate reactions to people and events, will strike a responsive chord in most people. But the long rhetorical digressions in which Biddle reflects on the decadence of the modern Greeks are apt to pall rather quickly, and his anti-Catholicism and priggishness will be offensive to many. The real danger, however, is that the modern reader will misapprehend the purpose of Biddle's work and the circumstances in which it was created. It will not do simply to read these materials as if they were written just yesterday, as if they should somehow automatically appeal to modern tastes in travel writing. They belong to a particular historical context, and they obey certain conventions that are no longer fashionable. It is this context and these conventions that have to be understood. Biddle's journals are, in short, period pieces that must be approached with caution and respect.

Much modern tourism in Greece is inspired, as any Greek will admit, by the search on the part of pale northerners for a convenient venue for enjoying sun, sea, sand, and sex. The presence of ancient monuments might add to the attraction; but nobody is under any illusion that the pursuit of Culture is the basis of the country's appeal to the mass market. What irks the Greeks even more is the tourists' indifference to the modern inhabitants of the country: only the odd scholar comes to inquire into Greek manners, Greek history, or the Greek language. Few people, that is, come to learn. To sit at a restaurant after a strenuous day's sunbathing and to eat souvlaki from the hands of a Greek waiter is about the limit of the tourists' involvement with the country or its people.

Two hundred years ago there were no Club Meds dotting the Greek landscape, and foreigners were few and far between. Even getting into the country was a major challenge; and once a person was there, he faced dirt and danger on all sides. As a remote and poverty-stricken outpost of a barbaric state, Greece offered little in the way of European amenities. Threatened by pirates at sea and brigands on land, annoyed by a host of insect vermin, struggling on occasion to find enough food to keep body and soul together, subject to the vagaries of Turkish despotism, and menaced by the ever-present prospect of putrid fevers and endemic plague, the traveler to Greece before the Greek Revolution had to be a very hardy individual—and he had to have some good reason for putting himself into great discomfort.

The attraction even then was not the actual state of the country or its people, both of which almost everyone found appalling. It was its ancient monuments and its ancient history. The traveler came to familiarize himself with the soil and the relics of the ancient Greeks. The tourist's motives were purely antiquarian. Having done his homework before setting out, he directed his steps to those places that were famous in history and legend to commune with the spirits of antiquity.

From the middle of the eighteenth century, and to an even greater extent from the time of Napoleon, Greece was a part of the Grand Tour.[18] An English lad just down from Oxford or Cambridge who needed a few years' polishing before he inherited his ancestral acres would go to the Continent in company with a tutor and with others of his own kind to sow his wild oats discreetly among the cultural attractions of Paris and Rome. On occasion, these offspring of the British wealthy class, the aristocracy and gentry, would venture into Greece when the journey became more practical. What is noteworthy about these travelers is their extreme youth. They were generally no more than about twenty and very immature. The whole point of the Tour was to impart to them some degree of worldly wisdom through contact with the outside world. The Tour functioned therefore as a kind of

18. William Edward Mead, *The Grand Tour in the Eighteenth Century* (Boston, 1914), esp. chapter VII: 103–39, "The Tourist and the Tutor," which describes the attitudes of the English abroad; Paul Franklin Kirby, *The Grand Tour in Italy, 1700–1800* (New York, 1952) 5–6: "A young cavalier still travelled to enlarge his comprehension of manners, customs, and government, and to see classic lands; but his journey was also a quest. He was expected, as in the days of chivalry to inure himself to weariness, hunger, perils, darkness, high winds, women, nakedness, death, and so on. He did this by going over the seas to ascend difficult hills and struggle through sloughs and over boiling deserts in Italy, where he encountered the monsters Pope and Pagan, and a hundred other 'Carnal Cogitations,' as he stalked among stupendous shells of antiquity or advanced with unflagging courage through the labyrinth of art." The term Grand Tour occurred first in Richard Lassel's *The Voyage of Italy* (Paris and London, 1670); Geoffrey Trease, *The Grand Tour* (New York, 1967); Jeremy Black, *The British and the Grand Tour* (London, 1985).

rite of initiation. To visit Paris, Rome, and Athens, absorbing what foreign nations had to offer and learning something in the process, was the goal. In actual practice, of course, many of these young men merely frittered away their time in the fleshpots of Europe, agreeably cultivating each other's company, and returning home more British than they had been before. But at least the Tour had a genuine didactic purpose.

It is within the context of the Grand Tour that we should understand Biddle's visit to Greece. His whole sojourn in Europe was a Grand Tour, but one taken by an American and including England itself. Still much under the impress of British culture, the wealthy elite of the new United States, who in the states of the mid-Atlantic and New England tended to be merchants, wanted the appropriate education for their children. Biddle's family could afford to send him to Europe; and in the best British tradition, Biddle followed the southward road like many Englishmen.

But though he was conscious of the didactic goal of his European, and specifically of his Greek, trip, Biddle was not just another ephebe on garrison duty. As his journals make abundantly clear, in three important respects he differed from his contemporaries: he was already remarkably, even precociously, mature; he was marked by a sense of moral earnestness, or serious purpose, far beyond anything usually associated with the Grand Tour; and he showed a truly American spirit of independence and initiative.

In the course of editing the journals and letters I had to decide which portrait of Biddle I wanted to use for the frontispiece of this book. Of the many that exist (the earliest of them done in Paris in November 1805), I chose Longacre's watercolor because it shows Biddle in middle age. Biddle's Greek journals do not give the impression of being juvenilia. It is in fact hard to believe that they were written by a twenty-year-old. Their tone is that of a perceptive and inquiring man who traveled to learn and who learned a lot, deciding in the process what he wanted to do with his life, and yet who managed to remain remarkably calm in the face of the annoyances and the obstacles that lay in his path in Greece and some of which every traveler, even now, has to confront. I do not mean to say that Biddle never lost his temper or never had a hard word for the Greeks. But his occasional fit of temper pales into insignificance beside his usual maturity and poise; and one would have to search long and hard in the journals for any hint of a boyish prank or even a boyish attitude.

One of the most striking characteristics of Biddle on tour was his sociability and at the same time his unsociability. Acutely conscious of his own youth, he tried deliberately to act and look older than he was; and one side of this habit was his general avoidance of traveling companions of his own age. He did meet such people, for example, Savy on Malta and four Englishmen in Greece; but he avoided continued contact with them because he thought that he had little to learn from them. Their company only dampened his own mental acuteness and need for inquiry. He therefore traveled alone, or with only a servant or a dragoman (interpreter). When we consider the dangers and difficulties of travel in the Aegean at this time, it is all the more amazing to see the young Biddle managing the journey by himself. He did not seem to need the moral support of a band of fellow travelers.

But he could probably dispense with such support precisely because he was an intensely social person who found acquaintances wherever he went. He hated to pass a man without talking to him. Already evident in the journals is his lifelong habit of mixing easily in the company of important people. Biddle was one of the major social lions of his time, and his journals show us a very precocious lion cub. Aided by his quasi-diplomatic status, Biddle invariably sought out interesting and prominent people whose company he thought would profit him. On the voyage to Sicily he found the American consul Barnes, who was apparently already a family friend. On his arrival in Malta, he took his letters of introduction straight to Governor Ball and immediately fell into the governor's social set. The American naval squadron winding up the war with Tripoli was still at Malta; and Biddle wandered into their company as well. In the Ionian Islands and Greece he passed through the doors of a succession of British consuls and Greek magnates. It comes as no surprise to learn that at Delphi he discoursed, as he himself says, with the Bishop of Chryso, in whose house he was lodging, or that while at Athens he wandered over the ruins with Fauvel and Lusieri and made a point of seeing anyone else in town who was worth seeing and even some people who, in his view, were not. Biddle loved to talk and would bend the ear of anyone who showed an inclination to reciprocate. So far from insulating himself from contact with foreign cultures, he actively sought to plumb their depths, developing in the process his own ability to speak foreign languages. French and Italian he spoke well, and he seems to have had some facility in German and Dutch. Clearly he was not fluent in modern Greek (even a Biddle does not learn this difficult language in two months' time), but at least he made the attempt to understand the language and was firmly convinced that the modern pronunciation of the Greeks themselves was the only sound basis for the pronunciation of the ancient language.

Though Biddle searched constantly for new information, he did not in

any sense go native. The object of his trip was his own intellectual forma-
tion and never simply a surrender to foreign values or customs. He was and
remained an outsider—an American on tour, carrying not just physical
baggage, but intellectual baggage as well. He might dine with a Turk (the
story of the customs inspector whom he met on first entering the Morea) or
sail in a Greek boat (his final voyage through the Ionian Islands to Trieste),
but he always did so with a critical eye for cultural differences; and his own
values are very much a part of his description. Indeed the contrasts he
draws between himself and those whom he meets are the most interesting
parts of the journal.

Biddle seems to have been for the most part a good-natured and amiable
traveler. By the end of his stay with the Greeks, however, the inconve-
niences of the country and the character of the inhabitants were beginning
to wear down this good nature. He, like many another traveler, was only
too glad to slip back to the civilized life of the West. Peace he may have
craved when he set out for Greece; but his final boat ride up the Adriatic
convinced him that dodging cannon fire in Napoleon's Europe was preferable to continued association with the ignorance and superstition of which
he said he had seen too much.

The man who emerges from the pages of these journals and letters is very
much a child of the Age of Reason. In Biddle's hardheaded view of the
purpose of travel and the state of Ottoman and Greek society, there is
almost no romantic sentimentality about the glories of the state of nature or
the bucolic scene. His nearest approach to what might be called a sentimental view of nature is to be found in his remarks on first arriving in the
Peloponnesos. Wandering out of the customs house at Chiarenza, he walks
to a nearby ruin and describes a shepherd, his flock, the sunset, and the
seascape before him in a kind of "mood-piece" that shows nature working
powerfully on his feelings. This attitude is rare. When Biddle traveled
through Arcadia, he was under no illusion about what he saw. Shepherds
had a hard and dirty life, and there was nothing refined or esthetically
pleasing about their habits. Repeatedly Biddle praises the benefits of civilized life; and though he is ready enough to note the continuity of past and
present in Greece (at one point he describes Odysseus as a common pirate),
his constant lament is the degeneration of Greek society because of its
enslavement to an alien and despotic master. He was fully convinced of the
superiority of his own Western point of view, and the reader will never find
him trying to describe modern customs in any sympathetic way. Though
he grants, for example, a certain dignity to the Turks and prefers them to

the Greeks, he does not describe their customs as an anthropologist might, by trying to probe the reasons for Turkish behavior. And rather than accommodate himself when occasion demanded to the Greek fasts and pursue camaraderie with the Greek sailors who were transporting him to Trieste, Biddle complained about their behavior when he insisted on eating as usual. If he sometimes got himself into a social impasse, he had only himself to blame.

As is evident so far, the element of the personal bulks very large in Biddle's journals: his own doings seem to be the item of most importance. This impression might seem to be reinforced by the form of the journals. Apart from the start of the first journal, the entries are cast into the form of long letters to his brother Thomas. But appearances can be deceiving because there is much in the form and even in the substance of the journals that is strictly conventional. Biddle sometimes said just what others said, and he sometimes said it in the same way. Since travel writing in the eighteenth and nineteenth centuries was a regular literary genre (and a highly popular one at that), there were certain conventions that everyone observed; and Biddle too followed these rules.

A travel account had to give information, and it had to give pleasure.[19] This neoclassical ideal, drawn straight from the Roman poet Horace, aimed at both. But an author should not talk too much about himself. Indeed he should efface his own personality, adding only enough of his own doings to convince the reader of the truth of the narrative. As the nineteenth century advanced, this ideal tended to break down; and books were written either purely for entertainment or purely for use. In the latter category were the Baedeker guides. But before this parting of the ways, instructional books of travel were customarily written as letters, the autobiographical journal, or as essays on special topics. In the best work the two types of writing were combined. Casting his material in the form of letters, or a succession of letters, gave the writer's account just the necessary touch of immediacy and accuracy. It was also the rule to show one's classical learning by larding the narrative with quotations in Greek and Latin. This practice helped to fulfill the public's demand for information. In conveying observations, or facts, and reflections, or one's view of the significance of the facts, the author could take any of several conventional poses, or personae. He could pose as a scientific or philosophic traveler who listened and collected information.

---

19. Cf. Charles L. Bratten, Jr., *Pleasurable Instruction: Form and Convention in Eighteenth-Century Travel Literature* (Berkeley and Los Angeles, 1978), passim.

He could be the splenetic traveler, showing himself independent of the attractions of foreign manners. Or one could be the sentimental traveler, displaying ecstatic feelings or emphasizing the virtuous characters whom one met. With the approach of the nineteenth century there came a shift toward more strictly autobiographical accounts. But even with the new emphasis on the personal, it was incumbent on an author, if he wanted an appreciative audience, to obey the conventions of the genre.

Though Biddle did not write his journals for publication (if he ever had such an idea, he gave it up), and though he may never have reflected consciously on these fashions, they certainly molded his ideas about the proper writing of a journal. As we might expect in the case of an early nineteenth-century work, the author takes a prominent place, together with an emphasis on his feelings in a foreign setting. But the older conventions still apply. Biddle is very much the philosophic traveler in quest of information, and he travels for the sake of his own education. He offers his observations, especially on manners, generally avoiding the picturesque and any subjective treatment of the landscape; he stops to reflect on their significance; and he adopts the epistolary form.

It is the passages of reflection that are apt to offend a modern audience. Highly adorned pieces of conscious rhetoric (Biddle loved to turn a phrase when he could not engage someone in conversation), they refer constantly to the theme of the corruption of ancient grandeur, the degeneracy of the modern Greeks, their bad character, and their slavery to the Turks. There is nothing new is these sentiments, because almost every other traveler echoes the same ideas. What is new is the rhetorical dress. But since Biddle was infatuated with oratory, it is hardly surprising that he wanted to exercise his talents in that line.

What is also new is the relative lack of classical quotation. Discussion of the significance of one's observations, whether philosophical, moral, political, or esthetic, was usually accompanied by extensive quotation in the original languages. But Biddle had few classical books with him, apparently only some Cicero. Not having a library on which to draw, he is much more sparing of quotation than one would expect. But he does quote Latin when he has the chance—and even in a journal kept only for his own amusement. He also quotes from memory, and therefore not always accurately. So powerful was the force of custom.

On the whole, however, there is very little borrowed learning or experience in Biddle's journal. He focuses his attention on what he actually sees and shows us how his attention is actively engaged by the real world through which he moved. But Biddle was no Romantic and no rebel against the Roman legacy of reason. He has little emotion for wild places, because he went to the Mediterranean to learn and not to feel. He was not interested in the primitive or the bizarre for its own sake, but only as a means of learning what true culture was. He was also no besotted antiquary. It is not strange that his geographical and archaeological observations are almost always perfunctory. He, unlike many of his contemporaries, had no interest in acquiring artifacts to take home with him, perhaps at least in part because he had little money. As he himself says, what mattered to him were men and not stones; and the value of his journal lies in its investigation of the world of the living and not that of the dead.

Perhaps the best way to set Biddle's journals and letters within the context of the literature of travel is to compare them with the work of his contemporaries.[20] The most comparable work is, like Biddle's, a book that was not published by its author in his own lifetime. John Bacon Sawry Morritt, of Rokeby in Yorkshire, stayed in the Aegean for over a year in the course of his Grand Tour of Europe in 1794–96. As a young man of twenty-two, he dutifully sent back to his mother, his, sister, and his aunt a series of letters based on the journal he kept. An edited selection of these letters was published in 1914.[21] Morritt was a man of means and could afford comfort. He hired a draftsman to keep a visual record, the standard practice before the advent of photography. The resulting drawings he took back with him to Rokeby, together with the collection of antiquities that

20. The phenomenon of the traveler to Greece is a subject that engages the increasing interest of scholars. Three recent books look at the literature of travel from different perspectives. Robert Eisner, *Travelers to an Antique Land: The History and Literature of Travel to Greece* (Ann Arbor, 1991), gives a summary of travel books from antiquity to the present, emphasizing works in English and addressing the general question why people went to Greece. Richard Stoneman, *Land of Lost Gods: The Search for Classical Greece* (Norman, Okla., 1987), devotes his attention to the birth of archaeological interest among western Europeans and the race for antiquities. Helen Angelomatis-Tsougarakis, *The Eve of the Greek Revival: British Travellers' Perceptions of Early Nineteenth-Century Greece* (London, 1990), tries to see what can be learned, apart from topography and archaeology, about the social and economic state of European Turkey. She treats the travel books as primary historical sources, noting the strengths and weaknesses that arise from the foreign perspective of their authors. The American contribution to the literature of Greek travel is surveyed by Stephen E. Larrabee, *Hellas Observed: The American Experience of Greece, 1775–1865* (New York, 1957), esp. 11–19 (for Biddle), and by Marcia Jean Pakake, "Americans Abroad: A Bibliographical Study of American Travel Literature, 1625–1800" (Ph.D. dissertation, University of Minnestoa, 1975).

21. J. B. S. Morritt, *A Grand Tour: Letters and Journeys, 1794–96* (London, 1985 [1914]).

he either bought or stole,[22] to provide amusement for his guests before dinner. Needing someone who knew both Turkish and modern Greek, he also hired a dragoman, or interpreter. His entourage, including the requisite tutor, comprised a party of from six to nine. Until he reached Turkey, he traveled in his own carriage. Thereafter he rode on horseback and hired Janissaries for protection. In short, Morritt went in style.

His letters are simple and straightforward accounts of his own doings. Chatty, descriptive, and full of wit, they bear few marks of the conventions that shackled books of travel prepared for publication. They are the spontaneous productions of a man who had no interest in parading his scholarship or providing his readers with a fund of miscellaneous information. Morritt was very much interested in Morritt, and he makes no attempt to efface his own personality. His observations and reflections on the country and its inhabitants are hardly profound, and his reactions are those of a proud Englishman easily amused or enraged and apt to complain about the lack of beefsteak and porter. One can almost see him putting his glass to his eye and "quizzing the natives." Morritt was much addicted to society, or, as he phrases it, "good company," which engrossed his attention. After leaving Austria, he was rather out of his element and was happy to return to Italy and the court of Ferdinand of Naples, where he could hobnob with the beau monde. Perhaps it was just as well that Biddle had no entrée to this particular set, since it was composed, or so Morritt tartly claims, of rogues and whores. A rather straitlaced young American like Biddle would not have found this company congenial, though his comments on it might have been just as amusing and penetrating as his observations on King Ferdinand, whom he did see.

The following extracts (pp. 179–81) from Morritt's account of his stay in Athens indicate the tone of his narrative:

> It is very pleasant to walk the streets here. Over almost every door is an antique statue or basso-relievo, more or less good though all much broken, so that you are in a perfect gallery of marbles in these lands. Some we steal, some we buy, and our court is much adorned with them. I am grown, too, a great medalist, and my collection increases fast, as I have above two hundred, and shall soon, I hope, have as many thousands. At this rate I have got some good ones,

22. Lord Aberdeen's two sculptures from Amyklai, which Biddle discusses in detail, Morritt tried but failed to carry off in 1795.

and mean to keep them for the alleviation of Sir Dilberry's visits, as they will be as good playthings as the furniture and pictures for half an hour before dinner.

We are very well with the Turks here, and particularly with the governor of the town, who has called on us, sent us game, made coursing parties for us, offered us dogs, horses, etc., and is a very jolly, hearty fellow. We often go and smoke a pipe there, and are on the best of terms. I shall really grow a Mussulman.

The Greeks are, you will see, in *très mauvaise odeur* with us; and I would much rather hear that the Turks were improving their government than hear that the Empress had driven them out, for I am sure, if left to the Greeks in their present state, the country would not be passable. We have just breakfasted, and are meditating a walk to the citadel, where our Greek attendant is gone to meet the workmen, and is, I hope, hammering down the Centaurs and Lapithae, like Charles's mayor and aldermen in the "School for Scandal." Nothing like making hay when the sun shines, and when the commandant has felt the pleasure of having our sequins for a few days, I think we shall bargain for a good deal of the old temple.

If Biddle quizzed the natives, at least he did so with much less arrogance and with a more consciously articulated educational purpose; and his notion of society was apt to be far wider than the aristocratic Morritt's. But he and Morritt do share a spontaneity and a freshness altogether missing in the massive published works of their contemporaries Edward Dodwell[23] and William Martin Leake.[24] Dodwell left the Peloponnese in early April 1806, on route to the Ionian Islands, whence he sailed for Sicily and Rome in mid-May. Thus he just missed Biddle. Leake for his part spent most of the first decade of the century rambling over the Aegean in the guise of a tourist, though he was actually a spy for the British Foreign Office. Leake and Biddle too never met each other. The books of Dodwell and Leake not only abandoned the epistolary form, but appeared long after the travels that

23. Edward Dodwell, *A Classical and Topographical Tour through Greece during the Years 1801, 1805, and 1806*, 2 vols. (London, 1819).

24. William Martin Leake, *Researches in Greece: Remarks on the Languages Spoken in Greece at the Present Day* (London, 1814); *The Topography of Athens, with Some Remarks on Its Antiquities* (London, 1821; 2d edition, 1841); *Journey through Some Provinces of Asia Minor in the Year 1800* (London, 1820); *Journal of a Tour in Asia Minor* (London, 1824); *Travels in the Morea*, 3 vols. (London, 1830); *Travels in Northern Greece*, 4 vols. (1835).

inspired them. The interval in each case gave their authors a chance to draw upon libraries and the learning of others. The resulting books are a mine of information but tend to lack personal interest and also reflection.

Dodwell's book is the product of a British expatriate who lived much of his life in Rome. When the French descended on Italy, he found himself trapped there, but secured permission, on giving his parole, to travel in the Aegean. He was not a particularly keen observer of the society he found there. He moved from place to place, intent on identifying classical ruins and virtually ignoring the current inhabitants. He did provide a certain amount of miscellaneous information about the natural landscape, about food and prices, and about questions of topography; and on occasion he could tell a good story. But even these stories are apt to be full of the condescension that runs all through his book. Like most travelers from the West, who had imbibed the thought of the Renaissance, Dodwell could cheerfully ignore what did not fit his picture of antiquity. The result is a concentrated look at ruins and at little else. The Greeks and Turks who lived among them Dodwell simply dismissed as irrelevant. But in doing so he merely followed the consensus. His readers wanted to know what had happened to the remnants of antiquity, and the sociology and politics of the contemporary Aegean were not for them a high priority. Illustrative of these attitudes is his description of his dinner with the bishop of Krisso, or Chryso, a scene well worth comparing with Biddle's account of his own visit to the same house:

> We had a letter, from Mr. Nicolas Strani, to the Bishop of Salona, who resides here; we passed the night in his house; and nothing could be more miserable! He lives with all the simplicity of the primitive Christians; there was nothing to eat, except rice and bad cheese; the wine was execrable, and so impregnated with rosin, that it almost took the skin from our lips! An opportunity however was now offered us of seeing the interior of a Greek house, and of observing some of the customs of the country, which are curious and interesting. . . .
>
> We dined at a round table of copper tinned, called, in the Turkish language, *siny*, supported upon one leg or column, like the *monopodia* of the ancients (Livy, b. 39. c. 6). We sat on cushions placed on the floor; and our dress not being so conveniently large as that of the Greeks, we found the greatest difficulty in tucking our legs under us, or rather sitting upon them, as they do with perfect

ease and pliability. Several times I was very near falling back, and overturning the episcopal table, with all its good things. The Bishop insisted upon my Greek servant sitting at table with us; and on my observing that it was contrary to our customs, he answered, that he could not bear such ridiculous distinctions in his house. It was with difficulty I obtained the privilege of drinking out of my own glass, instead of out of the large goblet, the κυλιξ φιλοτησια (Dion Cassius, b. 58. c. 3), or poculum amicitiae, which served for the whole party, and which had been whiskered by the Bishop, and the rest of the company, for both the Greeks and Turks use only one glass at meals.[25]

Another passage shows even better Dodwell's use of borrowed learning; and, despite its top-lofty tone, it is also rather uncharacteristically perceptive:

In travelling through Greece it is sometimes necessary to bluster and speak loud, in order to obtain the provisions which are requisite to support nature. We were always willing to pay much more than the value, but even with this were sometimes obliged to produce our ferman, and insist on being provided. This is however very rare, and on such occasions we found, that clamorous impatience was more useful to us than submissive tranquillity. It would appear from Plutarch (Life of Cato Minor), that the travelling through the Grecian states was formerly very much like what it is at present. Cato, in travelling in Asia Minor, used to send his servants on before him, in order to get lodgings and provisions; and when there happened to be no inn (πανδοχειον) in the town, they demanded hospitality from the magistrates. As Cato's servants conducted themselves with modesty, and not in the usual threatening and overbearing manner, they were little attended to, and Cato frequently found nothing provided for him; and even when he arrived he was neglected as a man of little consequence, from the patient quiescence of his people, and the contented manner in which he used to seat himself upon his baggage. The effects of outward appearance upon the ignorant is well expressed in Terence (Eunuch. act 3. sc. 2. line 31), where we see Thraso despising

25. Dodwell, *A Classical and Topographical Tour through Greece*, vol. 1, 155–57.

Phaedria, on account of the meek behaviour of the servant Parmeno, who modestly addressed himself to Thraso—

"Verum, ubi molestum non erit, ubi tu voles,
Ubi tempus tibi erit, sat habet si tum recipitur."

Thraso:—

Apparet servum hunc esse domini pauperis,
Miserique."[26]

Perhaps even more disturbing for a modern audience than Dodwell's cultural arrogance is his almost total lack of reflection. He tends not just to ignore the current scene, but also makes no comment on the significance, for himself or anyone else, of the ruins he does describe. Why did he bother to go to Greece? He never says. He was ready enough to describe the discomforts of travel (the dirt, the insects, and, above all, the difficulties of dealing with the people), and he spent much time drawing views of the ruins and the landscape with the aid of his artist and his own camera obscura. But what was the point of all this activity? At least Biddle had a reason for travel; and he had views, albeit conventional, on the relationship between antiquity and his own age. But Dodwell gives no evidence of having considered this issue for a moment. If in some respects Dodwell's book is a greatly expanded version of Biddle's journals, in others it falls far short of those journals in philosophic insight. As young as he was, Biddle had a much more intelligent and probing mind than Dodwell; and for this reason, if for no other, his account is much more interesting than Dodwell's.

If Morritt, Dodwell, and Biddle all remained outsiders, the same cannot be said for Leake, whose long sojourn in the Aegean gave him a far better opportunity to become well acquainted with both people and places. Covering the land on horseback, some of it several times, and keeping his watch always in his hand to measure distances, he acted as a spy, sending back reports to the Foreign Office that helped the British handle the Turkish Question. But there is one problem—a discontinuity between what Leake saw and knew and what appears in his books. Despite his obvious familiarity with the country and its people, his books show little evidence of his

26. Ibid., vol. 1, 530–31.

knowledge of these matters. His massive topographical researches, which
are valuable even now because of their detailed analysis of the land and of
the ancient sources, almost never say anything about the current political or
economic state of the country. Vivid hints here and there (for example, his
casual notice of a murderer impaled beside the road) lead us to believe that
Leake knew far more than he chose to say. But he too was still restrained by
some of the old conventions of travel writing. He did not consider it his
job to do what we would now call sociology, anthropology, or economics.
Blinkered like almost everyone else by the prevalent passion for the antique,[27] he could discuss the most minute topographical questions, bring to
bear upon them massive citations from ancient authors, without ever ad-
mitting the existence of the current population or its current problems.
Though he wrote far more than Dodwell, he managed to say a good deal
less about the Greeks, Turks, and others who inhabited the landscape he
described so meticulously. Perhaps in keeping with the increasingly posi-
tivist ideas of the nineteenth century and the consequent rise of science,
Leake cast aside any pretense of philosophical, political, or social reflection,
or commentary, and wrote what for us look like vastly enlarged Blue
Guides. He saw his job as purely topographic and was utterly untouched by
the eighteenth-century convention that demanded the union of observation
and reflection. This convention is still traceable in Biddle's journals; but by
the time Leake published his books, the split between the two goals was
widening into an unbridgeable gulf. By providing information, Leake may
instruct us; but no one ever would accuse him of trying to delight us. The
old classical ideal of Horace was now quite dead, at least for him. How
valuable soever his ponderous discussions may still be, they are almost unreadable. They have none of the spirit or the spontaneity of Morritt, Biddle, or even Dodwell in his rare lighter moments. In short, Leake the
man is almost impossible to discover. A sample passage shows his over-
whelmingly topographical and antiquarian interests:

> March 15.—From Argos to Anapli [Nauplia]. Leave the house of
> Kyr V—at 1.51: at 2.3, the last houses of the town;—2.11, cross
> the river Banitza;—2.31, pass through Delamanara, where, in a
> ruined church, are several ancient squared blocks and other rem-

27. A significant exception to the general run of travelers was David Urquhart, *Turkey
and Its Resources* (London, 1833), and *The Spirit of the East*, 2 vols. (Philadelphia, 1839).
Despite being an insufferable poseur, he made a genuine effort to understand an alien
culture and to convey that understanding to his audience.

nants of antiquity, and by the side of a well the shaft of a small Doric column, hollowed to serve as a trough for cattle. Hereabouts stood a pyramidal monument, which was the common sepulchre of the Argives who were slain on either side in a drawn battle between Proetus and Acrisius. It was adorned with representations of Argolic shields, in memory of the tradition that on that occasion the two kings and their followers were for the first time armed with shields (Pausan. 1.2.c.25). At 3.1 I arrived at Paleo-Anapli, as the ruins of Tiryns are called.[28] [There follows a long and detailed description of these ruins.]

We can probably be grateful that Biddle never published his own journals. If he had, he might well have followed in the footsteps of Dodwell and Leake, making his work far more informational, far more scholarly, and far less revealing of his own personality. That the journals are already conventional enough in their own way is a point that needs to be repeated. But their charm lies in the degree to which they transcend convention and show us the man behind the mask.

IV. Provenance and Description of the Journals and Letters

Whether because his father urged him or because the keeping of a journal was considered at the time to be every traveler's duty, Biddle recorded his activities right from the start. His first European journal begins on September 4, 1804, the very day of his departure. Apart from the first Greek journal, which covered the period from March 25 to early June 1806, and which, since it was handed down from father to son, has never disappeared, and apart from several letters drawn from his journals, this record was unknown until 1977. In that year, in an outbuilding at Biddle's home of Andalusia, there appeared a trunk containing all, or almost all, the journals that Biddle had kept during his European trip. There are fourteen of these journals, one of them being the second Greek journal [Figs. 1 and 20]. There is no journal for the month of March 1806. Is it missing, or was it

28. Leake, *Morea*, vol. 2, 349–50.

never written? An undated intruder into this genuine collection of Bid-
dliana, probably for August and September 1805, describes travel in
Switzerland and is the work of James West, Biddle's sometime traveling
companion. In 1978 all these newly discovered journals were committed by
Nicholas B. Wainwright to the care of the Historical Society of Pennsylvania in Philadelphia, where they now reside in Box 15 of the Biddle Family
Papers.

These journals are an odd assortment of small notebooks, no one identi-
cal in shape to any other. When he finished one, Biddle apparently bought
another wherever he happened to be. Some of them are written in pencil,
some in ink. Some are in English, some in French; and some are a mixture
of both languages. The information and reflections in some of them are
detailed and extensive, in others scrappy and disjointed. They describe his
visits to famous sites, to libraries, to art works, and to people and show us
what Biddle thought about them. The collection as it stands is in some
disorder due to Biddle's own slapdash methods and the episodic nature of
his journal keeping. The journals are not named or even numbered. Three
of them are not dated. Apparently he did not keep a journal when he was
settled for long in any one place, but only when he was on the move. On
the whole the collection looks like a personal diary that its author would
certainly never have wished to see in print in its present form. The two
Greek journals, however, are the most complete of the lot and the most
representative of the level of literary quality Biddle could attain. They
might even be called the heart of the collection. Since the trip to Greece
was, as Biddle himself says, a turning point in his life, it is hardly surprising that the entries in these two books are particularly full and satisfying.

Biddle's first Greek journal is now in the possession of Nicholas Biddle,
Jr., of Penn Valley, Pennsylvania, Biddle's great-great grandson. This journal passed to Biddle's eldest son, Edward, and then to Edward's descendants, until at some point (no one seems to know exactly when) it was
given on temporary loan to the Historical Society of Pennsylvania. It was
removed in 1980 together with a large number of other papers. In 1919
some extracts from it were published by William Nickerson Bates, who did
not, however, say where the journal was or who had it.[29]

This journal is a small pocket book 5 1/2 by 3 3/4 inches in size. Bound

29. William Nickerson Bates, "The Greek Journal of Nicholas Biddle," *Proceedings of the
Numismatic and Antiquarian Society of Philadelphia* 28 (1916–18): 167–83.

in stiff brown paper boards now sadly worn, it consisted originally of
ninety-six leaves (or 192 pages), in six gatherings of sixteen leaves each.
The first leaf is unnumbered, and on its reverse is a series of short mem-
oranda. The leaves thereafter are numbered on front and back from page 1
through page 187. There are two pages 107 and two pages 108. A Delphic
inscription appears on page 184. Pages 185 and 186 are blank; and on 187
is a diagram of the Pnyx at Athens, followed by two more smaller diagrams
of the same place on the next unnumbered pages. On the back of the
second to last leaf something was once written that was afterward torn out,
so that only half the leaf remains, on which there are a few traces of the
missing writing. On the back of the last leaf is written the following address: Mr McKenzie, No 26 Upper Guilford Street, Christ Church, Oxford. Thebes, 1806. Preceding this address are six words of modern Greek,
in some hand other than Biddle's, which are the name and "address" of the
Turkish customs official at Chiarenza who wanted Biddle to write to him.

The second journal is a vellum-covered notebook, or pocket book, 7 5/8
inches long by 4 3/4 inches wide. It consists of sixty leaves, or 120 pages
(twenty leaves each in three separately sewn gatherings). The last (or first)
page of one gathering has been torn out and is missing. Both gray end-
papers are unmarked, though Biddle started to write "So" for "Souvenir" on
one of them. One cover has the signature "Nich Biddle," written twice, in
addition to several faint doodles, apparently attempts to draw the figure
that appears on page 247. On the other cover the same signature appears
once, again with the same faint sketches. The inside of one cover is inscribed, in Biddle's handwriting, "Souvenir de la Gréce."

The notebook is divided into two parts, each paginated separately. In the
first part, the continuation of the first journal, the pages are numbered
191–267; and numbers 258–267 are blank. Entries begin on Saturday,
June 7, 1806; and they end on Wednesday, July 23. Preceding the first
page of this part, and written upside down in relation to it, are a series of
short reminders Biddle wrote to himself.

The pages of the second part are numbered 1–49, of which 40 through
49 are blank. Page 1 has the heading "Continuation of a Few Notes on
Athens." All this material is undated, and some of it may have been written after Biddle left Athens, when he was spending time in quarantine in
the lazaretto in Trieste. To make the entries in this second part, Biddle
flipped the book upside down, keeping the bound edge on the left, so that
the two sets of entries not only run toward each other from opposite ends of
the book but are upside down in relation to each other.

Apart from the two years (1978–80) when they lay in the same deposi-
tory, the two journals have had quite different histories. It is strange that
only one of Biddle's many European journals, and this the first Greek journal, should have remained above ground. Why was it not packed away
with the others and similarly forgotten? Whatever the reason for its continued circulation in the family of Biddle's son Edward, it has had a much
more checkered career than its companion. It was the second journal, however, that went to Boston to be part of an exhibit at the Fogg Art Museum
held from mid-December 1979 to mid-January 1980, to mark the 100th
anniversary of the founding of the Archaeological Institute of America.
Andrew Oliver, who organized the exhibit, gathered together a number of
portraits, letters, diaries, and actual antiquities to document American exploration and archaeology in the eastern Mediterranean before the founding
of the AIA in 1879. In late June 1979, Oliver had seen what he now
thinks to have been the second Greek journal in the library of the Historical Society in Philadelphia, where it had come to rest a year before. For
some reason, perhaps because he was guided around the library by Nicholas
B. Wainwright, who had just turned over the second journal to the Historical Society, Oliver did not see the first journal, which, because of its status
as part of a temporary loan, was not in the same box. In any case, it was
only the second journal that he exhibited in Boston.

Of the letters Biddle wrote to his family and friends in the course of his
trip to Greece, only four are now known. That there were other letters or
notes is clear from Biddle's own remarks in his first Greek journal when he
was on the point of leaving Malta and from a comment or two he makes in
the existing letters about enclosures for people other than the person to
whom he happens to be writing. His Maltese letters may yet come to light.
Whether there were ever any other major letters from Greece than the
existing four is at present an open question. Biddle himself remarks how
difficult it was to find a secure means of communication with Europe.
Except in Patras and in Athens, he may well have found no means of
sending a letter; and in any case he was on the move most of the time and
probably would not have had the leisure to write letters.

The four existing letters fall naturally into two groups on the basis of
their present location. The two long letters in the Library of Congress, both
of which were revisions of entries in the journals, are part of a large collection of about fifteen thousand items that are now collectively called *The
Papers of Nicholas Biddle* and that were the bequests of Charles and Edward Biddle between 1909 and 1955. The letters are in container no. 125,

the contents of which are available as microfilm (reel no. 48). At some point all these original materials were bonded to transparent paper so that they could be bound in a series of large folios.

The letter from Patras comprises folio pages 336 and 337, as well as 385 and 386, of book 125. In the binding process the end of the letter was unfortunately divided from its beginning, perhaps because the size of the sheets is not uniform. The material on 336 and 337 is 12 3/4 inches long and 8 inches wide; that on page 385 is 9-7/8 inches long and 7-7/8 inches wide. Page 336 is the original enclosing sheet, 10 inches long and 7-7/8 inches wide, and addressed to Charles Biddle Esquire, Philadelphia. The folds are still visible. In what would have been the upper right-hand corner of the folded "envelope" is the numeral 392. In red ink are two stamps, one saying just "Ship," another (a circular one) "New York, Feb. 13." The numbers 6 and 117 are written on one side of the back, as well as the phrase "Arr. Feby 14, 1807." The sealing wax and the paper to which it was attached have disappeared.

The letter from Trieste comprises folio pages 342 through 347. All pages measure 9 9/16 inches long and 8 1/16 inches wide.

The two letters in the Firestone Library at Princeton University (Miscellaneous Manuscripts CO 140, folder 2) were purchased by the Library in June 1943 from the American Autograph Shop. They are written on 17-7/8 by 10-inch sheets, folded down to 7-15/16 by 10-inches. That is, Biddle took a single large sheet and folded it in the style of a folio, leaving the fold to the left and giving himself four pages on which to write. The letter to his brother (Athens, June) is a fragment, lacking one or more large folded sheets. All the sheets of both letters are the same size, and there are no page numbers. Neither letter has an address sheet. Conservation work, presumably done at Princeton (no one knows for sure) consisted in "silking," and thereby stiffening and yellowing, the paper and in reinforcing the left-hand fold and the outer margins with paper tape. This process is old, but apparently reversible.

Were these two letters drafts, or were they actually mailed? There do appear to be traces of folds in the usual places. But the letter to his brother is not dated precisely, nor does Biddle specify in the salutation which brother he wants to address. There are several instances of alternative wording written between lines, and between two paragraphs appears a list of items that Biddle apparently intended somehow to expand. As far as it is preserved, this letter is a turgid rhetorical exercise, the very thing Biddle says he did when he had time on his hands. The letter to Watts, again with no proper salutation, contains a fair number of corrections (strikeouts and alternative wording) and looks rather more carelessly written than usual. Is this letter the one Biddle says he enclosed in the large letter of July 25, 1806, written from Trieste?

With the journals and letters of his European trip, Biddle established a habit of writing and an interest in literature that he would continue for the rest of his life. Quite apart from serving as editor of the *Port Folio* and contributing anonymous articles to it, he wrote a certain amount of poetry. But most of his effort went into letters, of which there are thousands still extant. Biddle saved everything: school essays, household account books, library inventories, odd receipts, journals of various sorts, and of course letters to him and from him. When he retired, he put his correspondence in some order, withdrawing only letters to and from his wife. The result was a mass of material that is now scattered in many libraries (much in the Library of Congress) and in private hands; and most of it, sad to say, is still unedited. The surprising thing is that, literary man though he was, Biddle himself never published anything under his own name except for occasional letters to newspapers. The journals of his European trip would have probably sold quite well if he himself had put them into finished form, because the literature of travel, especially when it concerned the more remote lands of the Levant, was highly popular in the early nineteenth century and became more so with the Greek War of Independence. Why did Biddle not publish his journals? That he was capable of producing something extraordinary is evident from his edition of the journals of Lewis and Clark. Perhaps the answer lies in the social position that Biddle assumed to be his: in his time a gentleman simply did not write for profit. To have one's name on the cover of a book did not carry the social cachet it now does. Or perhaps Biddle was just modest about his abilities, because he says in one of his letters that he had not the talent to write a travel narrative for an audience beyond his own family. In any case he turned his attention to politics and finance, and the European journals were packed away out of sight and mind.

V. Editorial Procedures

The editing for publication of journals and letters almost two hundred years old entails certain problems. Biddle, as he himself says, never intended these materials to circulate beyond the limits of his own family, at least in the form in which they now exist. Though his father urged him to keep a journal as a possible means of making money to defray the expenses of his trip, and though Biddle sent back accounts of his activity, which were eagerly received by his family, he himself never edited either his journals or his letters. It is therefore up to the modern editor to decide upon a plan of action that will do justice to the literary quality of the originals and, at the same time, make them accessible to as wide a modern audience as possible.

The composition of that audience is perhaps the single most important constraint upon an editor. The Greek journals and letters, though they should be of special interest to classicists and archaeologists, for whom the documentation of ancient sites before the arrival of digging scholars is a pressing concern, deserve a wider circle of readers. As a key figure in U.S. history in the first four decades of the nineteenth century, Biddle deserves more attention than he has hitherto received. Together with the papers from his years at Princeton, the journals and letters of his European trip, and especially the Greek journals, are the basis for the construction of Biddle's intellectual biography. If more of Biddle's written work were in print and available to American historians (at present we have only McGrane's selection of correspondence dealing with national affairs, and particularly the affairs of the Second U.S. Bank),[30] this man's contribution to his country's growth would certainly be easier to assess. But even apart from his importance to the political scene in the Age of Jackson, Biddle was, as I have already argued, a splendid example of neoclassical man and instrumental in furthering classical ideals and in adapting them to the New World.

Since there are, then, at least three prospective audiences for these journals and letters, it seemed best to avoid any editorial procedure that is unduly doctrinaire. Though inclined to the model of the diplomatic edition, or the type facsimile, a method whereby the handwritten page is set in print with absolutely minimal editorial intervention, I decided that in practice these documents could not simply be reproduced by setting down exactly every letter, every word, and even every mark of punctuation. On the other hand, a thoroughly modernized and sanitized version seemed equally repugnant. The course adopted is a compromise, but a compromise that leans heavily in the direction of the type facsimile.

In deciding on this procedure, I looked into the collected papers of other

---

30. Reginald C. McGrane, ed., *The Correspondence of Nicholas Biddle Dealing with National Affairs, 1807–1844* (Boston, 1919).

early Americans to see how this material was handled by its respective editors. The recent edition of the papers of Benjamin Latrobe and the latest edition of the journals of Lewis and Clark are the models I have followed.[31] The journals of Lewis and Clark are particularly relevant not only because they are exactly contemporary with Biddle's own journal, but because Biddle himself was the first to edit Lewis and Clark's work. It is useful, in other words, to see what Biddle himself produced (and what he might therefore have done with his own journals if he had published them), and to compare this production with modern editorial practices. Biddle's work was a thoroughgoing renovation of the original materials. Much was omitted, especially scientific information; and the whole was recast in a uniform literary style. The resulting text reads very well, and it is a superb adventure story. But is certainly not Lewis and Clark.

Nowadays we prefer the raw original to the elegant renovation, or paraphrase. In conformity with this preference, I will let Biddle speak in his own voice. This edition attempts to produce a reliable and definitive standard text, indeed a critical text, of the journals & letters as they actually exist. It tries to be as faithful to the originals as possible. I have not altered the original language or inserted my own opinions under the pretext of reproducing Biddle, and I have tried to avoid cluttering the text with an excess of editorial apparatus.

In practice, this austere ideal has been relaxed in certain ways. Biddle himself often supplemented a paragraph with an additional note on some other page of his journal. These scattered bits had to be brought together as Biddle intended. Thus it proved impracticable to reproduce the journals page by page: there was no reason to keep the original pagination or even to indicate it. By way of extending this practice of putting together what belongs together, I have repositioned one large segment of the second journal. Biddle's summary of his reflections on Athens seemed to require a major displacement. Rather than leaving this material at the very end of the second journal, where it now stands, I inserted it, under Biddle's own title ("Continuation of a Few Notes on Athens") after the entry in the second journal for June 9, 1806, and before the entry for June 13, when Biddle arrived in Corinth. Thus all the Athenian material will be found in one place. With one other small exception, a Delphic inscription that Bid-

31. Edward C. Carter II and others, *The Papers of Benjamin Henry Latrobe* (New Haven, 1985–); Gary E. Moulton and others, *The Journals of the Lewis and Clark Expedition* (Lincoln, Neb., 1983–91).

dle copied at the end of his first journal and that I have positioned in his account of Delphi, I have not displaced any other material, though I might have done, if I had wanted here and there to improve the flow of the narrative. Abrupt changes of subject and afterthoughts that might belong elsewhere but that Biddle did not himself correct have been allowed to stand. Because of the high quality of Biddle's writing, however, the reader will rarely notice problems of this sort.

The editorial treatment of orthography, punctuation, and syntax is equally conservative. My rule has been to avoid intervention or modernization if at all possible; but I have also not scrupled to make an occasional correction, or rather addition, rather than let the text, because of its peculiarity, call undue attention to itself. Part of the charm of Biddle's narrative is his own orthography and punctuation, both of which are remarkably modern and remarkably consistent. He, like Latrobe, but unlike Lewis and Clark, offers few obstacles to the modern reader. All punctuation is therefore Biddle's own. Only occasionally have I added a mark, generally a mere comma, to prevent the reader from having to reread a passage to get the sense. For the same reason I have here and there added a word in brackets to fill out the meaning when the text seemed to call for such an addition, when, that is, Biddle left out, whether carelessly or not, something that can readily be supplied from the context. All editorial intrusions except added marks of punctuation and except the odd correction of a clear mistake on Biddle's part are easily identifiable.

I have regularized the use of capital letters. Biddle sometimes wrote "greek" and sometimes "Greek," and so with other proper adjectives. Obvious errors and slips of the pen have, as I said, been silently corrected; but old spellings, including variant spellings of the same word, have been retained. Random lines and dashes have been omitted or replaced with periods, and some superfluous underlying has been omitted. Superscript letters have been lowered to the line. The paragraphing follows the author's original wherever his intention is clear. On occasion I have silently indented when I thought that doing so was appropriate. Abbreviated and contracted words, especially the names of towns and certain military titles, are spelled out wherever they might be misunderstood. Biddle's own cross-references have been replaced with bracketed cross-references to the printed text. The following are the only editorial symbols used in this edition:

[*italics*]:	Editorial remarks
[roman]:	Editorial expansions or additions

[roman?]:   Editorial conjectures
[..]:   A blank space in Biddle's text

I have not used [*sic*] to mark peculiar grammar or spellings. Unless I have made some mistake in transcribing the materials (always a possibility), any apparent grammatical errors or lapses in sense, of which there are very few, should be presumed to be Biddle's own.

Accompanying the text are footnotes, which are in all cases my own attempt to explicate whatever needs explication. In the hope that this book will find its way into the hands of interested readers who are not classical scholars, I have explained not only archaic and unusual words, together with variant and unusual spellings, but also Biddle's allusions to people, places, events, books, and ideas that may now be generally unknown. Though he was only twenty when he wrote these journals and letters, Biddle was amazingly well read even for his time, especially in classical authors. His erudition in this area would put a modern college student to shame and might even raise a blush on the cheeks of some professional scholars. But since fashions in learning have changed considerably since the early nineteenth century, it is best to err on the side of inclusion rather than to assume that anything Biddle mentions is now an object of common knowledge. Almost all people whose names occur in the text are identified, insofar as identification is still possible. The general index can be used to trace repeated mentions of a person, place, or object.

It remains to note one major exclusion from the edited text of the journals. Biddle drew a number of sketches to illustrate points of architecture or topography. Though these sketches could easily be reproduced by halftones and inserted into the text at the appropriate points, they invariably provide no new information; and they have absolutely no artistic distinction whatever. Biddle himself lamented that he had no talent for drawing, and his sketches amply confirm his modesty on this score. Wherever a sketch has been omitted from the text, a footnote will call attention to its existence in the original journals and, if necessary, will describe it briefly. In place of Biddle's own sketches, I have included a carefully chosen selection of contemporary and near contemporary illustrations from the works of other travelers and artists. The early nineteenth century was the great age of the topographic watercolor, the engraving, and the lithograph; and the landscape and monuments of Greece were splendidly represented in these media. Including illustrations of this sort will not only enable a modern reader of Biddle's work to see what Biddle himself saw, but will emphasize the very great difference between the appearance of Greece under the Turkocratia and its present appearance. Ancient sites looked very different before archaeologists appeared on the scene to strip them of their medieval encrustation, and readers of the early travelers need to be reminded of the great changes that scholarship and the Greeks' own national independence have caused in the landscape.

First Greek Journal

I had long felt an ardent desire to visit Greece. The fate of a nation whose history was the first brilliant object that met my infancy, & the first foundation of my early studies was so interesting that I had resolved to avail myself of any opportunity of witnessing it. The soil of Greece is sacred to Genius & to letters. The race of beings whose atchievements warm our youthful fancy has long disappeared. But the sod under which they repose; the air which listened to their poetry & their eloquence; the hills which saw their valor are still the same. The men of Greece are the descendants of the people who enlightened their country by their virtues, & who gave by the reflection of their science & their arts the empire of the world to Rome. Shall I be insensible to the pleasure of treading on the ground which had felt the footsteps of Epaminondas of Plato of Demosthenes? May I not be permitted to pluck a flower from the garden of Academus[1] or to repose under the Stoic portico?[2] And perhaps I may offer my feeble homage to him whose eloquence rendered him in the first of sciences, the first of men.[3] I am now able to gratify my curiosity. Absent from my country from which a long & varied distance separates me, alone, unencumbered, I feel myself

1. In the sixth century B.C. the Athenians founded three gymnasia outside the city where young men could receive military training and education: the Academy, to the west of the city; Kynosarges, to the southeast of the city by the Ilissos stream and near the Kallirhoe spring; and the Lyceum, somewhere to the east of the city. Plato taught at the Academy and Aristotle at the Lyceum.
2. The Stoic philosopher Zeno (335–263 B.C.) taught in the Painted Stoa, a public hall built on the north side of the Athenian marketplace in the mid-fifth century B.C. and noted for its murals. Zeno's followers took the name of their school from the building. In Biddle's time the remains of the building were buried under houses, and its exact location was unknown.
3. Presumably Demosthenes.

peculiarly fortunate in my position. To travel alone connects itself in the minds of most men with many an image of listlessness & ennui. But habit and a love of being alone have fortified me against any such sentiments, which if I have ever felt them, have approached me rather in the moments of society than of solitude. Society & travel must to be useful, be very delicately composed. The lessons & the experience of an old & a judicious man will be doubly [effective], because practically unprepared, on the mind of a young & willing companion, and such a man is always desirable. With females you can never see the whole of anything. The courtesies of society distract attention, & tho' many objects are seen more agreeably when seen with females, yet all are seen less profoundly & perhaps less usefully. But the most useless & unprofitable of all society in travelling is that with persons of your own age & standing in point of improvement. Rarely [do] such persons ever agree because they have rarely the same objects mutually interesting. They therefore spoil each other. They form a society between themselves which saves at once the trouble & the great advantage of cultivating that of the country where you travel. I have therefore always found the tone of my mind relax the most when accident threw me into the society of my young countrymen. I say, my countrymen, for difference of country operates like difference of age, there being in almost every nation a stream of knowledge peculiar to itself; & that of different nations & languages, forms a better society than countrymen.

I was not therefore to be deterred from my intention by the idea of being alone. I was activated also by another motive. I had just seen Italy. No man can be indifferent to the light of these objects which have commanded the admiration of the world, & surely Italy combines almost every possible inducement that can interest. Yet Italy has been so often seen that the sight becomes less interesting from its frequency. A traveller looks on nothing which has not already been looked at by a hundred thousand before him, which has not been measured & criticized by men whose only pursuit in life was to illustrate them. At the sight of these things, do you wish to enquire to look for yourself? You labor; put down your measures & your heights & your criticisms, & then find that all you have said has been anticipated by some cicerone, some venerable antiquary who has grown up on the spot, & occupied himself with these things from his cradle. The holy waters of antiquity are indeed refreshing, but all that we can now taste has been so sifted & so often tasted that the palate is discontented. The walks of curiosity are so crowded that one is elbowed out of his road by the herd of brother pilgrims all hastening to drink at the same fountain. It may perhaps also be an unsocial principle, but knowledge is doubly valuable when it is exclusive. All that we do know is indeed so small that we must be contented sometimes to build our reputation on the ignorance of our neighbor. A man of 1000 pounds a year is richer in America than in England, and a learned chemist in Russia much wiser than he would be in Paris; for knowledge like wealth is all comparative. When therefore we find out something of which others are ignorant, we are proud not so much on account of the intrinsic merit of the discovery but because we alone are acquainted with it. A man therefore will gain more by a voyage in Greece because that voyage is less frequently undertaken than that of England or Italy. The reasoning may be fallacious but it is at least consolatory.

I was fortunate enough, whilst thinking on my future plans to make the acquaintance of a Venetian gentleman who was about to embark in the vessel which had already been pointed out to me.[4] It required little time to make me intimate with a man of worth & of letters, and we therefore embarked from Naples on Friday the 28th of March 1806 on board of the polacre brig[5] *Themistocles* belonging to Zante[6] & commanded by Demetrius.

My friend Major Barnes of Virginia,[7] consul of the U. S. for Sicily, & another American or rather Englishman (for education is much more decisive than birth) named Semple accompanied us. The crew of the vessel were all Greek. There were also some passengers for Sicily where we proposed stopping on our way to Zante. We sailed from the bay of Naples about 4 o'clock on the afternoon on Friday. As we left the bay we had time to admire it as one of the most elegant of the world. A large amphitheatre [is] covered with little towns which glitter on the coast, crowned by the Vesuvius whose dark & threatening sides contrast agreeably with the surrounding verdure, bordered in part by a populous city defended by the two castles called Castello Nuovo & Castello d'Ovo, with the majestic castle of St Elmo which seems to hang over it from the clouds; these are some of those beauties which have rendered Naples so much admired. Towards the sea the island of Capraea ridgy & unequal breaks the uniformity generally so unfriendly to sea views. The weather which had been fair at starting became in the course of the night very rough, & the next morning Saturday 29 we found ourselves in the bay & under the port of Baiae with the wind

4. As Biddle later tells us, the man's name was Savy.
5. A three-masted Mediterranean merchant vessel carrying a square sail on the mainmast and lateen sails on the fore- and mizenmasts.
6. Anc. and mod. Zakynthos.
7. Joseph Barnes, U.S. consul at Palermo, 1802–6.

against us. Disappointed as we were, we determined not to lament our being windbound in a spot which had once received the pious Aeneas. We therefore descended went ashore & amused ourselves in walking along the hilly country around the Elysian fields which still bear that name.[8] Nothing can be more rich than the soil of that neighborhood. The manner of cultivation is also beautiful & I can readily imagine how enchanting must have been that spot. Over the grain which grows abundantly, hang the grapes which are attached to the elm or the poplar & lead from one to the other forming a festoon over all the surface of the ground. Yet the Elysian fields are now very small, & tho' covered with the marks of tombs & niches would not have been able to contain many inhabitants. We also went along the shore to examine & admire the temples I think of Venus Mercury & Apollo & the immense ruins which are seen on the borders of the shore.[9]

Another day Sunday 30 was also occupied by looking at the Piscina Mirabile (the great reservoir to supply the fleet of Misenum)[10] the prisons of Nero,[11] & afterwards dining on the lake Fusaro at a charming spot, a house in the middle of the lake appropriated to the King[12] who had the exclusive right of fishing here. The banished king has left all these enjoyments to the French generals. After dinner we visited again the baths of Nero after which we returned on board. How much little events effect the heart! I was sensible of the force of it on seeing on the shore an American seaman who having been shipwrecked near Leghorn had been induced by want to go on board of a French privateer. In spite of his unfavorable situation, there was something interesting in the appearance of the young man who knowing that I was a countryman came to tell me his history. His name was Morrison; he had been apprenticed to Mr Emerick a baker at Philadelphia and

8. The Phlegraean Fields is the name of the volcanic region between Naples and Cumae. Its character suggested both the horrors of the Tartarus, or underworld, where the souls of the damned were forced to abide after death, and the beauty of the Elysian Fields, which in Vergil's *Aeneid* (Book 6) is the underworld land where the souls of the blessed dead reside. Biddle seems to be confusing the literary landscape of the Elysian Fields with the actual landscape over which he walked, and which had been the resort of wealthy Romans, who, like Cicero, built their villas here. But this area did not, and does not, bear the name of the Elysian Fields.

9. These so-called temples were part of a whole bathing complex, an imperial palatium from the first centuries A.D. that comprises the present Scavi de Baia.

10. The reservoir and the aqueduct that supplied it were built in the time of Augustus (end of the first century B.C.) to provide water for the Roman fleet of the western Mediterranean, which was based on the harbor of Misenum.

11. These so-called prisons were actually an imperial bath.

12. Ferdinand IV, Bourbon King of Naples from 1759 to 1825.

might have been a clerk to a Mr Moses Levy. But his family had all been sailors and it was impossible for him to resist his [father's] wishes. He had some education and felt strongly his disgraceful situation from which he hoped soon to escape, as his time had nearly expired. My good wishes and my advice were received thankfully and given cheerfully, and with the hope that he may profit by them. The necessitarian doctrine (tho' I think it dangerous to society) has still many seductions. On principle I think it utterly indefensible. I reasoned lately with one of its supporters who insisted that altho' between different objects I had the liberty of balancing, yet that after a decision from the preponderance of motives, it was impossible that I should have decided otherwise, and that therefore our liberty of choice was only imaginary & all our acts were necessary. My reply, and I think it unanswerable, is, that all metaphysics is false unless it can bear the test of feeling. It must at last, in spite of ingenuity of refinement, be reduced to this. Now I have always felt within myself a consciousness that my choice was perfectly free. I naturally consulted in making my decisions, the strongest reasons, that is to say the strongest motives; but my choice was not the less arbitrary. Feeling therefore, or knowing, that I had this freedom of choice, I did not consult nor believe a philosophy which comes from the clouds to apprise me that the dictates of my nature are all erroneous; that altho' I & all mankind may be conscious of such liberty, yet we may rest persuaded that it is all an illusion, & that from the cradle to the grave, a concatenation of events (for such is their language) carries us through a series of actions which we can neither choose nor control. I will not dispute any man's pretensions to superior gifts from nature, but I will certainly, tho' I hope not necessarily, disbelieve them; & when I am told of the deceptions of my nature, I must first see that of my informer before I submit to his authority. The rays of intelligence from above are perhaps apportioned to the walk of life which they are destined to enlighten, but I shall never throw away my little lantern in hopes of superior sight from another's lamp until I can see its brilliance. As we advance in life we become every day more skeptical. I shall perhaps one day take my stand in the work shops of the chemists, & putting every human opinion in my crucible, let the dross and the smoke escape, & believe only what I see at the bottom. I think too that I shall always reject this doctrine of necessity, which tho' it takes from us our regrets for what it is impossible to avoid, yet by taking from men their power to decide destroys the distinction between vice and goodness, makes all penal laws unjust, & would pour upon society a flood of licentiousness and disorder. But to return to what I mentioned, the history of the world often gives it countenance. The young sailor whom I had seen was established with his wife and property and family at home, and might have flourished. But he was obliged to leave them. And I too! Have I not a family who loves me and whom I adore with the softest and tenderest affections? Have I not friends whose society would console and instruct me? Have I not prospects the most brilliant that my country could offer to ambition? Yet I wonder. Who would have thought this year since that this day should find me where I am; that eighteen months since when my only prospects were those of completing the routine of my profession, pleading the defenseless cases of vice and misfortune, & then dying like a mushroom on the soil which had seen me grow, that I should now be bending my devious course among foreign nations & lighting my lamp at the fires of distant people, without a relation to guide, a friend to console, or sometimes even an acquaintance to speak to me. I will not say that destiny has brought me thus far; or that destiny still impels me forward. Before us all is uncertain, behind us all perplexed & mysterious. But let me not say that I wander. My footsteps are indeed unsteady, & my path sometimes weary & irregular; yet my eye is fixed undazzled & undiverted from the polar star which must conduct me to safety. In the promiscuous intercourse with man, the mind is always strengthened, the heart is often ameliorated. Our first study should be ourselves. We come, says the Poet, into the world only to look about us & to die.[13] The wider the horizon of our view, the more we have seen of man, the more have we snatched from the night of darkness which is soon to envelop. Every good citizen owes himself to his country & his family, & I feel that at every step of my path, I become a better citizen. The more I have seen of nations the stronger has become my attachment to the institutions of that country which bears in its bosom the sacred principles of freedom, where all my hopes & my ambition tend. The more I have learned the condition of men the more have I blessed that family in which my early weakness was protected by maternal tenderness, where my mind was bent to the purest sources by the soft hand of a father's affection & a brother's love & where, placed in a station which protects me from the degrading distinctions which fetter the social systems of other nations, I have been equally exempted from the power of want, and the alluring treacherous smile of luxury. On these tender objects imagination has often thrown her softest ray where solitude & distance have mellowed its shade. They are still the

13. Alexander Pope, *Essay on Man* (1733–34), Epistle I, 4.

objects dearest to my heart. Let me go on then. Let me soothe my heart with the prospect, that when my range[14] of man is finished, I shall go home to the bosom of my family, & by an ardent devotion to my country & the tenderest filial affection atone for a long & cruel separation & for many an error into which everything but my heart has betrayed me.

The next day Monday 31 we amused ourselves with a walk on the celebrated Monte Nuovo the strange appearance of which in 1538 has been the wonder of naturalists. The scholar will be less pleased with its barren sides, the cultivated verdure at the bottom of the crater, & that delicious view from its summit, than with the sad idea that it has covered the country house of Cicero, that seat of lettered repose, the resort of learning and leisure which almost personified philosophy herself. Descending the mountain we went over to Puzzoli to dinner. Our Captain however sent after us to let us know that we should sail immediately because the wind was now fair. We contented ourselves for the spoiling of our idea with the hopes of getting under way. We might indeed have done so almost every [hour] since our stay at Baiae. The Greeks I am well informed, are good sailors, but very poor navigators. They rarely leave the Mediterranean; they go along from land to land; if they lose sight of their landmarks they are deranged in their voyage; they wait until the wind is directly in their favor, put into port whenever it ceases to be so, & in short have neither the skill nor the intrepidity of Englishmen or Americans. Their navigation resembles I should suppose that of the ancient Greeks. We weighed anchor with a favorable wind & night brought us the continuation of it. I had made myself intimate on board with a Greek priest who had been smuggled away from Naples. With him I began some lessons in his language. As I hope soon to know more of it than I do at present, I will only mention its similarity to the ancient language & the shocking pronunciation of it in our modern school masters. To Greeks our mode of pronouncing is unintelligible. I did a very foolish thing. Religious prejudices should rarely be contradicted, & never except with the hope of correction. With my priest I discoursed today on a variety of subjects & among others, on his religious [beliefs]. With regard to the necessity of fasts & mortifications I stated my doubts with tolerable skepticism, but when he grew warm, declared to have a piece of the true cross which would resist the flame, & secure him from ten thousand bullets, & above all when he related a miracle worked by a Patriarch of Constantinople who in an instant lighted with a touch of his

14. An obsolete use of the word, meaning "examination."

beard a room full of lamps which Satan had extinguished, I could not resist a loud & strong expression of my incredulity. I perceived he never will forgive me. I take from it a lesson for the future. Whatever may be our sentiments of religions we should avoid expression of them except to those who are liberal enough to pardon or to profit by them. The night brought us a continuation of good wind, & we passed in the course of the next day April 1st Tuesday the island of Stromboli and saw at a distance all the Lipari isles. This island of Stromboli is a natural curiosity. It raises itself from the midst of the sea in a conical form, & almost continually pours forth a stream of lava. On the sides which were presented to us we distinguished the courses of the several eruptions some of which came nearly to the borders of the sea. Such a desolate picture would scarcely offer to society many allurements; but man with his usual disregard of danger or his usual folly has not diverted Stromboli, but along aside of the lava, & as it were in the midst of desolation, has built his habitations & planted his vineyards whose appearance whilst it gratifies the eye, afflicts the heart of a spectator. In the course of the afternoon we were visited by a British frigate. I was fortunate enough to induce the officer not to come on board for had he done so, we should have suffered a quarantine of 14 days at Messina, for such is the ridiculous law of quarantine; a law which demands much correction, as do indeed most all of the existing quarantine laws. Late in the evening we reached Messina; and the next morning Wednesday April 2d after waiting a long while at the health office were permitted to go ashore. Before we were at liberty we were however conducted to the Governor who sees all passengers before anyone else. Mr. Barnes happening to be well acquainted with him, we were detained but a little while, and after finding lodgings &c sat down with the idea of occupying the few moments of our stay in seeing what was curious at Messina. Alas! Alas! We must not now be told of the weakness of man or his feeble insight into futurity. Fifteen anxious days of discontent of ennui & of oeconomy were not spent, but melted at Messina. When I growled at the dreadful idea of 5 days detention at Nice and lamented the sad delay of a Genoese felucca, I did not anticipate that I should one day linger in Sicily while reposing a confidence in the honor of a Grecian. But who could suppose that a descendant of Socrates could have been treacherous. Our man of Zante landed us at Messina with a declaration that he could not possibly remain there longer than four days. Believing him and unwilling to lose our passage we declined going to see Etna and Syracuse, two objects which we were very anxious to have visited. Four days however passed. They still remained and we believed the *"dopo domani"* the day after tomorrow which was the constant point of departure, would at last arrive. But unfortunately the holy week came on and no office would then be open for business; afterwards came the Greek fast days, and then if ten thousand offices had been open the Grecian would not have started. It all passed, & we hoped that as the wind was fair, we might at length be in motion. We laid our provisions, & went aboard on the 9th day after our arrival, having received a message that we would sail in an hour. Arrived on board some excuse was made to detain us a day & the next morning a proposition being made to the Captain for a cargo, he changed the whole plan of his voyage & we were obliged to leave him. The very day after I had taken my things from on board, by some strange caprice he weighed anchor suddenly and taking my Venetian friend Savy with him set sail without me and Semple.[15]

During all this time we were losing our money & our patience at Messina. It is a handsome place, situated at the bottom of a long ridge of hills, with a noble port, wide deep & secure & able to contain a 74 gun ship at 50 yards from shore. It was surrounded by a rampart, has a strong citadel & is defended by forts planted on the adjacent heights. The town itself is small, but the foreign troops now here[16] give it some appearance of gaiety or at least noise. It is just resuming its wealth after the famous earthquake which did it so much injury.[17] The most striking effect of it which is now seen, are the ruins of the palace which extending for half a mile along the marine or street fronting the port, three stories high and of a handsome architecture must have been once a beautiful building. But it was overthrown by the earthquake. It is now a melancholy mass of ruins. The fear of another similar disaster has made the inhabitants build their houses of only two stories which has a very pleasing effect & is conformed, if I do not mistake, to the ancient mode. The town consists principally of two long

15. Who was capricious, Biddle or the captain? As actually written, the sentence says, "The very day after I had taken my things from on board by some strange caprice, he weighed anchor." But I suspect that Biddle meant to say that it was the captain who weighed anchor because of some sudden caprice. Bates in 1919 suggested that Biddle had made himself unpopular by his tactless behavior with the Greek priest, and that therefore the captain was looking for a way of getting him off the ship. Unless Biddle is hiding something, the text does not seem to support this reading of the situation. Did the new cargo oblige the captain to change his destination?

16. British troops were holding the island against the advance of Napoleon's armies in Calabria. The Bourbon court of Ferdinand IV had evacuated Naples in January and was under British protection in Palermo.

17. The earthquake of 1783.

streets which cut each other nearly at right angles. The suburbs without the city are extensive & chiefly formed of little one story cabins, built for the moment, at the time of the earthquake & afterwards abandoned.

It is however a dismal place. The people are wretched, the streets crowded with beggars who are more numerous and more unfortunate than in any place I have ever been not even excepting Naples. I never had an idea of human misery until I saw Messina. The last state of wretchedness, the most degraded kind of humanity is to be found here. Man is really very little superior to a brute, & I have often examined whether these wretches who meet my eye at every moment have really anything in common with Newton or Rousseau. The sad & piercing exclamation of *"moru di fame,"* (I die of hunger)[18] assails a stranger at every avenue, whilst he in vain averts his eye from some miserable being tottering under infirmity, covered with rags, eaten up by vermin or almost expiring with disease. These sights steel the heart. Tho' I have never seen so much misery, I have rarely given so little in charity. What indeed can I do? I cannot extinguish and therefore will not whet the flame. I can do so little against the calamity that I content myself with doing nothing. But why is not the government which tolerates, which feeds & which almost encourages such a system, swept from the earth as unworthy to occupy its surface? The host of priests who eat up the profits of the land, & intercept from want the alms of the munificent is a great cause of the evil. The souls of purgatory, to be redeemed by mercenary psalms, a sturdy Capucin, & some nun who instead of adding to the number of her country's defenders, occupies herself with beads & ceremonies & prayers, these are the objects of bounty because they attack the meanest through the strongest of our feelings our credulity. And even at this moment of impending ruin instead of assisting the unfortunate, or boldly preparing to save their country, the wealth of Messina is idly lavished in ridiculous ceremonies of religion, in pretty curtains which hung from the windows dazzle his royal eyes, in pretty fireworks to amuse Majesty, & stupendous skyrockets to demonstrate Sicilian intrepidity with gunpowder. Government is in all things like man. He begins with his rattles, which follow him to reason & maturity and which he resumes when age and weakness announce his approaching ruin.

The commerce of Messina is greater than that of any port in Sicily. Its situation makes it central & gives it an easy access to the produce of Ca-

18. Standard Italian would be *muoio*. Biddle wrote "mori," which I have corrected to show the real Sicilian dialect form.

labria. The articles of its trade are olives, fruits, grains, silk, sulphur &c & the ports with which it has most intercourse are those of the Levant, the ports of France (Marseilles particularly) & Leghorn. To this last chiefly its produce goes & waits there in deposit; it formerly went to Naples also. There is very little direct trade with Sicily from America. We have three consuls there one at Palermo, at Syracuse, & at Messina.[19] The people of Sicily have a character of cunning & wit. They laugh at the Neapolitans as we do at the Irish, & with much more reason, the Neapolitans being dull in comparison with them. They make all of their Buffoons & Polchinellas come from Naples. They are a good deal oppressed & taxed. They do not like their government, but are devoted to the English. The soil is very rich and well cultivated in spite of the mountainous nature of the country.

I have never tried to understand the formalities of the Catholic church. Had I admired them I should have been gratified by seeing those which passed during my stay at Messina which happened to include the Holy week. But I looked at a quantity of processions & forgot what I did not wish to see. What struck me most was a ceremony of which I saw only the preparation. A machine was erected in one of the streets & was to be hauled about in procession thro' them. It consisted of a quantity of circles like hoops in a conical form, and at different parts of the hoops were wigs & heads for angels. The hoops diminished constantly to the top which was more than 50 feet high. Here was to be seated a strapping boy clothed in magnificent robes & representing no less than the Deity himself. On his right hand was a girl equally well dressed & personifying either the Virgin Mary or the Holy Ghost. Beneath the two were placed on the hoops & joined to the figures of the angels a quantity of little children. All these lashed well to the machine were to be dragged about on a sort of wooden scaffold drawn by men. The poor creatures suspended at such a height must have been dreadfully alarmed, & I should not have been surprised to see the whole family in tears at their dangerous position. And this religious mockery was to supercede all business.

There are many convents for women & for men. I went to see two of the former with Mr Barnes, who happened to know a young lady in one of them. She was a very handsome well behaved sensible girl, the sister of the

19. The records of the U.S. State Department show that there were three consuls in the Kingdom of Naples: Barnes at Palermo; Frederick Degan at Naples (1805–9?); and John Broadbent at Messina (1805–27?). The last two were local residents, possibly British subjects. Abraham Gibbs, probably another British subject, was consul at Palermo (1805–16?). What was the relationship of Barnes and Gibbs?

Marquis of Palermo. His name is Thomasso di Palermo. She sighed, she candidly confessed, after her freedom, but until somebody came to marry & relieve her she was obliged to be contented. As I could not rescue her in that way I could only pity her. Are these monasteries injurious? Strictly speaking nothing which secludes man from society from his duties should be tolerated. But I am not sure whether in the present state of Italian manners, these institutions be not of some utility. The whole estate of the family goes to feed the pride & the luxury of the eldest son. The daughters retire into convents. Had they remained out, the looseness of manners & their wants might probably carry them to prostitution. These monasteries, beside, give retreat & protection to age & infirmity, tired of a world in which they can no longer gratify their passions, & in which their departed friends have left them without hope or enjoyment. Whilst therefore the present manners exist, I would leave them as the retreats of female virtue. But I would drive from their haunts of unbridled licentiousness & hypocritical corruption the vile & hateful race of monks & friars & banishing them from a retirement of which they have not learnt the value, send them to some useful labors. I would strip from the Capuchin his beard & his sack, & make him atone for his mendacity by some trade which would restore to society what he had begged from it. I hope that all these things are not distant. Society has at the close of the last century received a great & glorious movement which promises to become general.

The Messines are an illiterate race. I looked in vain thro' all their bookstores for some books of which they scarcely knew the names. Even the most celebrated works of Italian literature are wanting. The language of the people is worse than that of Naples. At least I understand it with less facility. It is a brutal harsh dialect always accompanied by a cant which defies a stranger.

At Messina I saw for the first time a body of English troops. They are the finest looking men I have ever seen. They are indeed too fine, the men being so nice in their dress & the officers so handsome & without a beard, that they are rather to be looked than shot at.

Here too I had the pleasure of seeing Ferdinand the King of Naples. I saw him with some degree of satisfaction and of regret, of satisfaction because as I love to see man under every phase, the King who had just lost half his empire was an interesting object of speculation; of regret, partly for his meanness & partly from his misfortunes. It is indeed hard to condone any man on account of incapacity for a situation into which fortune alone had placed him. But if the King of Naples is to be judged by the ordinary standard, he is really incapable & unworthy of reigning. Nature had placed in him the blood of his father, accompanied it by the same indolence, the same weakness, the same love of hunting which were the most striking traits of the character of the late King of Spain.[20] He had received an understanding which his friends declare was not originally barren, but uncultivated by education & unweeded by controul, it soon became as useless to his countrymen as unprofitable to himself. He soon left to his wife[21] the care of governing his empire, of which he felt too strongly the burden. When he came from Palermo, he did not appear either in the marshal style which announced a resolution to retrieve his misfortunes, or in the modest unobtrusive manner which should have painted his feelings for them. I had stood in expectation at the door or rather at the window of the British Vice Consul to wait his arrival from 12 until nearly 5 o'clock. My uncourtly appetite gave me many hints against royalty, but I bore them patiently until the arrival of his Majesty. I at last saw him, not like the angel of the Revelations a man upon a white horse, but a white man upon a bay horse. At the head of a few shabby troops, not quite rabble nor yet soldiers he forced his way with difficulty thro' the crowd who formed around him with the most servile humility.

He is an old man whose physionomy certainly never destined [him] for the throne. A large nose, in some sort a characteristic feature of his family, is his most striking trait. His face is vacant, but foolish & good, & no man who sees it doubts of the propriety of his title King of the Lazzaroni.[22] His eldest son, indeed his only one, possesses the character of his royal parent. Yet his talents have not taken so liberal a direction. His only distinction is that of being a good cheesemaker, a reputation acquired by thirty years ripening & by the sacrifice of all the more noble titles to honor. The daughter is the wife of the Emperor of Germany. The queen of Naples is acknowledged by her enemies to have been an amiable & pleasing woman. But these qualities, to which may be added the doubtful virtue of liberality to her dependents, could not screen her from the native failings of a woman. She was capricious arbitrary & tyrannical. Her former prime minister was a Frenchman, the actual one an Irishman General Acton a sensible man.

The govt has been particularly favorable to America. Genl Acton told Mr Barnes whilst I was at Messina that altho' the American govt had never

20. The Bourbon Charles III (r. 1734–59).
21. The Hapsburg princess Maria Carolina, sister of Marie Antoinette of France.
22. This term indicates the poor people of Naples, with whom the king liked to identify himself.

been officially made known to their court since its independence, yet they had overstepped this breach of etiquette & were willing at any moment to receive from America any public agent qualified to make commercial arrangements. These I believe might be made to great advantage, & Commodore Rogers[23] afterwards mentioned to me that the court of Naples has behaved to the Navy better than any other of the Mediterranean, & he concurred in thinking that an embassy there might be made very serviceable. But at present the country is in a state of too much uncertainty.[24]

The only excursion beyond the suburbs of the city was on the top of the mountains which surround it when I saw distinctly the bay & town of Milazzo[25] on the opposite side. Here too the famous rock of Scylla may be seen to advantage. It is a high perpendicular rock at the foot of the mountain from which it is detached by a channel of water. It is washed by the sea & there is a tower on the top of it. The famous Charybdis is no longer to be seen unless you pitch upon any particular meeting of currents to be that celebrated whirlpool. The distance from Calabria to Sicily is about 5 or 6 miles, & it may be crossed in less than 3 quarters of an hour. There is always a current which meeting the sea produces a difficult & sometimes a dangerous navigation. I should imagine that one of these eddies formed by the current was the frightful Charybdis.

I do not know whether the lessening of the danger anciently apprehended is owing to the improvements of navigation or to a separation (still wider) of the island from the continent. It is still a difficult passage & vessels usually take a pilot.

My time in Messina had been occupied in reading Cicero,[26] getting from Savy knowledge of Italian, walking about & seeing sights fireworks processions &c.

---

23. After training in the merchant marine and service in the naval war against France, John Rodgers (1773–1838) was in the Mediterranean from the fall of 1802 until the summer of 1806 under Commodores Morris and Barron; and he then commanded the squadron on his own while peace was being made with the Barbary state of Tripoli, with which the United States had gone to war in 1801.

24. This is one of several passages in the journals that indicate Biddle wrote at least parts of his account retrospectively.

25. I have corrected Biddle's "Malaza." By "the opposite side" he did not mean Calabria eastward across the Strait of Messina. He was looking northwest to the Tyrrhenian coast of Sicily, where on a clear day Milazzo is visible from the heights above Messina. This town and harbor, ancient Mylai, was the site of the first Roman naval victory over the Carthaginians in 260 B.C.

26. He bought a copy of Cicero's *Orationum Selectarum Liber Unicus* (Patavii, 1715), which he autographed at Messina on April 6, 1806, and which is still in the library at Andalusia.

My dear Tom

I have a long account to render to you. Let me begin by observing that man soon becomes accommodated to his situation. By repining at my long delay at Messina I exhausted my ill humor & as my confinement increased I became each day less sensible of the burden of it. I however was at last delivered not by miracle or sword, but by a Spirenaro.[27] The vessel in which I came from Naples having sailed & carried with it my friend Savy my only resource was to go over to Malta. Accordingly on Thursday the 17 of April 1806 I got on board of one of the boats which trade between Malta & Sicily. These are very small of about eleven tons & 9 or 10 [yards?] long, with one mast forward assisted occasionally by a mizen. On the foremast they put two sails on each side & afterwards one on the top of a triangular form which seems to hover like a hawk over the rest. Aft there is a little canopy for passengers. The boat is very low in the water, the deck being always under the the level of the water; I say deck tho' strictly speaking there is none. On each side are little holes resembling portholes which let in the water into a sort of long trough & afterwards let it out again; so that when a heavy sea comes the water rushing in the bark in some degree yields to it [&] prevents too heavy a shock. They are said to be remarkably good boats. Instances of their being lost are very rare! As we left the harbor & got into the straight which separates Calabria from the island the views became extremely interesting. The strait is about 5 or 6 miles wide. On the Sicilian side it is bounded by the hills which overlook Messina, & the left offers the Calabrian shore which is richer than that of Sicily & covered even to the tops of their highest hills with luxuriant verdure & diversified by the towns on the coast. A passenger declared that the entrance of the Dardanelles resembled it exactly & I remember that the same sentiment was expressed by Major Weer.

The weather continuing good we made our way with the boat; & in the afternoon passed Catania at the foot of Aetna. We had already seen the mountain on turning one of the points which enclose Messina but the view of it after passing Catania is much more beautiful. It is indeed a noble mountain. Nothing can be more gradual than its graceful rise from the sea

27. Speronara is the standard Italian spelling for this small coastal sailing vessel once found in the waters off Sicily and Calabria, so named from an extended prow inherited from the beak or ram of the ancient warship. Certain aspects of Biddles's description of this low open boat, which could also be propelled by oars and which was used for small commerce, dispatches, and passengers, are puzzling. By "portholes" he must mean scuppers. Lateen-rigged, the speronara seems to have been a variant on the common tartana.

gradually up to a single point. In this respect it is much superior to Vesuvius whose neighboring summit The Somma shares the admiration. The
top is covered with snow & at the present season is inaccessible (I may add)
except to Americans; for Commodore Rogers has just gone to the summit
across the ice, at some risk & to the no small astonishment of the Sicilians.
On passing Catania I had to renew my regret at not visiting that place, as I
knew of a large collection of curiosities which one of its inhabitants, a
Prince, possesses. We continued our course & reached in the evening the
port of Syracuse. I was of course anxious to go on shore, & had prevailed on
the Captain to wait until next day at noon. In the course of the night
however, he changed his opinion, & at daybreak (Friday April 18) declared
it impossible to wait, & therefore sailed. I was obliged to content myself
with a sight of the port which is perhaps the fairest in the Mediterranean.
The entrance is narrow, the bay capacious & secure, situated to the south
west of the town. We sailed on until about noon when we went in to Cape
Passaro,[28] the sailors wishing to observe the weather before venturing across
the channel. We therefore went ashore to a small place called Terra Mobile[29]
where we found but few conveniences of life, the town being inhabited
chiefly by fishermen. We endeavored to amuse ourselves with walking &
seeing if any thing curious was to be found. In the evening, we returned on
board the boat & slept.

The next morning Saturday April 19, finding the wind too strong for
sailing, after a sufficient portion of grumbling, Mr. Semple & myself
walked along shore, & having procured hammers we discovered a number
of marine petrifactions incrusted in the hard stone intermingled with lava.
The greater part were plants of which we found some beautiful specimens
in high preservation, which we were careless enough to forget on leaving
the island. This part of Sicily must I judge be very interesting. We got at
least an appetite by our labors & slept in the town on a good bed; but so
preoccupied that a host of gentry alarmed at our intrusion treated us as
invaders.

Another day Sunday April 20th was to be lingered out at Terra Mobile. I
was occupied by bathing, by walking, by eating, by reading & speech
making (my usual remedy against misfortunes of this sort). I succeeded
until night. I could not but smile at an odd remark made by a sort of
merchant or shop keeper with whom I talked on the subject of religion & of

28. Capo Pássero, anc. Pakhynos, southeastern tip of Sicily.
29. Presumably the mod. Porto Palo.

America. He wished to know when the stipulations would be finished so that we might begin to build 74s[30] for he had understood that England in ratifying our independence had bound us not to build ships of war till after a certain term of years. Such are the strange ideas which the people of this country entertain of Americans.

The Monday morning April 21st we left Cape Passaro & went across the channel. The passage was made in 9 hours, the wind being good, tho' passages are often made in a shorter time. About four o'clock in the afternoon we reached the island of Malta.

Malta April 30. 1806.

My dear Tom

My last informed you of my having reached this place. The detail of my motions since will be the subject of this letter. As soon as we entered the harbor & had been boarded by the boat of the health officer, we were conducted before the board of health & then permitted to go where we chose. The first place was naturally an hotel which was that of Smith, a Scotsman. We dined, & feeling myself fatigued, in order to relieve myself I went to the theatre. The acting was miserably bad tho' as the house is handsome, & as this is the only Opera & an Italian one better might be expected. During the play, some of the officers of our navy came in & sat immediately behind me. Among others I thought I recognized the face of an old neighbor T. Brown.[31] As we were rising to leave the theatre, one of the officers after seeing my buttons asked politely if I were of the navy of the U. S. I answered no—of the army.[32] I then asked about our squadron particularly if there was any chance of finding our dear James.[33] I was much disappointed on finding that he was not here. On returning to the tavern, I

30. Ships of seventy-four guns.
31. Thomas Brown (midshipman 1801, lieutenant 1807, master commander 1815, captain 1825, died 1828).
32. Before Biddle departed for France, Governor Bloomfield of New Jersey had made him a colonel in the state militia—with the right of designing his own uniform! Biddle was also a brevet captain in the U.S. Artillery on the strength of a family relationship with General James Wilkinson.
33. Nicholas's brother James (1783–1848), who was to have a distinguished career in the U.S. navy (lieutenant 1807, master commandant 1813, captain 1815), was aboard the frigate *Philadelphia* as a midshipman when it was captured at Tripoli on October 31, 1803. The crew was held for nineteen months before being ransomed and returning to the U.S. by way of Malta.

found Hunt[34] whom they roused from his sleep & who finding who it was got up, & made me go with him on board of his vessel, a bombard. We there slept, or rather chatted the greater part of the night.

The next morning Tuesday April 22d after breakfast Mr Hunt & myself waited on the Commodore of the squadron.[35] He received me with a great deal of plain politeness & invited me to a dinner given by him today to his officers. We then came on shore, & I called on Govr Ball with my letter from Major Barnes. I found him just going out to ride, & remained but a little while with him. He asked me if I were a relation of the gentleman who was here some time since. I mentioned my being his brother, & said the gratitude which myself & all the family felt for his attentions to him. He seemed much gratified by these sentiments. He invited me to dinner the day following. At 4 o'clock I went on board of the *Constitution* to dine. I found there besides the Consul Pulis[36] & Dr Cutbush,[37] the officers of all the gunboats &c. Hunt, Smith,[38] Izard,[39] Laurence,[40] Crane,[41] Sinclair,[42] & several other gentlemen.[43] The dinner was agreeable & I found the Commodore next to whom I was seated a pleasant & polite man. The dinner was not protracted unnecessarily. When we rose I went with Mr Smith & Dr Cutbush to see the gunboats. The people of this country are astonished to hear that such little vessels have ventured across the Atlantic & yet the

---

34. Theodore Hunt, a lieutenant aboard the *Philadelphia* when it was captured in 1803 and commander of one of Rodgers's bomb ships, resigned from the navy as a master commandant in 1811. For unknown reasons he left the sea, and he died in St. Louis in 1831.

35. John Rodgers.

36. Joseph Pulis, U. S. consul at Valetta (1805?–15?), was not a U.S. citizen and apparently did not even speak English. An odd choice for a consul, he apparently hindered communication between Preble and Bainbridge by hoarding the mail. Since he had formerly been consul for the bashaw of Tripoli, perhaps his loyalties were divided.

37. Edward Cutbush (surgeon 1799, resigned 1829).

38. The reference is probably to midshipman (acting lieutenant) William Peters Smith, a native of Philadelphia and nephew of Judge Richard Peters. He resigned from the navy in 1809.

39. Acting lieutenant Ralph Izard, Jr., of Charleston, South Carolina (midshipman 1799, lieutenant 1807, resigned 1810).

40. Acting lieutenant James Lawrence (midshipman 1798, lieutenant 1807, master commandant 1810). As captain in 1813 of the frigate *Chesapeake* in its fight against the British frigate *Shannon*, Lawrence, mortally wounded, uttered the famous cry, "Don't give up the ship!"

41. William M. Crane (midshipman 1799, lieutenant 1807, master commandant 1813, captain 1814, died 1846).

42. Acting lieutenant Arthur Sinclair (lieutenant 1807, master commandant 1812, captain 1813, died 1831).

43. Presumably this list of names includes only some of the officers of the sixteen gunboats in Rodgers's squadron. I have punctuated the lines as Biddle wrote them.

young commanders of them declare that they are as safe as 74s. As you have probably seen them I will mention only that the double bowsprit & the turning cannon are improvements highly valuable. Their construction is much admired & being of about 70 tons burden & carrying 40 men they are much superior to all other gunboats. In the evening I returned and went to the theatre.

The next morning Wednesday April 23 was employed in walking about the city of Malta & seeing what was curious. The object most striking is its position. Religiously built upon a rock & between two arms of the sea both capable of containing vessels it is almost impregnable on the sea side. It is on the land side equally strong, the fortifications being very ruinous. It is regularly built; that is there are three or four long streets which run the whole length of the town and are the principal ones inhabited. The ascent from the wharves to the high part of the town is very fatiguing as you are obliged constantly to mount by steps. The houses are in general hand-somely built and of a particular whitish stone easy to be worked but after-wards hardening, & the whole has the appearance of great neatness. The principal part of the town is separated from the rest by the large port which is subdivided into two or three arms. The port is very secure. The entrance is however very difficult with certain winds. The houses in which reside the Governor & the General are very handsome. The church of St John[44] is not at all remarkable on the outside, but within it is richly decorated. I think there is a profusion of ornaments, some of them not very judicious. What is most admired in sculpture is the baptism of Christ by John.[45] I do not know who is the author, nor do I care for I really do not think the piece fine. The decollation of John by Rubens[46] is handsome, but in a bad light. The chamber in which the Grand Masters were placed during the year after their death is small & dreary & will probably contain no more Grand Masters. The botanical garden a little out of town is a fine collection of plants which shows the goodness of the climate, for the tropical & northern plants grow within 50 yards of each other by giving them northern & southern exposures. It has been made by the present govt.

44. Until 1798 the conventual church of the order of the Knights of St. John of Jerusalem, the building was erected between 1573 and 1577; and most of the Grand Masters of the Order are buried there.

45. In the apse of the sanctuary is the colossal marble group the *Baptism of Christ* by Giuseppe Mazzuoli (1644–1725).

46. The painter was actually Caravaggio. Biddle may be confusing this painting with the late seventeenth-century tapestries that adorn the walls of the nave and are based on paintings by Rubens and Poussin.

Having seen the town, talked of Tripoli [Fig. 2], bought some things &c, the time came for going to dinner. I therefore went to the govrs where I found Commodore Rogers, Dr Cutbush, Mr Blodget[17] & Misters Higgins & Dyson, the first our navy agent here, the second at Syracuse.[18] A number of officers soon arrived & we sat down to dinner with a large company. I sat between Captain Pierce of the British navy & Mr Dyson. The talk was about France & altogether table talk tho' not so wise as Selden's.[19] After dinner (which was accompanied by music from a band in an adjoining room) other company arrived & began to play cards. During this time Commodore Rogers and myself retired into a corner and afterwards walked, holding high discourse on naval matters.[50] After a good deal of talk he spoke of Preble,[51] & had just said I do not hesitate to say that Preble is no officer—I do assert it,[52] when Sir Alexander Ball called me on one side to introduce me to Dr Sewall the Judge of the Admiralty here. With him I walked & discoursed for a long time on a variety of subjects. He is a good man & a sensible one too. I am to dine with him on Sunday. I then after having left him talked with Sir Alexander until the hour of going. I went home and found Hunt who brought an invitation from Izard to dinner tomorrow, & with whom I slept on board of his bombard. In the morning Thursday April 24 I was occupied in looking out for a passage to Greece & some little matters.

47. Samuel G. Blodget, drowned, a lieutenant, in 1812.

48. The merchant William Higgins was appointed by Preble in 1804 to look after American interests on Malta. In this way Consul Pulis, whom Preble could not remove from his post, could be neutralized.

George Dyson was, as Biddle says, the American naval agent at Syracuse. In November 1803, Preble decided to establish a base here for stores and for a hospital rather than continue to rely on Gibraltar or Malta not only because he wanted to be closer to Tripoli but because he preferred to be less dependent on the British and to make it more difficult for his seamen to desert to British ships: he needed a harbor that the British did not dominate.

49. The English jurist John Selden (1584–1654) is best known for his *Table Talk* (1689).

50. Such close talk between Rodgers the commodore and Biddle the tourist is not so strange as it may appear. Rodgers himself was only thirty-three at the time, and most of his officers were in their twenties.

51. Edward Preble (1761–1807) commanded the third naval squadron sent against Tripoli in 1803. Before his arrival in Syracuse, the frigate *Philadelphia* had been captured at Tripoli with its captain, William Bainbridge, and the entire crew. Preble first assaulted Tripoli in August 1804. He was superseded by Samuel Barron, who accomplished little. Barron, however, brought Tobias Lear (see note 61) as consul general to settle affairs with the Barbary states.

52. I hope that my interpretation of this sentence accords with Biddle's meaning. He actually wrote, ". . . and had just said I do not hesitate to say that Preble is no officer I do assert it, whenever Sir Alexander Ball called me." Rodgers, that is, says and asserts that Preble is no officer.

Among other things I saw a Mr Noble a merchant here, to whom I had a letter of introduction. He was very intimate with Lord Nelson[53] on board of whose ship he once remained 7 weeks. He was also his agent. He speaks of him in very high terms. He has a number of letters from him. Among the rest some begun by Nelson, continued by Lady Hamilton[54] & finished by Nelson. One began by expressions of the friendship Nelson felt for Mr Noble. "So you do, my dear lord," continues a female hand (that of L. H.), "and so do I too." After some time the parenthesis closes with "Now go on, my lord," & Nelson finishes. He gave me a little note of Nelson's closing some letters from Gibbs at Palermo. I have sent on this little curiosity to our dear brother James & you will therefore see it. Any remains of a great man are sacred. A love for relicks is the most pardonable side of superstition, for the mind finds a relief at the most trifling monuments of things which were dear to us & which are lost forever. Mr Noble adores the late Lord Nelson. He says that Nelson often used at Palermo to make him disguise his handwriting, sometimes make him dress himself like a servant and send or carry money hidden in a basket to persons in distress. Sometimes even people who dined at his own table used to be supplied in that way for Nelson said he knew they must be in want and would not ask. No one except Noble himself used to know of these charities. His acquaintance with Lady Hamilton was he thinks perfectly innocent. He loved her more than he did any other woman but his love was quite Platonic for he thinks that in a long intimacy & after living with them both seven weeks on board a ship he should have discovered if it were otherwise.

He was not fond of gambling, detested cards, on board of his ship never permitted them except for the sake of gratifying Lady Hamilton. Noble has been on board when she & the royal family of Naples were there. When they played pharo the stake [was] limited to half a dollar. Nelson however lost a great deal of money or rather Lady H lost it for him, for she used to hold the cards whilst he was on the sopha. Nelson was very attentive to commerce [&] used to say that he claimed no [benefit?] from protecting it for without the navy [it] would fall & he shewed me one of his letters to that effect & even with those expressions nearly.

His wife received him very well at first & even went with him & Lady H to the theatre, but her friends or rather N's enemies made her oblige him to give up either her or Lady H. His pension to her was very handsome.

53. Horatio Nelson (1758–1805), the victor of Trafalgar.
54. Emma Hamilton (1761?–1815), wife of Sir William Hamilton, diplomat and archaeologist, who was British envoy to the court of Naples from 1764 to 1800. Nelson's famous liaison with Lady Hamilton, whatever form it took, began as early as 1793.

He was a very great man, particularly in cases of difficulty when he rose superior to them.

I heard Sir A. Ball mention that altho' Nelson understood French very well he would not hazard himself in it as beneath his dignity to speak imperfectly a language.

You see my dear Tom I send all these little anecdotes of this great man. I went to dinner on board of gunboat No 2 with Mr Izard. We were Hunt, Laurence, another gentleman, whose name I do not know, & Mr Blake 1st lieutenant of the *Constitution.*[55] He is the most gentlemanly American officer I have seen in point of manners. He was formed at Paris where he lived with Mr R. Ca[d?]man. The talk was of a variety of things. In the evening I returned to my house where I remained.

The next day Friday April 25 having changed my lodgings I started from my lodgings to see our Consul, but meeting Hunt who mentioned his being absent, H & myself went to see the library. This is a collection of about 30,000 volumes, begun I think in 1760 & gradually augmented by donations. They never buy, so that they are behind hand for the new books. It is open from 9 to 12 & from 2 to 4. There is however another garrison library. Besides the books there is a little statue of Hercules about the antiquity of which there are many doubts. I will not decide, but judge it modern & besides I never admire a little Hercules. The god of strength should always I think have a size corresponding with our ideas of force. A long stuffed snake, a little baby of a mummy, an inscription found here which has served to fill up two vacant places in the Phenician alphabet, some vases, a mammoth's tooth sent from America by Dr Barton,[56] & one or two handsome editions complete the circle of curiosities. Having gone round it I took up a book & Hunt went off. He returned however soon after, & brought with him Commodore Rogers & Captain Hull.[57] I again visited the curiosities with these gentlemen, & after we had finished Commodore Rogers asked me to go & take a ride with him. I agreed & we went to Higgins's. You my dear Tom who remember my want of horsemanship will imagine my ideas at the sight of a fine horse which I was to mount.

55. Joshua Blake (lieutenant 1800, resigned 1809).
56. Dr. Benjamin Smith Barton (1766–1815), Philadelphia physician and naturalist, much interested in herbal remedies.
57. In the war against Tripoli, Isaac Hull (1773–1843) served in Preble's squadron in 1804 and cooperated with William Eaton's assault on Derne in 1805. Promoted from master commandant to captain in April 1806, he commanded the frigate *Constitution* in 1812, when it captured the British ship *Guerrière.* He died in service in 1843. Masters commandant were really junior captains and were always addressed as captain.

Much as I dislike equitation, there was no declining. We rode out about a circuit of 8 miles. During this ride he spoke with great frankness on all the concerns of the navy. Of Commodore Truxtun[58] his opinion is very high indeed; he knows his eccentricities but is equally sensible to his good qualities. He says he used often, in going down to tell him the occurrences of his watch, to find him asleep with his arms akimbo in his usual story telling position. But he separates his pride from his talents & declares that altho' he should be perhaps the greatest sufferer by it, yet he would be very glad if T would enter the navy tomorrow. He says that T has a great many enemies among the elder officers of the navy, but that it all arises from jealousy & is shameful disgraceful animosity. He thinks Robinson who served under T, who was very well treated by him, & who afterwards took occasion to say all that was bad of him, an ungrateful & worthless officer & he would break [him] if ever he could, should fortune place R under his command.[59] He resumed the subject of Preble's conduct of which he spoke strongly. He thinks P has many good qualities but he has treated him shabbily. When he came into the Mediterranean he hoisted a broad pennant (the sign of a Commodore) before he had seen Rogers whom he was to supercede. R might have punished him for it, but the service requiring accord among the officers he submitted, tho' giving P to understand that they must come to an explanation when they meet.[60] He has understood that P. blames the treaty with Tripoli. Rogers himself laments that a treaty was made at the moment because it deprived him of a glorious chance (the best he ever had) of distinguishing himself; for his force was adequate to destroy Tripoli & his plan laid. But Lear[61] having made the treaty, he did

58. A privateer in the American Revolution, Thomas Truxtun (1755–1822) became a captain in the new U. S. navy in 1794, served in the naval war with France in 1798–1800, and was to command the second squadron against Tripoli. But the actions of the Jefferson administration caused his withdrawal and retirement. He was later influential in the politics of Philadelphia.

59. Thomas Robinson, Jr. (midshipman 1798, lieutenant 1799, master commandant 1804, resigned 1809).

60. Rodgers was already serving in the second Mediterranean squadron, commanded by Richard Morris. When Morris, because of his dilatory conduct, was relieved of duty and ordered home, Rodgers took over the squadron as acting commodore until Preble could arrive. At this time commodore was not an official rank but only a title of courtesy used to designate the officer commanding a squadron. When Preble entered the Mediterranean in September 1803, Rodgers actually had seniority over Preble, though he was his junior in age. Rodgers waived his rank and agreed to serve under Preble since Preble had been appointed to the command and Rodgers had been ordered home.

61. Tobias Lear (1762–1816), an intimate of George Washington and his personal secre-

not think it his duty towards the prisoners to decline sanctioning it. He thinks a treaty might have been made without any money paid.

Of Eaton's[62] conduct he disapproves highly—thinks his debt a private one & that he laid a trap to ensnare Morris.[63] Morris he thinks has been ill used. He told him so & that if he would conduct himself like a man, he (Rogers) would not only speak but fight for him. Morris however declined doing so, & R would not be of the C. Martial.

He then spoke of his own enemies whom he knew were numerous. He had been unfortunate in that respect. When he became Commodore all the officers except one or two disliked him, but he had done always what he thought best without party or affection. I took occasion to compliment him on the unanimous good wishes of all his officers which he possesses in the highest degree, & mentioned my own surprise at it for I had always a different idea of him from what I now have.

---

tary from 1790 to 1799, was appointed by Jefferson consul general at Algiers (1803–12) with the authority to adjust affairs with all the Barbary states. Between 1803 and 1805 he made treaties with Morocco, Algiers, and Tunis; and finally, after Preble's repeated attacks on Tripoli in the autumn of 1804, he concluded peace with Tripoli in June 1805. This last treaty provided for the ransoming of the crew of the frigate *Philadelphia* for $60,000, a controversial issue. Rodgers had taken full command of the squadron from Preble's successor, Samuel Barron, in May 1805.

62. William Eaton (1764–1811), U. S. consul at Tunis from 1796 to 1803, with the approval of Jefferson and the grudging acquiescence of Commodore Barron (1804–5), had concocted a filibustering expedition to establish Hamet Karamanli as the legitimate ruler of Tripoli in place of Hamet's younger brother Yusuf, who had usurped the place of bashaw. Setting out from Egypt, his expedition marched westward across Libya and, in the face of overwhelming odds, captured the eatern Tripolitanian border town of Derne in April 1805. The successful capture of this town was widely hailed as a brilliant military feat and was a strategic success since, partly because of it, Lear was able to convince Bashaw Yusuf to conclude a treaty of peace. Barron and Lear, however, between them hoped to frustrate the expedition by keeping it short of men, money, and supplies. Eaton therefore spent his own resources and on his return laid the bill before Congress, which ultimately paid part of it.

But it does not seem as if this is the conduct of which Rodgers disapproves here. It is more likely that he is condemning Eaton's earlier dealings as consul at Tunis. While there, Eaton had excoriated Commodore Morris's dilatory prosecution of the war against Tripoli; and he finally annoyed the bey of Tunis so much that the bey insisted on his departure. Morris appointed George Davis as acting chargé d'affaires. Eaton had also spent his own resources on the conduct of his diplomatic business, and he therefore expected to be reimbursed by the State Department. In February 1803, Morris had actually been arrested in Tunis because of what he thought was Eaton's financial ineptness in dealing with the bey. Thus there was bad blood between Eaton and Morris.

63. Richard V. Morris (1768–1815) was given command of the naval squadron in the Mediterranean in place of Truxton in 1802–3. Though authorized to superintend all negotiation with the Barbary states, their continued hostility and his own lack of success resulted in his recall and a court of inquiry, which condemned his conduct. He published a vindication of his conduct and then retired into private life.

Nicholson of Boston is, he thinks a poor devil.[64]

We then talked of the conduct of the British towards us. It had been very friendly, all the discerning men of their navy seeing how manifestly it was their interest to conciliate us. A part of their late conduct showed it also. Sometime since Collingwood[65] took from one of our boats at Gibraltar four British sailors. Laurence her commander behaved with a great deal of spirit, but could not obtain their restitution. Rogers issued orders that in future all such attempts should be resisted, & that when ever an officer came to complain to him, the only evidence he would admit of his having done his duty would be the loss of his nose & his ears. He had soon occasion to put his own doctrine in practice. Three of his seamen, Englishmen by nation, deserted & went on board of a British ship. They were claimed & refused to be given up as being British subjects. They soon after sent to demand of Rogers some seamen who deserted from their ships. The one could not be given up without the other; Rogers wrote a strong & sensible letter, & declared to the Commanding British Officer that unless his men were given up he should consider the insult as personal & desired to meet him at a place designated. The men were immediately given up & an arrangement made by which deserters are to be mutually surrendered, & even Englishmen shipped in America even if they have previously been deserters from the English service, and all American impressed seamen are [to be] given up. Americans entering voluntarily are not demanded from the British. These terms are certainly very favorable, such as I am persuaded we could not have obtained from negociation, so much better is firmness than argument.[66]

General Villette who commands the troops here is not liked particularly by the Americans. He treated Rogers shabbily. He called & left his card twice at Gen. Villette's who never returned his call. R will not speak to him now.

64. This is probably a reference to Samuel Nicholson (1743–1811), senior officer in the American navy from 1803 to the time of his death. His main achievement seems to have been supervising construction of the frigate *Constitution* in Boston harbor from 1794 to 1798.

65. Admiral of the British fleet in the Mediterranean. This event had taken place on June 12, 1805. Lieutenant Lawrence, in command of Gunboat #6, was forced off Cadiz to surrender three sailors.

66. The problem of impressment, one of the causes of the War of 1812, was a complicated issue because seamen signed aboard a ship regardless of its nationality. Thus there were apt to be large numbers of foreign seamen aboard any merchant ship or warship in this period. There were Americans on board Nelson's *Victory* at Trafalgar, and perhaps as many as a third of the *Philadelphia*'s captured crew were in fact British. The Americans had no proper system of naturalization, and the British in any event refused to admit that an English citizen could change his citizenship. This situation was bound to cause ill will on both sides.

Whilst speaking in this open familiar frank way, we reached town, & as I had occasion to see our Consul, the Commodore walked with me to see him. Afterwards being nearer his ship than my home, he invited me to go & eat a family dinner with him. I did so. Before dinner he shewed me from his letter book several letters on the subject of his dispute with the British on account of his seamen, & spoke of almost all his officers. Blake he said had more talents for his profession than any man he knew. He liked Hunt on account of his honesty, asked about his father & property. Izard had very excellent talents for an officer. Bainbridge he said must have something to say to Preble who in his dispatches speaks of the frigate's having surrendered without the loss of a solitary man.[67] Cutbush is a good physician. [I?] asked what sort of a man was my old college acquaintance Dr McCallister.[68] He received a letter from R. Jones[69] which he shewed me, & spoke of him as a young man of merit family a nice sense of right & wrong [of] spirit of honor & said other things highly flattering. Lear was a plain good man & he & the Commodore always agreed in their opinions on the several matters. We talked about Mr Fenwick,[70] whom he believed to be irreproachable, & of Madame Tallien,[71] Beau Dawson[72] &c.

67. William Bainbridge (1774–1833) commanded the frigate *Philadelphia* when it was captured in Tripoli harbor on October 31, 1803. Already having reached the rank of captain because of his exploits in the quasi-war with France, Bainbridge was sent to the Mediterranean, first with Richard Dale and then with Edward Preble. Though he and his crew were captured, his efforts were partly responsible for the peace treaty of 1805. He later had a distinguished career in the navy, fighting in the War of 1812 and undertaking diplomatic missions in the Mediterranean.

In a letter to the Secretary of the Navy in December 1803, Preble had seemingly censured Bainbridge's conduct by saying that the *Philadelphia* had been captured "without a man on either side having been killed or wounded." Rodgers seems to echo the tone of Preble's letter. Though Bainbridge was formally absolved of any dereliction of duty in the loss of the frigate, there were many who looked on his character with some suspicion.

68. Surgeon's mate Dr. Thomas Gates McAllister, of Fort Hunter, Pennsylvania, son of Archibald McAllister, cruised the Mediterranean in *John Adams*, *Constitution*, and *Enterprise* from early 1805 to July 1807. Worn out and desperately ill from his voyage, he died at home in January 1809.

69. Richard R. Jones of Pennsylvania (midshipman 1802, resigned 1808). Jones was later U.S. consul at Tripoli (1812–19) and consul general at Alexandria (1852–53).

70. John R. Fenwick, adjutant (first lieutenant in the Marine Corps from 1801, captain from 1809, resigned in 1811).

71. Thérésa Tallien (1773–1835), wife of the French revolutionary Jean-Lambert Tallien, who helped to overthrow Robespierre, kept a salon and a stable of lovers. After divorcing Tallien, she married again in 1805.

72. John Dawson of Virginia (1762–1814), called "Beau" because of his dress and manners, was originally opposed to the adoption of the Federal Constitution but served in Congress from 1797 to 1814 and was an ally of Jefferson.

After dinner [I] returned home & occupied myself with books &c; R. Jones came to see me & remained at the house all night.

The next morning Saturday April 26 I occupied myself in different ways amongst the rest by a visit to Govr Ball with whom I had a long conversation, who gave me a book, the history of the revolution of Venice, & who asked me to go with him today to see his garden at St Antonio.

I omitted to mention that yesterday, after our ride Commodore Rogers & myself visited the Armory, one of the principal curiosities of Malta. It is a large collection consisting of about 16,000 stand of arms, partly French, partly English. The French musquet is longer by about 3 inches than the English; the calibre also is different, & one of Villette's aides mentioned that the French he thought better than theirs; the English bayonet is longer than the French, so that with fixed bayonets there is little difference in the length. There is some old armour, & some cannon, amongst the rest a leather cannon, that is a brass tube cased with leather, some Turkish muskets & swords & pistols, a most enormous head piece which must have served for some giant, a number of ancient swords. The cut & thrust is the best sword; it is the ordinance sword of G. Britain. We also saw the Arabian horses here. When an Arabian mare has a daughter, says R, a feast is made as we would at the birth of a child, & the animal is branded on the neck & under the tail. Very difficult to procure Arabian horses since the French & English were in Egypt. (He mentioned at the same time a story of a Mameluke servant who had orders not to sell is horse. An Englishman asked him how much he would take for the horse. The Mameluke told him to put down money until he told him to stop. The other began & increased the sum until the Mamelouk fearful that such an amazing sum should destroy his fidelity finally burst into tears & and galloped away as fast as he could.)

To return, at two o'clock I went to dine with the officers of the *Constitution* at Blake's invitation. There were a number of officers both of this & of the other ships. There was much gaiety but very little drinking, for I believe (what indeed Rogers mentioned) that our officers are much more temperate than the British. They are very clever sensible men.

At four I left them & went to the governor's into whose carriage I got with Lady Ball & Mr & Mrs Lang. The ride is of about an hour. The country is intersected by large stone walls which tho' necessary to preserve the soil have an ugly appearance. The soil appears in general gravely. And yet by cultivation it yields corn & clover both excellent. The subsistence of Malta is provided for by the Levant from which they bring 40 quarterns of corn annually & other grain proportionally. Malta is calculated to yield about a fifth of its consumption says Commodore Rogers. From Sicily it has not latterly derived much supply. St Antonio is the country residence of the Govr. His garden is very handsomely arranged & abounds in good fruits. Among other things is the blood orange peculiar to this country & resembling blood in color. I do not however think it so good as some of the other kinds. After having walked over the garden & house we got in & drove to town to the Palace where I remained to tea. The talk was about France & indeed a variety of things.

The laws of Malta have been unaltered by the British, so that the Maltese enjoy the security of the British flag without any inconvenience, particularly as all the civil offices are in their hands, there being not more than four or 6 British civil officers in the island. The only objection made to their law was in the case of torture to extort confession. They had an example some time since of this when the Maltese council of the govt recommended their administering it, but he refused, & suggested the plan of making one King's evidence. It succeeded for they discovered the criminal, three men being accused of murder.

An odd law of Malta is that when a stranger marries a Maltese woman he must leave the island, as they feared to overstock it.

In Malta they have the same prejudices as in Italy that when a person dies of the consumption not only all the furniture of the house is to be burnt but the walls scraped.

In the evening I remained at home.

The next day Sunday April 27 was occupied in the first place by going to the chapel at the Governors with Mr Blodget & R. Jones. I there heard for the first time since I left America the English service read & an English sermon. There is a wonderfully attractive decency in our religion, something very different from the prostrated meanness of Catholicism. The Protestants ask favors of God with a decent but submissive firmness. A Catholic upon his knees & striking his bosom is unworthy from his meanness of the very blessings he solicits. The sermon was from a good rosy Irishlooking young man who taking his text from Job gave a comfortable dissertation on the greatness of the Almighty & the duty of prayers, one of those sermons which neither alarms the confidence nor improves the understanding, which is heard & forgotten. The rest of the day I occupied by writing letters home & at five o'clock went by invitation to Dr Sewalls. The company consisted of Mr & Mrs Sewall Mr & Mrs Hilliard Commodore Rogers & Captn Hull[73] of our navy and Captn Stewart of the British. The talk was

___

73. After "Captn Hull" I have excised the words "& Lieut[t?] Hull]." Aside from Isaac

altogether of the table kind. In the evening arrived some other company. Whilst they discoursed, Commmodore Rogers & myself retired into a corner where we talked politics &c. We supped & as the Commodore expected to go tomorrow he asked me to go on board & breakfast with him before he went off. Accordingly Monday morning April 28 at 8 I went on board & breakfasted. The talk was various; he brought out a quantity of curiosities which he had collected from all sides. After breakfast I took my leave of him, & occupied myself by preparing for my voyage & writing my letters.

Early on Tuesday April 29th I went on board of Hunt's vessel to deliver him my letters & bid him farewell. He went, but as the ship in which I was to go did not sail I went on board of the *Constitution* to take my leave of some of my acquaintances. Just as I arrived the Commodore happening to come on deck saw me & invited me below. I went & found there Mr & Mrs Hilliard who are going to Gibraltar in the ship & Mrs H's father. We there remained for a considerable time during which Commodore Rogers got out his letter box and we looked over a deal of correspondence on the Barbary business.[74] From all that I see the Commodore has acted with great spirit and firmness. It seems that during the blockade of Tripoli he took one or two Tunisian vessels going into that place. The Bey had demanded restitution and it was denied. Fearful of difficulty Rogers determined to go over there and arrange it. The Bey, being apprised by Davis[75] of Roger's coming declared that if he did he should declare war immediately, and Davis himself was so well persuaded of the truth of the declaration that he came off in a boat to meet Rogers and advise him to retire. Rogers would not but went to Tunis and wrote the Bey that having heard of his declaration he gave him 36 hours to make up his mind on the business. The Bey was in a furious passion & in his speech to Davis he expressed sentiments of pride and dignity worthy of a greater pasha worthy of a greater prince. The Tunisians distinguished themselves (or the descendants of the Carthagin-

Hull, there was no other Hull in the Mediterranean squadron. Either Biddle meant to write "Captn Hull & Lieut [*some other name it is not now possible to conjecture*]" and, by a slip of the pen, repeated "Hull" instead, or he is referring to marine second lieutenant Edward Hall, who resigned as a captain in 1809.

74. It is very odd that Biddle says not a word about Rodgers's dealings with Commodore Samuel Barron, who, because of illness, had to turn over command of the squadron to Rodgers. Rodgers's own ambition was frustrated by Barron's dilatory conduct of the war against Tripoli and by Lear's apparent domination of Barron. Despite what Biddle says about Rodgers's agreement with Lear "in their opinions on the several matters," there is evidence that Rodgers disapproved of much of the diplomacy that ended in the treaty of peace.

75. George Davis, American chargé d'affaires at Tunis. Rodgers was at Tunis in late July and early August 1805.

ians) from all the other Barbary powers to whom the Bey in his speech affects great superiority. He reminds us of our having nearly solicited the interposition of Algiers and of our having offered ten thousand dollars tribute to him, facts with which I was unacquainted. Threatening still to declare war, Rogers fired upon one or two of his vessels entering the port and made such a formidable appearance that the affrighted Bey sent out to beseech him in god's name to stop and to let him send an ambassador to America. Which he did. Davis it seems had a very erroneous idea of the business for he told Rogers that if he came he pledged his honor there would be war in 24 hours. Rogers says he knows that people & even the government thinks him rash in the way he resolved that they should hear at once of his rashness and his success, for if the Bey had declared war he says that he would in two weeks have taken his town made him ask Peace on his knees and defray the expenses of the quarrel, or else he would never have returned to America. One of the ambassador's objects is to solicit the recall of Rogers.[75a]

At twelve I left the ship and he invited me to dinner at three. On my return at that hour we dined with Mr & Mrs Hilliard her father and Mr Higgins. He was all this while trying to get under way but could not. We remained until 10 at night. Talking of seamen Rogers mentioned an instance of their generosity which occurred sometime since at Gibraltar Bay. One of our boats in which was a lieutenant was upset in consequence of carrying too much sail. The boatswain I think had told the lieutenant that they had too much sail but the other calling him a rascal declared that he would throw him overboard if he said a word. When they upset this man and another who could swim declared that they would not desert their officer who could not swim & in spite of his request to leave him & save themselves they would not but sank with him. In the same boat a sailor was swimming on an oar and seeing another sailor who was also swimming without one, he called out to him. Here, says he, I can't save myself; with this oar you perhaps can as you swim better than I do. He shoved him the oar & sank cooly forever.

I left Rogers (he desiring me to call & see him again should he not go tomorrow) & returned home in the rain. He also mentioned a case of one of his men who fell overboard & who was swimming after the ship without

75a. The very amusing story of the ambassador's visit to the U.S. is recounted by Louis B. Wright and Julia H. Macleod, "Mellimelli," *Virginia Quarterly Review* 20 (1944): 555–565.

saying a word when R happening to hear something ran on deck & had him picked up. Upon asking him why he had not sung out, he said he did not want to make a noise about it & R says he believed he would have drowned rather than call out for assistance. These stories were introduced in speaking of sailors being in general better than landsmen. I do not know how to decide. Their profession familiarizes them with danger & they fear it less than others but I do not know whether in the ordinary intercourse of life they are more honest. I much doubt it.

I was this day Wednesday April 30 1806 (see before) to have left Malta. The frigate sailed in the morning.[76] Our ship was also to have sailed but on my going down to the port I found that she had already set sail. I followed him out to sea in a boat, but finding that in spite of my signals he took no notice of my boat I was obliged to return with the loss of my passage. As soon as I got on shore I occupied myself in looking out for a second vessel, & found one about sailing for Zante on board of which I proposed to embark. I called in the course of the morning on the Govr, who sent me a quantity of seeds [&] invited me to dinner today. I went at 5 & found a large company. At table I sat between Major Waddell & Captain Schomberg a post captain an Irishman who commands the naval force at Malta. He is not more than 27 & is very polite & clever. The Irish are in general much more men of the world, more polite than Englishmen. A traveled Irishman is a very gentlemanly man.

There is a son he says of our Genl Burgoyne[77] here, an officer of artillery. In England interest may serve you in the navy until you get as high as post captain, after that all goes by rotation. In the evening came a quantity of people who played cards &c. I amused myself with talking to Captn Schomberg, Dr Sewall, an old French emigrant & Sir Alexander Ball. Sir Alexander speaks very highly of Mr King[78] whom he has seen even at the opposition tables in London, & who was at once firm in his conduct and much respected at the court. Dr Sewall mentions that the Admiralty court is composed of a single judge, one crown advocate one advocate for the

76. Rodgers left for Algiers and Gibraltar, where he turned over command of the squadron to Hugh George Campbell on May 29, 1806, and sailed home.
77. Biddle presumably refers to the British general famous in the American Revolution for being defeated. His son, Sir John Fox Burgoyne (1782–1871), was the eldest of four illegitimate children and served in the British army in the Mediterranean after 1800 in Sicily, Malta, and Egypt.
78. Rufus King (1755–1827), U.S. representative in London from 1796 to 1803, friend of Alexander Hamilton and unsuccessful Federalist candidate for vice-president (1804 and 1808) and president (1816).

people, [..?] proctors &c. I had seen the court in the morning & admired the gravity of the costumes, the judge & advocates having the long wig & gown which give additional force to all their arguments.

I must finish this letter by remarking on the politics of Malta. It cannot subsist alone and must therefore belong to the most maritime power. Her grainaries (which are subterranean & ample) contain I think about two years store. Her supplies are from the Levant & Sicily. The Grand Masters seemed to wish to make it dependent on foreign supplies that is on themselves as England does Newfoundland. The possession of Sicily by the French far from endangering Malta will render it more important & scarcely less tenable; altho' French cruisers may enter the trade, they cannot avail against a superior marine. Yet England will in that event be obliged to supply Malta from Africa or elsewhere—but with her navy, no matter where her supplies come from.

I close my darling brother this little journal which if it pleases you will reward me for the trouble it has given me. The hasty notes of a traveller will not bear nor do they incite criticism. You will therefore not exercise the talent which you possess but read kindly & believe I am your ever affectionate brother   N Biddle.

At sea May 5th 1806 Monday
afternoon.

The white hills of Zante, my dear brother are just appearing, & I must prepare for my long story by bringing up my history to the present moment.

The day May 1st (Thursday) following the date of my last was spent at the library in reading Spon & Wheler[79] & a work by a man of Marseilles named Guise on the manners of the Greeks a very interesting book which confines itself to the habits & customs of the modern Grecians which it treats with much judgement.[80] The afternoon was employed in a solitary walk upon the ramparts in which I thought only of you & our dear family. I began to feel alone after being in the bustle of acquaintances & visits. In the evening I enclosed the seeds sent me by the governor, with a note to our townsman Dr Barton. I was glad of any opportunity of shewing my

---

79. Jacob Spon, *Voyage d'Italie, de Grèce et du Levant fait aux années 1675 et 1676 par Jacob Spon et George Wheler*, 2 vols. (Amsterdam, 1679); and George Wheler, *A Journey into Greece* (London, 1682).

80. Pierre Augustin Guys, *Voyage Littéraire de la Grèce*, 2 vols. (Paris, 1771).

respect to so good a man. The packets I gave to Harridan one of our lieutenants commanding a gun boat.[81] I do not know whether he be not partial to his own service, but he declares that after having served in the English navy, fought the French & seen a good many actions he finds the Americans the greatest of them all. The next morning Friday May 2d I repaired early on board of our ship. The [ship] did not however sail & almost all day was lost on board. I have often remarked that sailors seem to know the value of time less than any other class of people. Two days [out of] a week is nothing to them. It is most provoking to a traveller whose time is his greatest treasure. To make it more so as we were about sailing, the custom house officer came on board & discovered some raw cotton which the Greek was smuggling, there being a duty on the exportation of unwrought coton in favor of the poor. The Greek said it belonged to the sailors who did not know the law. The officer said that he could not get the Governor's decision until Monday. Alarmed at this appearance of delay, I went to the Govr who was good enough to direct them to leave the goods & claim them on their return. This done, about 5 in the evening we left Malta with my stay in which I am much pleased owing to the particular attention received from Sir A. Ball, Dr Sewall & above all Commodore Rogers to whom I am very much indebted. Malta & Gozo form one government. The first contains 7999, the second 12829 inhabitants.[82] (Must read Bertol.)[83] They were given by Charles 5th to the Knights in 1530. Valetta built 1565 by G. Master of the same name. Taken by the French 1798. The same year the people revolted & shut the French up in the fortifications where they were blockaded by the people on the land side & the English by sea until the surrender in 1800, since when they possess it, tho' they stipulated to give it up by the Treaty of Amiens.[84] All that day & night we remained near Malta there being no wind but the day following Saturday May 3d we went on our course. My time was employed in reading Junius[85]

---

81. Nathaniel Haraden. Navy records show his promotion from sailing master to lieutenant in March 1807 and to master commandant in April 1816. He died in 1818.

82. Has Biddle reversed the figures?

83. This reference is a mystery.

84. By the treaty of 1802, which ended the war of the Second Coalition, the British promised to give up Malta, but kept it. After the word "Amiens" Biddle's text breaks off confusingly with the words "justified by." For some reason he does not explain, he seems to have thought the British retention of Malta justified.

85. In the London *Advertiser* from January 21, 1769, through January 21, 1772, appeared a series of letters bitterly critical of the British government and even of King George III.

Cicero & Anacharsis's travels of which I have an Italian translation,[86] & in taking some lessons of Greek from the seven island vice consulate at Malta who is a fellow passenger.[87] I find it easy & that my former studies will render its recovery very easy. We passed in the course of the morning a British convoy from Corfu[88] the only incident of today. The next [day] Sunday May 4th was passed in the same way. The weather pleasant, the wind fair but light. I occupied myself as yesterday; this morning Monday 5th brought us a continuation of the same weather & the same occupations. My Greeks tell me of a certain Rigas[89] a man of Thessaly, a scholar, & an author who had first lived in Vienna where he printed a paper which becoming gradually too French he was obliged to flee into Turkey where he wrote a poem to the Greeks, reminding them of their former glory & exhorting them to revolt & independence. It was ineffectual; he was taken & they say killed by the Turks or Germans. I have often enquired with a view to ascertain whether ancient monuments &c can recall a corrupt people to a sense of shame. It would seem that the govt of Ury[90] was right in their reply to the Abbe Raynal.[91] I think that the peasants of Switzer-

---

The authorship of these letters has never been definitely determined. For obvious reasons, they were quite popular in the revolutionary period of American history, and Biddle may have had a copy of the edition published in Philadelphia in 1795.

86. Jean-Jacques Barthélemy, *Voyage du Jeune Anacharsis en Grèce dans le Milieu du Quatrième Siècle avant l' 'Ere Vulgaire* (Paris, 1788). Biddle's Italian translation was probably *Viaggio d' Anacarsi*, 12 vols. (Venice, 1791–93), which I have not seen. He may not have carried these books back with him because he had already acquired the French version before leaving home. The seven volumes of the third edition (De Bure, Paris, 1790), with Biddle's autograph of June 1802, are still in the library at Andalusia. This remarkable production, now generally considered unreadable, was one of the most popular books of its time and was translated into many languages and went through many editions. It was almost obligatory reading for any young man on his way to Greece. A kind of picaresque novel, it is the record of an imaginary trip by a Scythian through late-classical Greece. He is supposed to be giving the reader a view of Greek life, including information on topography, politics, and customs. The frequent maps are a conflation of material from ancient sources and from the accounts of modern travelers.

87. The Septinsular Republic was formed in 1800 as a Turkish and Russian condominium from the former Venetian possessions in the Ionian Islands. Though theoretically free, it was garrisoned by the Russians.

88. Anc. and mod. Kerkyra.

89. Rigas Feraios (1757–98), a revolutionary poet executed by the Turks for urging a Balkan confederacy under the leadership of the Greeks.

90. William Tell, the legendary Swiss patriot whose deeds symbolized the struggle for freedom, is supposed to have come from the canton of Uri. Friedrich Schiller's play about Tell had just appeared in 1804.

91. Guillaume Thomas François Raynal (1713–96), French philosophe and historian. His

land felt & knew nothing about the monuments of Tell, that is they knew there was something curious because they saw strangers admired them, but the patriotic sentiment was lost. The Roman does not know that the soil which he dishonors was trodden by Brutus,[92] and this Greek reminded his countrymen of their former greatness in vain. During the last revolution,[93] some Roman (Ceracchi)[94] for instance harangued the people on these same subjects but unless a nation can meet an orator at least half way he will not excite them to great things. If the soil be not prepared, if words cannot take root—they are *ludibria ventis*.[95] Pain & common sense is a spark, but the tinder was all prepared. But we are approaching Zante & I therefore conclude with the customary but sincere assurance of my esteem   N B.

Zante Thursday May 8th. 1806

Soon after the date of my last we came in between the islands of Zante & Cephalonia and at night we go to the town of Zante [Fig. 3]. On my arrival that is to say the next morning, Tuesday May 6 I came ashore and waited on Mr Strani[96] for whom I had a letter. He is a very polite old gentleman & has procured me lodgings at a house kept by an Englishman (named Carlo a man who was once servant to J Adams at London & in Spain, and also to W Smith of New York). I also went to see the English

---

books, which popularized the ideas of the Enlightenment and were a form of democratic propaganda, were widely circulated in North America as well as in Europe before the French Revolution. In Biddle's Swiss journal for August 1806, Raynal appears again, this time as the builder of a monument to dead Swiss heroes at a chapel at Altdorf, where Tell is supposed to have shot the Austrian Gessner in 1307. What the government of Uri actually replied to Raynal I have been unable to discover.

92. Presumably Lucius Junius Brutus, traditional founder of the Roman republic in 509 B.C. Or does he mean Marcus Junius Brutus (85–42 B.C.), who joined the conspiracy to assassinate Julius Caesar in 44 B.C.? See page 112.

93. Biddle refers to the short-lived First Roman, or Jacobin, Republic, instituted in 1798 after the French army of Napoleon had invaded the Papal States and kidnapped pope Pius VI.

94. The peripatetic Roman sculptor Giuseppe Ceracchi (1751–1802), as famous in his own day as Canova, visited the United States from 1789 to 1792, where he made friends with such men as Washington and Hamilton. His bust of Washington in now in the possession of the Carolina Art Association/Gibbs Art Gallery. He returned to Europe in 1791–92, became a partisan of Napoleon, and was in Rome in 1798–99 at the time of the proclamation of the Republic. Later in Paris, accused of an attempt on the life of Napoleon, he was condemned to the guillotine.

95. "Playthings for the winds," a quotation from Vergil's *Aeneid*, 6.75.

96. Samuel Strani, brother of Nicholas Strani, British consul at Patras.

Consul. I then walked about to see & to learn. The map will apprise you of the position of this place which is on the eastern side of the island of the same name. The town is situated at the bottom of a range of hills which overhang the town, & which enclose it within a very narrow compass. It is long but not broad. The streets are small, their form circular, and there is no part of the town except the square of St Marc which is handsome [Fig. 4]. This square is however triangular, and the houses in the neighborhood of it are three storeys high and ornamented with a portico before them in the style of Bern. The rest of the houses are of two storeys only tho' they have the portico also. There is no port, all the vessels lying in the road before the town. It is this circumstance alone (their want of a port) which hinders Zante from becoming much more considerable. The town has few manufactures except one of cotton which being partly imported & partly native is here wrought & is sent out to Barbary in trousers &c. The commerce of this place was considerable with England and indeed almost all the southern parts of Europe. It consisted of an exportation of currants & oil. Their currants are famous. The growth is much more luxuriant than our currants & the fruit is indeed different. When preserved they are exquisite. The olives are another sort of fruit the staple of the island; a little corn & cotton and some wine the last of which is strong & tolerably good complete the list of their productions. All these are seen to great advantage in mounting the hill behind the city, where the whole plain which composes the island opens itself. This plain shut up by hills towards Cephalonia & spotted with villages & covered with the most luxuriant vegetation is one of the wettest islands which I have yet beheld. The soil does not seem to have been naturally good, but to be much improved by culture. The Zantiotes are indeed a very industrious people, an honest people & very much at their ease for labor is high, and the beggars are all foreigners. There is no other town of consequence on the island except this which contains 18,000 inhabitants. The island itself is about 30 miles in circumference and contains about 40,000. Zante is the principal island in point of riches of the republic of the seven islands. This republic was formed of a number of possessions which several nations desired and none could enjoy without injuring the others and therefore the only mode of settlement was for all to relinquish them. This government was formed in 1800, and I will give you from its own written constitution enough of its form for you to judge of its merit. (1st, It is aristocratic. 2nd, It is composed of all the islands inhabited & uninhabited on the coast of the Morea[97] & Albania and formerly

97. Anc. and mod. Peloponnesos.

belonging to Venice, the seven principal of which are Corfu Cefalonia Zante Santa Maura[98] Cerigo[99] Ithaca & Paxo. 3d, The Greek is the established religion but all are tolerated. 4th, A body of people in each island elects every two years a Legislative body of 40 & a senate of 17 members. The legislative body elects a President of the senate who is called Prince and has his office two years. The senate is the executive body. Each island is governed by a Regency consisting of a Pritano[100] or governor who must not be a native or resident of that island and he has a council of two regents men of the place. The Pritano is elected by the legislative body on the presentation of the nobles or Sincliti[101] of the island.

The judicial power is vested in a tribunal of the first instance in each island, four tribunals of appeal and one of cassation consisting of 7 judges chosen by the leg. body.

The criminal jurisdiction is in other hands & is divided into two branches correctional & criminal given to different tribunals.

Strangers are naturalized after ten years by signal service done to the state, the introduction of a useful even a mechanical art, by industrious or commercial establishment. They may also be naturalized after 5 years residence if they have large landed property, and any extraordinary skill in science or the arts; and by marriage with a seven islandress.

These are some of the provisions of their constitution. The very cursory look which I have been able to give of it lets me perceive that it partakes of the liberal spirit of the new political school but that like most of their work it is not sufficiently guarded against foreign encroachments. In fact it is declining. After the two first years, the senate without waiting for the nobles, reelected themselves & they say that the Principe[102] will soon alter either his name or his title. Indeed I look upon the whole as an hasty thing which will dissolve in its weakness or be overthrown when the govts of Europe have leisure enough to attend to other matters than their quarrels. The entire constitution which I hope one day to show you will enable you to judge of the new govt which has its capital at Corfu & which sends its ministers to Petersburg & Constantinople, & its consuls to many parts of the Mediterranean. Was there ever a govt in which jealousy did not find a place? Zante is jealous of Corfu which tho' larger & stronger has not say the Zantiotes so much riches so much substance. The gentlemen here I find

98. Anc. and mod. Leucadia, or Leukas.
99. Anc. and mod. Kythera.
100. This word is an Italianized version of the ancient Greek word *prytaneus*, or president.
101. Another Italianized Greek word.
102. That is, the Prince.

speak contemptuously of the govt. They think they have purchased sovereignty at much too great an expense. They have been forced & inflated into greatness which costs much more than it is worth. They now have 800 soldiers (Russians) in this city alone paid by Russia however. They laugh too at the constitution which is longer than their territory. It is a quarto. The people are fond of England because England is the first consumer. They are also not disinclined from the French who (says the B. consul) they like too much. The Russians are not liked. They are too hard too rough.

Of the usages of Zante little can be said, as their intercourse with Italy has imparted to them in some part the Italian character. Their dress is nearly that of Italy with the addition of the large trousers & mustachoes neither of which are used by the gentlemen. The women live very retired. The people do not much like to let you go into their families. A man may show you a great many civilities abroad, but he does not take you home to let you see his family. I for instance have seen a great deal of Mr Strani who has waited on me a number of times & with whom I have breakfasted twice & yet I have never seen his wife or any of his family. When they do out, it is always with a black mask which however they take off occasionally. I have seen some, but they were not handsome. They generally sit at the window whence thro' a blind or wicket they see unobserved what passes. The wife of my land lord is a very fair indeed quite handsome woman & may be considered as a specimen of the beauty of the island. Insular situation corrects the force of climate & these people are much whiter I think than the Italians.

But the B. Consul says they paint white & red. Is it possible that this habit supposed to be the offspring of the last stage of corruption, can have found its way here? On this subject I must mention to you two tombstones [Fig. 5] now here to be shipped for England which were found by Lord Aberdeen at Sparta & which will certainly be much talked of in London.[103] The coquetry of these ladies followed them to their tombs on which they placed a large square marble ornamented with all the instruments of the toilette engraved on them. This singular monument of vanity is very curious as it presents a strange detail. In the middle is the washbowl in relief (as are all the rest) at the bottom of which is the name of the lady. All the rest of the stone is covered with the *disiecta membra* of the toilette. A look-

---

103. These objects were not tombstones but dedicatory offerings either made by the priestesses Anthusa and Laogeta or made during their priesthood by attendants who cared for the dress or ornaments of a cult statue. Greek women frequently dedicated ornaments to some deity on a particular occasion.

ing glass, a shell (probably for paints), ear pick, slippers, combs exactly like our fine toothed combs, a purse, a number of boxes with the lids of which being opened shew the apartments as if for tooth powder &c, & a variety of things some of which I could not explain. I was struck by the resemblance of many of the articles to those of the present day. In particular the looking glass[104] which is like those now used & the purse also of modern adoption. The two stones are exactly alike except in size, the name of the lady, & some few of the articles but the plan is the same in both.

Zante cannot feed itself, does not grow 3 months provision [not bread?], [but] must belong to a maritime power. Zante is a mixture of all nations. There are even some descendants of old English families all of whom are now Greek priests a most sad schism from their Protestant sanctity.

There are some tar pits about ten miles from the town—very sulphurous said Mr Strani for I did not see them.[105]

Customs, & little ones too, keep their ground long after laws are forgotten. At a little village near the sea coast called Volimes[106] the people have the custom of putting a piece of money into the mouth of a dead man at his funeral. Being peculiar to that spot, or rather to some particular families there as it seems from the old custom of providing oneself with money enough to pay Charon's ferriage,[107] & as the only account these people can give is that it is the traditional custom, it is possible that some straggling settlement has formerly fixed itself there, and unknown to history. But it is singular and shows the tenacity of usages.

Tuesday as well as Wednesday & Thursday have been passed in waiting for a passage, in seeing the country and making some enquiries of which you see the fruit. I can only add that I believe our country might derive benefit by opening some channels of commerce, by making Mr Strani consul here (bye the bye the govt has declared that all consuls shall be foreigners, a law however originating in a quarrel with the Spanish consuls deputy and easily repealable) and by sending cargos of staves of [logs?] [& of] tobacco which is better liked than Levant *coffee* (W. India more agreeable than the Alexandria & Muscovada sugars). I don't know as to the *cotton*

104. A small drawing has been omitted.
105. The pitch springs (Herodotus 4.195) are located on the southwest promontory of the island.
106. Biddle wrote Volines.
107. In Greek mythology, Charon was the ferryman who conveyed the souls of the dead across the rivers of the underworld. To pay for the passage, the dead person was provided with a coin, which was put in his mouth.

tho' it might do. In return we might receive currants & oil from here (tho' their oil is not the best) & other Levant productions.

It would be worth an experiment. I start early tomorrow for the Morea and therefore put down my little quill & go to bed. Adieu my dear Tom

N Biddle

Zante May [8th] 1806
Thursday evening, 11 o'clock

In selling land the measure at Zante is by the bushel, that is as much ground as a bushel ought to be sown in. Something like Dido's cow skin.[108] [Rousseau leans?] upon tales.

Patras Sunday
May 11th 1806

My dear brother,

I have at last touched the holy soil of Greece. I retain the expression of the thousand sentiments which the name suggests & by continuing my notes will present you with the history of my arrival.

On Friday May 9th I left Zante in a small boat bound for the Morea. The passage which is 18 miles should generally be of about three hours to the most prominent point of that country. We however remained on the water nearly eight. As I approached the shore, I was eager to catch the manner in which Greece would first present itself. A long chain of irregular country, broken by bays, and diversified by mountains, whose tops are covered with snow, seen indistinctly from Zante gradually become more clearly discernable. A high hilly shore, for the most part barren, covered with shrubs with occasional spots of cultivation, enlivened by Castel Tornese (a fortress on a commanding eminence)[109] were the first objects which

108. Vergil's *Aeneid*, 1.365–368, alludes to the story in which Dido, arriving at the future site of Carthage, outwitted a local king. He offered her as much territory as she could cover with a cow skin. By cutting the skin into thin strips, she enclosed a substantial territory.
109. Built in 1220–23 by Geoffrey I de Villehardouin, Clermont, later named Klemoutsi from a neighboring village and then Castel Tornese, was the center of French power in the Morea after the Fourth Crusade and is still one of the finest examples of Frankish military

met the eye. The aspect was however barren and unpromising. We passed the little island of Caucalida (on which there is a single house) and arrived in the bay near which was Chiarenza the place of our destination. Presuming that this was a town I was surprised on a nearer approach to find that a custom house & two huts were all that represented the ancient city of Cyllene. As we got from the boat about a dozen Greeks & Turks sitting cross legged on the beach rose to receive us. For the first time I trod the ground of Greece. The letter I had brought for the custom house officer I found to be useless as he had been just superceded; however as the person with whom I came was acquainted with his successor I was under no embarrassment. We walked about forty yards to the custom house, a small building of which the upper story alone is inhabited all the lower part being only a wall. We went up a pair of stairs on the outside and passing over a drawbridge got into the little castle. It did indeed resemble one when upon going into the room we found a Turk in one corner upon a carpet, and smoking a pipe. His figure was not the most prepossessing. He was dressed in the stile of his country with a turban, jacket, and a sort of loose trousers, with a pair of red slippers. His long red mustachoes vied in fierceness with his pistols & dagger which he carried in his girdle. He was however in spite of his dress, a very good looking and a very excellent man. He received us with great kindness. There being no chairs he brought us a trunk as a substitute for one but wishing to please him I preferred his stile and for the first time I saw how superfluous an article a chair is. After some preliminary talk carried on by means of my servant, he asked if I would eat and immediately a sheep was sent for and killed for supper. Whilst it was preparing I went out to see the country & walked about a quarter of a mile to a little rising ground, which offered the remains of a Venetian fortress.[110] It was a beautiful situation. The sun was just going down. Around me was a melancholy picture of desolation. Over the ruins of the fortress where vegetation was contending against the fragments a groupe of cows & sheep were feeding. The shepherd leaning upon his staff stood wondering at

---

architecture. It later passed to the Byzantines, Turks, and Venetians; and it was finally ruined in the Greek War of Independence. The castle was sited on the promontory of Klemoutsi, the ancient Chelonatas, as a means of maintaining communication with the Adriatic and western Europe.

110. Anc. Kyllene, medieval Glarentza or Chiarenza, was the fortified harbor of the castle of Klemoutsi. Biddle seems to refer to the remains of a ruined castle at the harbor, one of the same date as the castle of Klemoutsi itself. Unfortunately he later bypassed, or passed without mentioning, Andravidha, French Andreville, the French capital of Achaia, the usual residence of the Frankish princes, for which Klemoutsi was the citadel.

the curiosity of this stranger. At a little distance the sea was calm, & the numerous islands which covered its surface gave it a beautiful variety. The eye rested upon Ithaca that little spot which is immortalized by the song of the first of poets & by the residence of the man who like myself was a wanderer. I now felt that I was in Greece. I felt that I was alone in a foreign country distant from all that was dear to me, surrounded by barbarians who yet occupied a soil interesting from its former virtues & its present ruin. I thought of my country my friends & of you. Unwilling to remain too long, I returned to the House. The Turk offered me a pipe, & seeing that he was a good fellow I sat down & smoked with him. I soon delighted him & before we left, he was my great friend, said that he was sorry to receive me so poorly as he did not expect company, but wished me to come again & spend a week with him when he would treat me better, & desired me to write to him to let him know of my safe arrival at Patras.[111] The supper soon came in, & we sat down to a round table of about *six* inches high. A soup a [bouillon?] & a roast were supplied at the expense of the sheep. My Turk eat the first with a wooden spoon & the second with his fingers. A cosmopolite would have been delighted with my accommodating temper. We sat & talked & smoked. He was quite a good hearted Mussulman. He had often treated the Zantiotes at his house but he complains that when he went to Zante no man either took him to his house (except Strani) nor said good morning to him. There was much of our Indian character about him. He was a pious man too. Just before dark as we were talking, he got up & having washed himself went to the window, & spreading on the floor his mantle, stood upon it & began his prayer. He sighed, & seemed moved, went upon his knees, then kissed the floor & repeated several times the same ceremony, then returned & resumed the conversation. As the night advanced I laid down on a bed along side of his & slept soundly till the morning.

Saturday May 10 we then rose, & having sent for horses, I bid farewell to the good Turk, kissed at him thro' the mustachoes, & left Chiarenza. This place after undergoing many revolutions was destroyed I think by the Venetians. Now the custom house is all that remains. We rode along the sea shore, following the circuit of the bay. At parting from Chiarenza the coast is barren covered with shrubbery. But we soon reached a rich cultivated country. Ancient Elis (the territory we now passed) was part of a large plain

111. The seven words of Greek on the last page of the diary, written in a hand other than Biddle's, must be the name and "address" of this Turk. See page 123.

which beginning at Patras extends all along the coast & is about one two or three miles wide in different parts. It is extremely rich & is in fact the best part of the Morea. Some parts lie waste, for want of inhabitants, but the greatest portion is beautifully cultivated. Large fields of rich grain without any enclosure are seen on every side.

In about two hours time we reached a little village called Le Kena[112] where we stopped to breakfast. It was a charming little place, each house being detached & scarcely distinguishable thro' the trees which were at once an ornament and a protection to it. On going into the house I looked around as usual for the books, & smiled on taking from the shelf a little dogeared dirty volume & finding it a Greek collection of Aesop's fables, Musaeus[113] & some other classic pieces. The learned pedantry of our Hellenists would have been very disconcerted at finding his boasted treasures thus degraded, & finding a ragged boy a better commentator than the disciplined pedagogues of Oxford. I had here strong temptation to go aside to ancient Elis about two hours inland from Kena, but it was growing late & I continued towards Patras. We passed thro' one or two villages or rather hamlets, all pretty & apparently comfortable. Chaminizza was the largest of them. There was here a wedding & we were regaled with the music & the sight of the bride. In all these places I was particularly pleased with the sight of the peasantry, a stout hearty lot whose dress which approaches very near the antique renders them still more interesting. They recalled because they resembled the ancient heroes of this country. They are not however numerous; as the country is thinly inhabited. I ought not to omit that for the first time I heard from a shepherd's boy the sound of a flageolet, that rural music so sweet so famous yet so little heard. I had never heard a note from a Swiss peasant whilst watching his fold. Instead of music they love only tobacco, & from their pipes nothing issues but smoke. We reached about eight at night the town of Patras and went to the house of the B. consul Mr Strani.[114] Having been nearly fourteen hours on horseback I was glad to eat some supper & go immediately to bed. It is a long ride to come in a single day from Chiarenza here. It is counted twelve hours, the only mode of computation in Greece.

The next morning May 11th today I reposed myself & looked about me.

112. Mod. Lekhaina.
113. This Musaeus was an epic poet, possibly of the late fifth century A.D., author of *Hero and Leander*.
114. This Strani, Nicholas by name, was the brother of the Strani whom Biddle had seen on Zante. The Zantiote Strani was not a consul.

Patras is a small town situated near the entrance of the gulf of Lepanto[115] on the declivities of a mountain. There are not perhaps more than about 2000 people all occupied in trade which is here more flourishing than in any part of the Morea.[116] It consists of grain, the currants of Corinth, & other small articles which go to Venice Malta England & sometime ago there was even an American ship. Patras is utterly uninteresting there being no antiquity of any sort. They have however discovered lately in an old wall or mound iron hooks for fastening ships to by which it seems that the sea has altered. These hooks have probably a connection with the story of Alcibiades in the Achaean council recommending them to prolong the port.[117] There is a large fortress (Turkish) which defends the city.[118] There is no port, but a harbor only which is excellent. The gulph is very fine—no instance of a vessel lost there. I will conclude with the declaration of my esteem						N B.

Chryso[119] Thursday May [15th]

I continue my journal. Another day Monday May 12th was spent at Patras to rest myself & to enquire. Mr Strani is an amiable man who understands well the position of the Morea about which we discoursed. But Patras itself is so uninteresting that altho' treated with much civility I was well content to leave on Tuesday May 13 morning & to direct my course towards the town of Vostizza.[120] We got post horses the post being regularly established thro' Greece. About 9 we left Patras whose fertile environs were very soon changed into a barren rocky soil producing scarcely anything & almost depopulated. The road winds constantly along the shore at

115. Anc. and mod. Gulf of Corinth.
116. Leake in 1805 estimated the population at ten thousand, saying that Patras was the most populous town in Greece south of Ioannina and the port for most European commerce with the Morea and the whole western coast of Greece. One-third of the population were Turks, the rest Greeks or Jews.
117. Leake supposed that the story of this wall and its rings, which can be found in Spon and Wheler, was a fable repeated from one generation to the next and that the wall was actually Roman. Biddle seems to conflate this wall with the story of Alcibiades' idea of building long walls to connect Patrai and its port in 419 B.C. (Thucydides 5.52).
118. The medieval fortress, repeatedly rebuilt by Byzantines, Franks, Venetians, and Turks, occupies the site of the ancient acropolis. The medieval city of Patras that Biddle saw was burned in the Greek War of Independence and then refounded on a grid plan.
119. Anc. Krisa and mod. Khrisso.
120. Anc. and mod. Aigion.

the foot of the mountains. In about an hour we reached the part of the road near the isthmus. Here are two forts which are called Due Castelli, one on each side of the strait which is about 3 miles wide, the entrance I believe good. The castles seem to be strong & are occupied by the Turks.[121] We continued our ride & passed one little village of which I forget the name & two hours before reaching Vostizza stopped to eat at a little Khan or tavern. The most common food of the people is sour milk or the Turkish dish something like sour craut except that there is nothing but milk & lemon in it. All the ride presented nothing antique or interesting. The road is extremely bad & is crossed by large torrents which are almost impassable in winter. But there is nothing antique as remains of any of those cities which composed the famous league.[122] Speculators love to compare it with our union, but what a comparison between twelve towns in a country which may be passed in 12 hours with the greatness & extent of our country. You know the history of the Achaeans who came here driven from Sparta by the Eraclidae.[123] Vostizza distant from Patras about 8 hours (24 miles) is the ancient Aegium. There is however nothing antique except I think some masses of stone on the sea shore which have the appearance of ruins. On my arrival I went to the house of the governor with a letter from Strani. Not speaking Greek,[124] his civilities consisted in furnishing me with a bed & something to eat. He felt his embarrassment & escaped from it in a way not very favorable to Greek good manners. After supper he went to bed without saying a word & in the morning when I started he having gone out I did not see him. I felt no regret, for tho' a sort of governor he was something of a beast & had never been to Athens tho' only 18 hours distant from him all his life. The only antiquity is an inscription on a stone making part of a wall. It is thus:

121. At modern Rion, on the south side of the gulf, stands the Castle of the Morea, built in 1499 by the Turk Bayazid II. Across the gulf, at Andirrion, is its twin, the Castle of Roumeli.

122. The Achaean League, reformed in 280 B.C. from an earlier confederacy, was a federal association of cities mainly on the northern shore of the Peloponnesos. It was dissolved by the Roman conquerors in 146 B.C.

123. The legendary Heraklidai, or descendants of Herakles, returned to the Peloponnesos and conquered it for themselves, carving out three kingdoms (Sparta, Argos, and Messene) and sending refugees in various directions. Cf. Pausanias 7.1.1–9. (This Pausanias was a Greek traveler who flourished in the mid-second century A.D. and who wrote an elaborate description of the Greece of his day devoted mainly to historical, mythological, and archaeological topics.)

124. It was of course Biddle who did not speak Greek.

ΕΥΡΥΛΩΝ
ΑΝΕΘΗΚΕΝ[125]

It formed part probably of some monument.

The next day Wednesday May 14 I embarked on a boat for this place. The distance is about 30 miles & the general passage is of 4 hours. The gulph is fine & large. I suppose 8 or 10 miles [wide], the waves like the sea. In the boat were a quantity of horses & one thing or another which were to be landed at different parts of Romelia[126] so that it was dark when he got into the gulph of Salona, in one corner of which we lay all night & for the first time I slept upon sand over which a sheet was thrown.

In the morning Thursday May 15 there being no wind we remained a long time on the water rowing and about 11 arrived at what is called The Scala of Chryso.[127] This is a little harbor & one or two houses at the bottom of the bay & fine gulph of Salona[128] & about 6 miles from the town of the same name.[129] This must be the ancient situation of Cirra or perhaps it was more easterly. As soon as we arrived we got a mule for the baggage & walked about across a rich & beautiful valley in which are two streams, one the ancient Plistos, & arrived here about noon, contented to find at last rest & shelter. Adieu   N B.

Delphos May 16. 1806
Friday

My dear brother,

Why have I not the pencil of an artist to transmit to you the scene before me? I am sitting amongst the ruins of one of the proudest cities of Greece. How sad & solitary a picture. This spot once the center of Grecian arts & religion where the genius & the superstition of the first of nations loved to display its power & its extravagance, now oppressed by a foreign people, its altars changed for a new religion, its monuments dispersed & ruined by barbarians, has [just?] scanty enough remains to indicate its position & proclaim its misfortunes. Yet the sense of its ruin mingles itself with the august & venerable remembrance of its renown & its greatness. These ruins

125. Eurylon dedicated [this.]
126. The pashalik, or province, north of the Gulf of Corinth.
127. The ancient town of Kirrha, or Krisa (two forms of the same name), lay near the modern port of Itea.
128. Anc. and mod. Krisaian Gulf, an arm of the Gulf of Corinth.
129. Salona: anc. and mod. Amphissa.

are indeed complete & desolating to the mind. This awful abode of the Gods this temple which contained his image[130] & presented to the admiring stranger the votive treasures of superstition & the brilliant productions of the Grecian artist now lies defaced, & mutilated.

The hum of his people has ceased. His oracle is silent. On the ruins of his temples the cross has been planted to triumph over his misfortunes & to proclaim the victory of a new religion. The race so honored, so proud whose oracle dictated to nations groans under the rod of a Turkish despot. I look in vain for the crowd which once ascended the mountain to bring the offerings & the hopes of every people. They are all all fallen, & the little village which now insults the memory of Delphos, has not a remnant of either its wealth, its glory or its spirit. [But?] shall we weep or admire the majestic masses of ruin which have defyed the fury of conquerors & the insidious, creeping hand of time? They still survive to convey an image of that greatness of which the substance is no more. Nature still smiles at the wreck. In spite of barbarism she still asserts her power. The rich & lovely [plain] which leads to Delphos is still luxuriant. The Plistus still winds along its little course & this territory once the cause of a fanatic & cruel war[131] now blooms to avenge itself on the ruins of its persecutors. So great is nature, so feeble is man. Yet let me separate my feelings from my narrations & tell you as well what I have seen & what I have felt. About 7 this morning we left Chryso and after about an hours ascent reached this place. After some conversation with the Turkish governor we arrived at the house of the priest. I could not but smile at the sad reverse which priestcraft has undergone. The high priest of Delphos is superceded by the humble poverty of a Greek curate whose beard is perhaps his nearest point of analogy to his predecessor, & his poverty & honesty the widest distinction between them. We went out accompanied by him to see the ruins. They are all situated on the declivity of a hill which beginning at the root of Parnassus descends to the plain. We first walked to the foot of the hill where was a fountain which seemed to be antique, & which he said was the Castalian.

130. The temple of Apollo at Delphi.
131. The people of the city state of Kirrha claimed the right to levy tolls on pilgrims coming to Apollo's shrine at Delphi, some five miles away. Because of this presumed sacrilege, the Amphictiony of Anthela, an organization of Greek cities that protected the sanctuary of Demeter and Kore near Thermopylai, waged war against Kirrha. The victory of the Amphictions resulted in the destruction of Kirrha and the organization of the city-state of Delphi, which now controlled the port city. Before 590 the people either of Delphi or of Kirrha managed the Panhellenic Pythian festival. It was afterward controlled by the Amphictions.

We however soon saw another which must be the real fountain, for the first was very small & the source not visible. This fountain issues from two sources at the foot of the large cleft which separates the two parts of Parnassus.[132] The one is large about 8 or 10 feet wide & 20 long. There are steps down to it for the persons to sit upon who wished to have cures performed by it (says the Parson) & a small room fabricated out of the rock which surrounds the fountain. The steps & the rock are antique. The other source is a little higher up & smaller, but they soon join. The water is very pure & very good. The whole fountain was covered (or rather the stream) by Delphic women washing dirty linen & who did not understand perfectly the object of my curiosity. The Parnassus, so famous in Grecian mythology, is a hill which to unpoetical eyes offers few attractions. It is barren of a bluish & grey appearance, & is almost perpendicular over Delphos which continued the descent to the plain. From Delphos the top of P which is obscured with snow & clouds is not discovered.[133] It is the most southern [part] of the ridge which is divided from the ridge on the coast by a little valley. At the point where the Castalian fountain issues, the mountain is divided into two by a large cleft of 20 or 30 feet probably caused by an earthquake & extending from top to bottom, so that there are two tops to Parnassus. It struck me that one of them should be destined to men of real genius the other to the race of pretenders "damned to everlasting fame" by the satire of the first. I could distinguish Virgil & Pope upon the one hill whilst Bavius Maevius[134] & the *Dunciad*[135] heroes squatted upon some sharp stone on the other grinning their teeth at their common enemy & at each other. Has not antiquity made this distinction?[136]

---

132. Since Biddle uses the word Parnassus in two senses and switches from one meaning to the other without warning, his description of Delphi is unnecessarily obscure. The ravine in which the Castalian fountain originates is separated by two great crags, anciently named Nauplia and Hyampia. It is these two crags that Biddle, in accordance with ancient practice, calls the two parts of Parnassus. But the massif of Parnassos rises behind the Phaidriades, a whole line of cliffs bounding Delphi on the north and of which Nauplia and Hyampia are a part. These cliffs are bare and hide the cloud- and snow-covered mountain rising behind them, which is a complex mass with two (!) main peaks of its own.
133. This sentence is an interlinear insertion in the journal.
134. Vergil (*Eclogues* 3.90) and Horace (*Epodes* 10) pilloried the Roman poets Bavius and Maevius, who they thought were hostile to them.
135. The reference is to the satiric poem written by Alexander Pope in 1728.
136. Parnassos was associated not just with Apollo, god of music and prophecy, but with Dionysos, god of wine and ecstatic religion, and whom Apollo partially displaced at Delphi.

Parnassus is not the highest mountain in the neighborhood, there being some covered with snow. The hill is too steep to be ascended directly at Delphos. Having no pretensions I knew that they would treat me as an intruder & therefore did not presume to attempt to mount. Near the Castalian fountain & making part of the room & steps around are other large ruins which may probably have formed the Temple of Apollo.[137] Against the rock is a recess or niche which might have served for a statue or the oracle itself. From this niche to the room over the fountain (a distance of 30 or 40 feet) is a subterraneous passage perceived thro' the stones under the room. This most probably served for the passage of the priests in order to assist the oracle. Indeed all the mountain is filled with these invisible roads as may be perceived by the echoes of the niches as well as by actual observation, they having discovered one which they were afraid to pursue. Immediately under the Parnassus is a sort of bowling green with a bench (in stone) round it serving (says the Parson) for music & amusement. The large ruins near it show that it belonged to some immense building. Lower down the mountain are other large masses of ruin some of which retain the form of houses, & evince their ancient majesty. In the rocks are a great many holes worked out & destined either for baths or beds. There is also a large plain about half down the mountain which must have been the gymnasium. None of the ruins do more than stimulate without satisfying curiosity. Temples to which no names can be assigned, & apertures in the rocks are all that remains. Yet I have seen few ruins so noble. The city descends from the foot of Parnassus down to the little stream & valley which shuts it up to the south. To the east & west are the apertures,[138] one going to Lebadea the other to the plain. Judging from the temples near Chryso I should suppose the city of Delphos to have been there (as we are told there were churches at the entrance) & to have gone over the little hills which

---

In Greek literature, one of the double summits of Parnassos was sacred to Apollo and the other to Dionysos. The distinction Biddle himself draws between good and bad poets seems predicated on the belief of some Roman writers that Parnassos was the source of poetic inspiration. Antiquity, however, did not distinguish between good poetry inspired by Apollo and bad poetry inspired by Dionysos. Biddle seems rather to have muddied the waters by his conceit.

137. The French excavations after 1891 disclosed the sacred precinct of Delphi to the west of the Castalian fountain. Apollo's temple formed the centerpiece of this sanctuary and was the place of the oracle.

138. That is, passes.

separate Chryso from the little town of Castri.[139] The most inhabited part
was under the Castalian fountain. The descent is divided in the middle by
the Castalian stream which loses itself in another at the foot of the hill. The
inscriptions are unsatisfactory. I have just been to see one which is in a
cellar, & after having annoyed some hens who were roosting we distinguished by the aid of a candle a great deal of writing on the stones of the
wall. I perceived it would have required a year both of much more light
both physical & moral than I had to examine them & therefore I contented
myself without looking at a number more in another house. There was one
however in a field which the Priest declared no one had yet been able to
explain. This piqued my learning & I therefore copied it but without
knowing if I can make sense of it.[140]

Λ · Μ Α Ρ Ι Ο Ν Ν Ε Π Ω Τ Α Α Ι Γ Ι Α Λ Ε Ι Ν Ο Ν Τ Ε
Τ Ε Ι Μ Η Μ Ε Ν Ο Ν Α Π Ο Τ Η Σ Κ Ο Ρ Ι Ν Θ Ι Ω Ν
Β Ο Υ Λ Η Σ Τ Ε Ι Μ Α Ι Σ Β Ο Υ Λ Ε Υ Τ Ι Κ Α Ι Σ Κ Α Ι
Α Γ Ο Ρ Α Ν Ο Μ Ι Κ Α Ι Σ Α Μ Α Ρ Ι Ο Σ Ν Ε Π Ω Σ
Π Α Τ Η Ρ Κ Ο Ρ Ι Ν Θ Ι Ο Γᵇ Σ Κ Α Ι Ο Υ Λ Ι Α Α Ι Γ Ι Α Λ Η
Δ Ε Λ Φ Η Τ Ο Ν Ε Α Υ Τ Ω Ν Ι Ο Ν Α Π Ο Λ Λ Ω Ν Ι
Π Υ Θ Ι Ο Ι

Delphos Friday May [16th]1806

I was soon besieged by men who had found coins. I was not desirous of
purchasing medals but those which they offered were unintelligible or uninteresting & what was most curious was a Russian coin which I might
have purchased on account of its preservation, had not my servant recog-

---

139. The village of Kastri lay over the ruins of ancient Delphi. It has since been moved to
permit the excavation of the site.

140. This inscription is here printed exactly as Biddle transcribed it. Many other travelers
also copied the stone, which was identified as lying in the village of Kastri. Biddle's attempt
to copy the exact form of the letters shows that the inscription belongs to the Roman
imperial period, as one might guess from the Roman names. A. Boeckh published an
articulated text as No. 1716 of *Corpus Inscriptionum Graecarum*. The inscription, which is a
fragment, reads: "A[ulus] Marius Nepos Aigialeinos, honored by the council of the Corin-
thians with the offices of counselor and magistrate. A[ulus] Marius Nepos, a father, from
Corinth, and Julia Aigiale, a Delphian, [dedicate this statue of] their own son to Pythian
Apollo." Biddle probably misread the initial alpha as a lambda, though others also read the
letter as lambda. There are also one or two other mistakes in his transcription that I have
ignored in the translation.

nized it as a Russian penny. I will in future lay but little stress on my learning in that way. I have now seen all that is curious in Delphos. Any enjoyment it is always my wish to transmit to you & should what I have written give you pleasure you know the joy it will inspire in yr. aff. brother

N B.

Chryso Friday evg.

Dear Tom

My journal of yesterday will announce to you my arrival. I knocked at the gate of the Despotes or bishop to whom Strani had given me a letter, and I was delighted to find a venerable man of more than 70 with a long beard, & withal one of the most amiable men I have ever seen [Fig. 6]. The cordial welcome, & the politeness superior to the littleness of forms, made me at once master of his house, & shewed the goodness of his heart. He was indeed a man whose lot was enviable. In the decline of a long life he found himself enjoying one of the first honors of his profession which brought at once the esteem of his people & an affluent provision for his old age. His retirement offered all that peace, respect & fortune could give. Of the world he knew little except from the report of passing strangers who all came to admire & enjoy his hospitality. To such a man a stranger was indeed a pleasure as it informed him of the agitations & quarrels of a world which tho' they could not approach his retreat, he still loved to hear of at a distance. Of my own country he made many enquiries. He had seen one other American Smith of Carolina who seems to have pleased him wonderfully, for he declares he had never seen such a man.[141] From him I learnt in

141. Apart from Joel Roberts Poinsett, who in the course of an extended trip through Europe and Asia in the years 1801–8 visited Sicily in 1802, Joseph Allen Smith, an elusive South Carolinian related to the Izard family, was the first U.S. citizen to visit Greece. In some fifteen years in Europe and Asia, he sailed through the Greek archipelago, visited the mainland, and spent some time in Athens. But we do not know when. He may have been in Athens in 1804, because he was in Constantinople in May of that year on his second Russian trip. Smith's brother William lived in Philadelphia, and his letters to William might have been shown to Biddle before the latter set out for Europe in the fall of 1804. Smith and Biddle may well have met in Paris; and both returned to Philadelphia in 1807. Cf. Roger Kennedy, *Greek Revival America* (New York, 1989), 170. Whatever Smith may have written to his relatives (and these letters, if they exist, deserve to be ferreted out), Biddle's is the earliest account by a U.S. citizen of an extended tour of Greece. Smith may have been the author of a short memoir entitled "Present State of Athens," which appeared in the *Literary*

my turn something with regard to the state of the country which is cruelly oppressed by the Turks. This little town of about 15 hundred inhabitants is placed on the hill which rises from the plain of Cirra. It is about 2 miles from the town of Castri & must have been near the suburbs of Delphos. The rich valley which it overlooks was the cause of the celebrated religious war. It is still very rich. I should suppose it to be about two miles broad & 6 or 7 long. It is well cultivated in grain & olive trees. Chryso has several ancient temples near it. Some of them have inscriptions but almost impossible to decypher. I observed on a large round stone covered with writing the name of φλαβιος[112] whence I presumed it to have been since the Romans were here.

Today Friday I went to see Delphos & in the afternoon returned to my good Bishop with whom I have had a long conversation. I shall leave this place in the morning & must therefore bid you good night.   N B.

Livadia,[143] Wednesday

My dear Tom

On Saturday May 17th following my last I left Chryso at an early hour & after a ride of 8 hours reached this place. On leaving Chryso the road follows the valley at the foot of Delphos & runs nearly the whole distance between the mountains. A part of the ancient road the Via Sacra is in the way and in excellent preservation. The Grecian is built of large thick stones, not so broad nor so smooth as the Roman. It is however very firm, and its excellent state shows how much more terrible are the passions of men than the ravages of time. She comes gently and imperceptibly but vandalism like the tempest roots up in a moment all that is fair & graceful. Had man spared the temples of Delphos how perfect would they now be where even a temporary road is unhurt after 2 or 3 thousand years.

The road is disagreeable in the beginning & the country barren. The only incident occurring was our having the company of a cutthroat looking Turk whose society gave me no satisfaction. We arrived however safe at

Magazine and American Register (Philadelphia, October 1807), 194–96. Seven of his letters to Rufus King were published by George C. Rogers, Jr. (ed.), "Letters from Russia, 1802–1805," *The South Carolina Historical Magazine* 60 (1959): 94–105, 154–163, and 221–227. These letters allow us to date his trip to Greece approximately, and they suggest something of his motivation for going there.

142. That is, the Roman name Flavius, written in Greek letters.

143. Anc. Lebadeia.

Livadia near which the country opens into a fine plain. Having reached the town I rode to the house of the Logothetis[144] to whom the Bishop of Chryso had addressed me altho' I had no letter for him. This induced me some embarrassment amongst the inferior officers in his family, but as soon as he entered (being absent at my arrival) I told him that hearing of his hospitality, I had presumed upon it to come to his house uninvited & unintroduced. He received me with the utmost openness & I found myself at home with him. The evening was past in seeing & enquiring among the family & supping & sleeping. The next morning Sunday May 18 I learnt much of Grecian politics and character. The spirit of the Greeks is bowed but not broken. Tho' oppressed cruelly by their masters they remember, that they were *men*. The people are disarmed, a Turk is a word of terror, and a refinement of tyranny seems to have been carried [to?] every subject that can interest the feelings of humanity. The people tho' poor hate their masters with the most noted enmity, and wounded as their feelings are the slightest spark (either foreign assistance or a favorable moment) is all that is wanted to inflame the whole nation into rebellion. The despotism of Turkey is proverbial, but I this day saw an example of it which enables me to appreciate the merit of the saying. A new governor of Negropont & Livadia has just been appointed. He was once at Cairo where tho' he became acquainted with & was fond of Englishmen he did not imbibe any of the liberal spirit of their country. After passing thro' Smyrna where he cut off a number of heads, on account of some delay in the contribution, he passed up to the Dardanelles then down along Turkey carrying fire & desolation with him. Superceding all the governors thro' whose district he passes (unless they be like himself Bashaws of three tails[145]) with a complete power over the life & property of any individual, and a power to levy unlimited tribute on the towns which are on the route to his govt, he is an object of dismay to his people. He was this day to enter into Livadia. The ceremony promised to be curious, & I went out to see it. I soon learnt a lesson of Turkish govt. I had scarcely walked about 50 yards from the house in company with the Chancellor and the Physician when a Turkish dragoon rode up after us and showing a billet of lodging demanded of the Chancellor where the house was. The Chancellor said he did not know the house.

144. The name Logothetis was actually a title indicating the manager of the revenues of the church and was used by other important Greek families elsewhere, for example, in Athens. The man's name was Ioannis Stamou Khondrodimas.
145. The *though*, or horse's tail, stained red and stuck on a pole with a gilt nob on top, was a military ensign. A man's dignity was determined by the number of tails he was allowed to have carried before him.

The Turk abusing him in the grossest way ordered him to take him immediately to the house. The Chancellor seemed indignant & inclined to resist.
The blush on his cheek was a tribute to manhood which like his country's
freedom passed in a moment. The Turk ran his horse up against him and
drawing his sword drove him before him like a dog. Luckily at some distance the Chancellor found a man who knew the house & undertook to
conduct the Turk who then let the poor wretch go. Such was the treatment
which a common soldier dared to give to an old man, a respectable man &
an officer. Until this moment I had never known the meanness of tyranny.
The unfortunate object of it rejoined us, walked on to his friends & told
them. What language will your indignation suggest for them? Did they
rise in arms & massacre every thing that bore the name of a Turk? Did they
demand the punishment of the wretch who had dared thus to insult their
friend & their countryman? By heavens they laughed. Their wretched de-
basement was matter of jest for them. Yet Livadia is an hour from Cheronea, four hours from Platea, ten from Thermopylae![146]

This incident did not excite my curiosity to see more of Greek slavery. I
sat down however on the grass amongst a crowd of Greeks. They all said &
openly that they had come to see their tyrant, that he would rob them of
their property & spoke of him with high indignation. Yet this is the way in
which they perceived him. Tho' bleeding under the scourge they were tick-
led with the pomp of their oppressor, and came out in the burning sun &
waited on the grass 3 or 4 hours his coming. He came at last. Preceded &
followed by a herd of savage cavalry & infantry, a band of music consisting
of a quantity of kettledrums & a flute or two, he received the elders of the
town who kissed his hand, & he then went on to his lodgings. He had
displayed all his troops, and his most brilliant ornament was a number of
horses without riders & with large gilt shields on each side of them. Having reached the city & assembled the chief governors he first made them
subsist[147] his 2 or 3 hundred followers, & then pay a contribution of 14
thousand piastres. It was in vain that the elders declared the poverty of
their city and that no former Pasha had demanded more than 4 or 5 thousand. He told them he must have it that if they did not give it he would

146. These were the sites of three famous battles in Greek history: the first in 338 B.C.,
when Philip of Macedon defeated the free Greek city-states; the second in 479, when the
Greeks defeated the land army of the Persians; and the third in 480, when the Spartans
under their king Leonidas, together with some of their allies, were surrounded and annihi-
lated at a pass that gave entry to Xerxes' army to southern Greece.
147. The transitive use of this verb is now obsolete.

cut off their heads and burn their city. They were obliged to produce the money which added to the expenses of three days lodgings for the troops cost the town 25 thousand piastres (somewhere about 7 thousand dollars). After the Bashaws arrival I amused myself with reading &c until bed-time.

On Monday May 19 the same scene was renewed. Unable to get horses whilst the P remains here I passed my time in reading and walking. Among others I went to see the oracle of Trofonius the only antiquity near this place. Of the celebrated seat of credulity & priestcraft you already know the history. It was formerly at a small distance from the town, & the rock & mountain covered with woods all of which made it very well calculated for its purposes. But the old town being destroyed, & the new one built on each side of the cave which is now in the middle of the city, it ceased to be terrible. It has become less so from the change of religion. The rock is at the bottom of a hill & near a fountain. A number of excavations in the rock are seen. One (I should suppose destined for the statue of Apollo) is large and in the form of a niche. Here is an aperture or rather a canal large enough to let a man crawl along on all fours, thro' which the wretch who came to sacrifice was probably obliged to go. Near the niche I mentioned Lord Elgin[148] discovered a staircase going down to water, but after digging some time the water stopped their labor and the staircase is now covered with earth. The cave recalls to mind all those images of hypocrisy & deceit which stained a religion in some things really great. Her deceitful arts are now discovered & detected, but the works are still objects of admiration. I was surprised today in speaking to a Greek priest to hear him defend the tricks of the Trophonian oracle and the formalities of the priests. He says they did their duty, they were the ministers of God (& as to their ceremonies if a Greek were now to see our forms he could think them equally as ridiculous as we do his). Is it then so? Are our ceremonies merely like theirs, or is their a real substantial difference between the two religions? This afternoon arrived here two Englishmen Misters Palmer & McKenzie from Constantinople.[149]

148. Thomas Bruce, 7th Earl of Elgin (1766–1841), was appointed ambassador to the Porte in 1798. His artists were engaged to study the archaeological remains, especially in Athens, from 1800 to 1806. In 1816 the British Parliament bought for the nation his collection of sculpture, much of it taken from the Parthenon in Athens.

149. Alexander Mackenzie (1781–1809) matriculated at Christ Church College, Oxford, in 1800, graduating B.A. in 1804 and M.A. in 1807. He was the son of John Mackenzie of

On Tuesday May 20 the two gentlemen left us & I was obliged to remain for want of horses. I therefore did nothing but read & sleep & walk.
Among other things I read almost all the *Confessions* of Rousseau which I
found here in the house. To be interested deeply in a man's memoirs either
you must have been acquainted with him or the subject he introduces must
be valuable. Rousseau seems to have thought himself much more eccentric
than he really was. His book is a good picture of a heart ignorant of the
world with some good qualities & passions mingled with a few base ones.
On the whole his story can be followed with tolerable attention on account
of the stile & the celebrity of the author. The next day Wednesday May
21st I was also obliged to wait for altho' the Bashaw is gone they having
carried with them all the horses it was impossible to stir. I however learned
something from inquiry among the people. Livadia the ancient Levadia is a
tolerably large town, built on a declivity of a hill. The houses are in general
mean the streets badly built, & there are few houses except that in which I
live that are decent. The Logotheti has really a charming house & I have
been quite well accommodated. The manner of living of the Greeks has
some charms. In the first place I admire their dress which is accommodated
to their climate, loose & cool. In their houses you find the rooms surrounded by a little bank on which are placed cushions on which you repose
[Fig. 7]. On entering a house you first are presented with a pipe then coffee
& sometimes a spoon full of citron & a bowl of water. The breakfast is
generally a cup of coffee; the dinner at noon & the supper at night are like
our own. They change plates & knives & forks very often, & always use the
plates one on top of each other as [*one or two words illegible*] with us. The
women are very handsomely drest. The hair is left to grow almost down to
the heels and has little bits of silver attached to the plaits. The ringlets also
fall over the shoulder upon the breast. The breasts are suffered to hang
down for a length always disagreeable & sometimes disgusting. I have seen
some handsome women, but the lower classes of the people are not so, tho'
the children are sometimes beautiful, [having] fine features fine complec-
tions, but [these are] soon spoilt by the sun. The women generally die their
hair & a light red [or] auburn inclining to red is the most fashionable color.
The dress differs in different parts. I think that of the country people is

---

Bishopsgate, London. After graduation he entered holy orders. He presented to the library
of Christ Church a statue of Aphrodite and Eros (a Roman copy of a fourth-century B.C.
Greek original) that he had brought back from Greece. A plaque beneath it bears the
inscription "A. D. MDCCCV. A. SE. PROPE. PELLAM. INVENTUM. D. D. ALEXANDER. MAC-
KENZIE. A. M. ALUMNUS." His companion, the clergyman Palmer, has proved to be elusive.

much more convenient & handsome than that of Switzerland so much boasted of. The jacket short & occasionally suspended on one arm, the open collar the hunting shirt coming like a petticoat over the thighs, the pantaloons girt under the knee by a black ribbon and the fancy colored shoes & slippers form a very pretty dress. The Albanese are more like our Indians than any other people whom I have yet seen. But I must close this letter with an affectionate adieu.   N B.

Livadia Friday night May 23rd

My dear Tom

We have seen the spots of Grecian superstition. Let me now lead you to the spot which is illustrated by their brightest virtue. I have just returned from Thermopylae. This celebrated place was too interesting to be passed & I willingly devoted two days to the pleasure of visiting it. Yesterday morning Thursday 22nd I left this place & after crossing the plain before it & then the hill which closes it, arrived in an extensive plain. The villages are on each side at the foot of the hills. The first of them is the celebrated Cheronea which gives its name to the whole valley. I did not turn aside to this town but continued thro' the valley of Cheronea which witnessed the last sigh of Grecian freedom. The Cephisus is a small river which when augmented by the winter rains & snows must be of a tolerable size. You must learn however to moderate your ideas of European rivers. The Cephisus would not in our country aspire to the name of a creek. Yet it would be unjust to measure importance by size, & the Cephisus waters a handsome valley tho' at present in many parts uncultivated. After stopping at a khan we continued & soon got into another plain more rich & extensive than the first. Here are a number of villages thro' some of which however we passed, & having reached the opposite side began the rising. From this spot to Thermopylae a distance of about 6 hours the country assumes quite a different appearance being mountainous barren & difficult to pass. The common road is by a town called Molo[150] on the sea shore. I however went across the mountains & arrived at Boudinitza[151] about 2 hours from Thermopylae. This is a little town where there is a monastery & a large fortress.

150. Mod. Molos.
151. Anc. Pharygai and mod. Mendenitza. The site is occupied by the Castle of Bondonitza, seat of a Frankish marquisate from 1204 to 1410.

This place I should suppose to have been anciently inhabited & were it not that Tronio[152] in the territory of the Locri is said to have been in the plain I should fix upon that as the spot. We left it & after crossing one or two hills we came on the old road which must be that of the pass. The road is narrow as are indeed all old roads but its size would not indicate the streight because it is not smaller than other roads. Indeed the whole face of the pass is totally changed. The sea has retired more than a mile & there is in fact no longer a streight. The marshy ground has become cultivated, the water as at Morgarten[153] has entirely left the hill & made Euboea quite nigh the continent. At two hours from Boudinitz we found the stream of warm water which serves to ascertain the position. A single stream coming from the hills is formed by two others at the foot which issue from the ground & after running across the road are lost.[154] The water is a tolerably high temperature, something more than lukewarm. Further on is seen the small hill on which was the tomb of Leonidas & still further the large mountain which encloses the valley of Thessalia and [forms?] the ridge of Mt Oeta. These objects the Phocian wall the tomb the stone of Hercules have disappeared & it would be idle to search for the path which treason pointed out to the Persians.[155] Indeed so totally has everything changed, that the only attraction of Thermopylae is the venerable sentiment of the actions it has witnessed. These remembrances are indeed interesting. History has perhaps exaggerated the number of the Persians, but the voluntary devotion of the free men of Greece against any number of adversaries is a sight the most impressive. These men were free. They obeyed nothing but the impulses of bravery & the proudest disdain of servitude. Yet man is always the same

152. That is, anc. Thronion, which lay to the southeast of modern Molos.

153. Morgarten, a mountain in Switzerland at the south end of Lake Aegeri, was the scene of a victory by Swiss peasants over the Austrians in 1315.

154. This sentence makes sense only if one has a map of the site. The single stream is the Spercheios River, which, coming from the west and draining the slopes of Oita, now flows into the Malian Gulf nearly opposite the old pass. In its course it collects the water of the two streams, each issuing from a hot spring, which flow across the road and into the marshy ground along the river.

155. The Phokian Wall, stretching from the cliffs of Mount Kallidromos to the sea, closed off the narrow pass of Thermopylai, so called from its hot springs, and the narrowest point of the main route from the north into central and southern Greece. When in 480 B.C. a Greek army under the Spartan king Leonidas tried to hold this pass against the advancing Persian army of Xerxes, a Greek traitor showed the Persians a path over the mountain; and in this way the attackers took the Spartans from behind. The story is told in Herodotus's Book 7. Leonidas's tomb was marked by a stone lion. The stone of Herakles refers to an altar anciently situated near the hot springs.

thing. The herd of Greeks who wander around Zeitun[156] and Molo do not know of the heroic valor which has signalized Thermopylae, nor have their imperfect institutions yet brought them to the refined & ardent love for freedom. But they are men. They have sense enough to feel their misfortunes but not spirit enough to remedy them. They may however one day (may that day soon arrive!) when aided from abroad, and stimulated by their sufferings act worthily of themselves.

The spring still has the name of Thermopylae & the valley which leads to the sea is very pretty. At the end of the farthest mountain is seen the village of Zeitun, the ancient Lamia. Having seen what was to be seen that is the springs which are suphurous & which in their course near the mountain turn a little mill for grain, all the ground around which is hollow & gives a strong reverberation I returned to Molo a little town situated in the plain about two hours distance, and near the sea. Here I slept in a miserable khan upon the floor and afterwards continued my journey this morning home. The route was somewhat different from that of yesterday. The little country of the Locri is hilly barren & must have produced a hardy race of men. We stopped at a shepherds encampment, at a little village in the grand valley, and afterwards at Cheronea. This place venerable as the birthplace of Plutarch is a very small village of about 30 houses in a little valley enclosed by two little hills & about two hundred yards from the road to Livadia. On the highest of the hills are the remains of a castle which must have commanded the town. The only remains of antiquity here are this fortress and a theatre that is the ruins of one. The steps are cut out of the rock in the hill & the shape of the theatre is still distinguishable. In the church is an inscription which seemed to be worth the pains of decyphering. I rode to Livadia where I found the two gentlemen returned from Delphos & about making the route to Thebes where I shall go in the morning. I will therefore only add that altho' fatigued my excursion to Thermopylae has given me much satisfaction. Adieu.

N B.

Thebes Sunday May 25. 1806

My dear brother

You must follow me with your ancient history in your hand thro' the ride of yesterday. We left the Logotheti of Levadia about nine o'clock. We

156. Anc. and mod. Lamia.

soon got into the large valley which is bounded by the ridge of Mt Li-
betrio.[157] As we rode along we saw Orchomenos at the side of the valley,
and afterwards the lake Copais which appears to have shrunk much. We
also saw for a moment the ridge of Mt Helicon. The spring of the Muses[158]
might have attracted us, but we wanted to go on, & in about 4 hours
reached the town of Pa[rapoungia] said to be Leuctra. On going further
about a mile we discovered ruins which show plainly that here must have
been an ancient city which could have been no other than Leuctra. It is
situated in a small plain & over the ruins of the town are the fields of grain.
You remember that at Leuctra Epaminondas defeated the Spartans.[159] There
are among the ruins none that can be worthy of attention. We therefore
rode on to Platea where we arrived in about 3 hours. Here we stopped to
examine the ruins of this famous city which is situated on a eminence at the
foot of the Citheron.[160] The modern village is called Cochla. The ruins are
wholly unsatisfactory.[161] The elevation where was the citadel is a fine commanding spot & is indicated by some ruins. Some traces still remain of the
walls of the town. Near the citadel is a prodigious large ruin in the form of
a large wall of immense large stones & two projections. This must have
been either a part of the wall or more probably of a large tavern destined for
those who came to visit & to sacrifice. Near the citadel & in the plain is a
fine fountain spoken of by Pausanias[162] and around it immense ruins of
buildings. In the neighborhood are some sarcophages. The tombs of the
Spartans are placed by Barthelemy on the wrong side of the town. This is
all that we could see of the celebrated spot where as you know the Persian
army of Mardonius was defeated. The plain which is commanded by the
town is large & rich but at present not in a high state of cultivation. All

157. As Biddle rode south out of Livadia toward Thebes, keeping Mount Helikon on his
right, the ridges on his left, which separated him from the Kopaic Lake, were Mounts
Lafistion and Libethrion.
158. The Valley of the Muses and its associated sanctuary and spring lay on Mount
Helikon, a mountain massif closing the Kopaic basin to the west.
159. The Theban leader Epaminondas defeated the Spartans and destroyed a good part of
their army in 371 B.C.
160. The battle of Plataia, described in Herodotus's Book 9, took place in 479 B.C.,
when the Persian army, retiring through Boiotia after the defeat of the Persian navy at
Salamis, was itself defeated by the forces of the Greek league commanded by the Spartan
Pausanias.
161. Most of the extant ruins postdate the famous battle.
162. Presumably the Gargaphian spring (Pausanias 3.4.3), which figures prominently in
Herodotus's description of the battle. Its exact location is still disputed.

Boeotia is indeed a charming country. I have never seen anywhere the ground so beautifully diversified by hill & valley & the soil is at the same time very rich. From Platea we went on to Thebes where we arrived at night it being about three and one half hours from Platea. Having reached the town we first waited on the Bashaw with three tails who had come on from Livadia here & where in spite of remonstrance he levied twelve thousand piastres & staid three days. This was more oppressive than the tax on Livadia which was more able to support it Thebes being a city of no more than 1500 or 2000 souls. The dark looking Bashaw received us with politeness, ordered that we should have our horses without delay. He is a very handsome man tho' brown, fine long beard &c. We found him smoking a large hooker, & surrounded by his Turks to whom we ought to have given a present, but, I do not know how, it was declined. The Pasha directed us to the governor who found us lodgings where we slept. This morning early we walked out to see the city. We were conducted to several temples in ruins or converted into churches. One only remained in preservation near the gate of Platea. One or two other gates particularly the Cadmean, that which led to the Cadmea or citadel we could also distinguish. The fountain which is the farthest of all from the citadel, & was called the Ismenian is a beautiful source of water with the ruins of buildings around serving to show that there must have been a temple there. Here says Sophocles the Thebans had their conversations & the boys came to play marbles. The situation of Thebes is delightful. The town must have been built in part on the hill & in part on the plain. The hilly part consists of several little mounds on the highest of which was the Cadmea. The plain is about 2 miles broad and six or seven long & has a charming affect. The ancients seem to have been connoisseurs in situations. Thebes the country of Pindar & the seat of war & freedom has forgotten the name of the poet & the spirit of its heroes. I am sure there is not a copy of his works at Thebes, & we all can see they are enslaved beyond the danger of addition.

Having seen all (the stadium the tomb of Pindar, the theatre we could not discover) we were willing to leave Thebes. Yet it seems that our not having feed the servants of the Pasha or some other cabinet reason made them remiss in their duty for our horses did not arrive. The fact is, as it will be under all tyrants that these dependents whilst they tremble before their tyrant have no fear as soon as he is absent, & as the Pasha went this morning the orders which he left behind him are not very well executed. Whilst waiting for the horses we formed our plans & for an analysis of the human mind it may not be amiss to record our resolution. Mr McKenzie wished to go & see the subterranean canals of the Copais[163] & had fixed to accompany the Pasha to Agripo (ancient Chalcis).[164] Mr Palmer intended to go to Athens with myself, but last night resolved to go with the Pasha also. In the morning the P went without them, & Mr Palmer resolved to go to Athens with me. On enquiry he found that we should lose only one day, & he therefore resolved to go to Copais & persuaded me to go with him. On still better information however it appearing that we should lose two days, I abandoned the journey to Copais, but after long persuasion & discourse on the beauties of Copais I joined them & we resolved all three to start tomorrow for Copais. Having made up our minds we got up to walk about the city. At the very door of the house we met the horses. We ordered them back for tomorrow. But the postillion declared that if we did not take them there was a Tartar[165] waiting for them; moreover that we could not go from here to Copais the road not being a post road, so that we should be forced to go to Agripo back to Copais & in this way lose three days. I immediately ordered my baggage on the horses. Palmer followed the example and we are on the point of leaving Thebes for Athens. Adieu. Yr. brother   N B.

I left Thebes then on Sunday evening & after crossing Mt Citheron exposed like Oedipus on the top of it at night, we reached a little village where we slept. This village is 4 hours from Thebes. We continued in the morning Monday 26 May our ride over a barren hilly country for four hours more. I did not think that Attica was so mountainous. Tho' some of the places where we past were excellent points of defence particularly at a spot where we saw a castle which is probably the ancient Phyle[166] & all along

163. In the Kopaic plain in Boiotia was a large lake, or swamp, much of which dried up in summer. Its natural outlets were swallow-holes, but these were not capable of draining the lake sufficiently. Hence at various times from the second millennium B.C. attempts were made to supplement the drainage system by means of dikes, canals, and tunnels. Biddle refers to the natural swallow-holes.

164. Anc. and mod. Khalkis lies on the island of Euboia opposite Boiotia and by the strait anciently called the Euripos. Negripont, or Negropont, was the medieval name of the island and the town. ΕΙΣ ΤΟΝ ΕΥΡΙΠΟΝ was corrupted to Egripo, or Agripo, or Negripo.

165. A military servant, presumably of some Turk.

166. The fortress of Phyle, one of a number of Attic border forts, dominated the ancient direct road from Athens to Thebes. Present remains are of the fourth century B.C.

which we saw the ancient road. After leaving this village at three hours distance from the city, we soon reached a fine plain covered with olive trees & grain tho' in some parts uncultivated which conducted us to Athens. Having descended at the house of a widow lady a madame Mina a Greek who usually accommodates strangers we found that two English gentlemen Mr Walpole[167] & his painter Mr Williams were at the monastery [Fig. 15].[168] Mr. Palmer a particular friend of Mr Walpole immediately fixed his lodgings with him. I preferred staying with the poor woman who lives upon strangers & who seems afflicted at the idea of our leaving her. With these gentlemen & Mr Lusieri[169] we began to see the town.

Athens

My dear brother

My heart beats as I date my letter from the venerable presence of the mistress of the world [Fig. 8]. I seize the first moment of leisure since my arrival to collect & communicate the sentiments it has inspired.

Having now seen many of the objects which distance & fiction have exaggerated into greatness, I am able to appreciate the value of Athens. On my arrival at Paris I was stunned with noise & overwhelmed with occupation. Rome gave only a mingled sentiment of melancholy. To the magnificent ruins of her temples no man can indeed deny his admiration & his sorrow. But the herd of degenerate Romans who surround them, the unblushing mendicity which assails us in the midst of them, the crowd of obtrusive strangers whose curiosity offends your own abstracts the mind. There was even something consolatory in the midst of these ruins. The

167. The classical scholar and clergyman Robert Walpole (1781–1856) toured Greece shortly after his graduation from Cambridge in 1803. He was the author of *Memoirs Relating to European and Asiatic Turkey*, 2d ed. (London, 1818), and *Travels in Various Countries of the East* (London, 1820). Both books are compilations of the work of earlier travelers and contain very little by or about Walpole himself. His painter Williams I could not identify. Whoever he was, he was *not* "Grecian Williams": Hugh William Williams (1773–1829), the Scottish landscape painter, whose sojourn in Greece came some ten years after Biddle's.

168. The Capuchins had established a monastery in Athens in 1658. In 1669 they purchased the Choregic Monument of Lysicrates and the surrounding buildings for use as a convent and a hospice for visitors. The Monument of Lysicrates served as a library.

169. Don Giovanni Battista Lusieri (d. 1821) was engaged by Elgin at Naples to sketch and paint the monuments of Athens. He remained in Athens until late in 1806, departed because of the Russian war with Turkey (Britain was an ally of Russia), then returned in 1809.

destruction of marble is infinitely less afflicting than that of mind. And the Italian people in spite of oppression & misfortune are still the first people of the world. The ground on which Brutus stabbed a tyrant to the heart is indeed disgraced by many a fawning sycophant & many an intriguing scoundrel. But there is still a lambent flame of genius round the Capitol. The Forum is still trodden by many a Roman capable of redeeming & regenerating his country. I therefore sought some more perfect [scene] of ruin & I have found it here. Rome gives but half the ideas of destruction, but Athens presents every visage of desolation & despair. When I walk amongst her ruins & first recalling her ancient greatness meditate on her fall, the mind sickens over the melancholy picture. When I see her citadel adorned with temples which have defyed not only the barbarian rage of conquest, but the shock of the elements, now degraded by the hand of violence or idle curiosity; when I see her temple of Theseus[170] which teaches us to admire the grand simplicity of a great people, her temple of Jupiter[171] the most stupendous of all ruins; when I see all this I feel for the decline of human greatness. Yet these are light when compared to the decline of man himself. Let us look around us. The voice of the Athenian people is silent. The crowded Areopagus[172] [is] a melancholy hill to which time has not left even a ruin. But the Pnix,[173] the holy spot where this great people assembled to hear their orators, to dictate laws to *themselves* & to indulge in all the license of unbounded freedom, here is the spot on which the fall of Athens is more acutely felt. Where are her orators? Gone forth to enlighten distant nations without a solitary ray for their country. Whilst erudition has lighted her lamp by their genius [&] their works, their very names are forgotten by their countrymen. Where is her people? Are these men, the wretches little superior to the beasts whom they drive heedless over the ruins, are these men *Athenians?* Where is her freedom? Here is the meanest

170. Overlooking the ancient marketplace on the west, this temple, dedicated to Hephaistos and Athena, was built in the mid-fifth century B.C. In Biddle's time, the ancient marketplace was covered by houses.

171. Started by the tyrant Peisistratos in the sixth century B.C., the temple of Olympian Zeus was continued by Antiochos Epiphanes in the second century B.C. and finally finished by the Roman emperor Hadrian in A.D 132.

172. A small rocky hill just west and slightly north of the Acropolis, the Areopagus was the site of the court of the same name.

173. The Pnix, usually spelled Pnyx, on the heights west of the Acropolis, was the site of the Assembly of the Athenian people. Until the end of the fifth century B.C. the northeast-facing slope was used as a theater, with the bema, or speaker's platform, at the bottom. In its later form, an immense retaining wall reversed the slope; and the bema, in which Biddle shows such interest, was carved out of the rock on the southwest side.

stab of all. To the justice of the collective people of Athens have succeeded the arbitrary desires of a cadi.[174] The deliberations of the people are succeeded by the firman[175] of a distant master, and on the citadel itself, the palladium of Athenian freedom, sits a little Turkish despot to command & to terrify her children. But is this all? Alas. One melancholy sail in the Piraeus.[176] The Athenian mind is still more degraded than the Athenian city. The Academy the Lyceum the Prytanaeum[177] have been superceded by a little school of elements which has never heard of Plato & the natural veracity of the people uncultivated by education has not yet produced anything worthy either of themselves or their country. I shall endeavor to give you as succinctly as I can, a description of this place.

Athens is situated in the midst of a very extensive plain. This plain must have been once extremely well cultivated. But the want of inhabitants and the general degradation of the country has injured without being able to destroy its excellence. It is still very rich, & as in ancient times is covered with olives. The city of Athens is towards the southern extremity of it. Nothing can be more beautiful than its position. Wherever you turn you discover little hills which diversify charmingly the country. To the south Hymettus to the east Pentelicus, to the northeast the Parnes & all around the city many little reliefs. The plan of the town is given with tolerable accuracy by Barthelemy except that he gives much greater extent than he ought to the walls, for they comprise only one half of the Musaeum &c.[178] The citadel is on a fine eminence overlooking the whole [Figs. 8, 9, 10, 11, 13, and 14]. It is here that we see the celebrated temple of Minerva[179] of which the remains attest the ancient magnificence. But as all the bas reliefs are taken away, and the statues also by Lord Elgin we can see noth-

174. A Turkish judge.

175. This document was a written order issued by the Porte that entitled the bearer to specified privileges. Foreign travelers used it as a passport to lay claim to post horses and to smooth away difficulties in dealing with local officials.

176. The port of Athens, some five miles to the west of the city's citadel.

177. The Prytaneion was the town hall of Athens. Located somewhere on the north slope of the Acropolis and the site of the city's eternal fire and a mess hall for those dining at public expense, it has not yet been excavated or identified with certainty.

178. The Mouseion hill, on the top of which is the monument of Philopappos, lies to the southwest of the Acropolis and was included within the fifth-century B.C. walls, which were like the rim of a wheel whose axis was the Acropolis.

179. The temple of Athena Parthenos, or the Parthenon, was built under the direction of Pericles and Phidias from 447 to 432 B.C.

ing but the columns which are of amazing grandeur & the fronton.[180] It must have been a wonderful building, when we consider the entrance or Propylaeum[181] which is now unfortunately encrusted in another building. Indeed so complicated are the little houses over the ruins that you see but little of the majesty of the temple not being able to see it close. What is still more unfortunate is that the Turks have a mosque in the middle which spoils very much the effect. The best points of view are at a distance where the temple appears to great advantage. The columns are of six or 8 feet diameter & of a noble Doric. In the neighborhood is the temple of Neptune Erechtheus & of Minerva Poliades [Figs. 11 and 12], a double temple built to these two protectors of Athens.[182] In a sort of portico belonging to the temple and adorned with some fine female statues was placed the famous olive tree which Minerva made to spring out of the ground & on Neptunes side the well. The figures are very much injured, & two of them have been taken away, one by Lord Elgin. On the citadel is the house where the Governor lives.[183] It is customary for strangers to visit him & make him a small present of some piastres. On the citadel somewhat below the Parthenon is the theatre of Bacchus[184] where the people used to listen to the works of Euripides, Sophocles, Eschylus &c. This is however a small theater by no means such as we would suppose for so large a people. Now the form only of the seats, the walls of the proscenium and the arches which were to support the building are to be seen.

The temple of Theseus (on a rising near the Pnix) is the most perfect building which is to be seen at Athens. Being converted into a church the

180. The pediment was a triangular space at either end of the temple above the columns and architrave.

181. As they now stand, the Propylaia, or entrance gates of the Acropolis, were built by Pericles' architect Mnesicles from 437 to 432 B.C. In Biddle's time the gates were incorporated into the Turkish defensive walls of the Acropolis.

182. The Erechtheion, built from 421 to 406 B.C., though devoted to many cults (hence its peculiar form), was the house of the cult statue of Athena Polias. The olive tree probably stood to the west of the building and not, as Biddle says, in the Porch of the Caryatids on the south side of the building. The olive tree and the well of saltwater were the gifts, respectively, of Athena and of Poseidon in their legendary contest for possession of Athens.

183. The Disdar, or military commander, of the garrison of the Acropolis.

184. Biddle is confusing the Theater of Bacchus, or Dionysos, in its present form a building of the fourth century B.C. and the second century A.D., with the Odeion of Herodes Atticus, built between A.D. 160 and 174, on the southwest slope of the Acropolis. The Theater of Dionysos lies farther to the east and had disappeared beneath the Turkish fortifications, though its site was suspected by some. In the great age of Athenian drama, the theater had little in the way of architectural embellishment, most of the spectators simply sitting on the slope of the hill and watching the actors perform in a circular orchestra.

ends of the interior are curved, the roof is vaulted & the shape of the inside quite altered, but the exterior is quite preserved. It is of a beautiful Doric simplicity. The reliefs which seem to be alto-reliefs are very fine.[185] The columns have many of them been affected by an earthquake which has made the pieces project one over the other. The same is the case with the temple of Minerva. Even the earthquake however spared these buildings. It forms a very striking object viewed from any point of the city. From the temple you go along a little rising ground, where are a quantity of foundations cut out of the rock, & which must formerly have been porticoes, & you then reach the Pnix. This is a small hill running east & west—where the assemblies of the people were formerly held. Formerly the orators spoke on the side of the hill looking towards the hill. But the thirty tyrants[186] changed it towards the citadel. Accordingly facing the city is a platform & a little flight of steps on which the orators stood to address the people. This is a very interesting spot. The people it would seem were not seated, the orators stood upon steps. In the rock near the steps are a quantity of little holes destined for *ex votos* which have been found there. The place for the people was not large. From the Pnix after crossing the little valley where the Piraeus wall passed formerly we reach the Musaeum now occupied by a single monument that of Philopappus.[187] From the Musaeum you walk to the temple of Jupiter Olympian that is to three rows of columns supposed to belong to the temple of that name. They form a most majestic sight, the columns being larger than any other at Athens & the foundations of an astonishing size. The Areopagus lies between the citadel & the Pnix. It is small hill where justice used to be rendered by the people. There are no ruins here. The cave of Pan is a hole in the rock of the citadel near the place of the ancient scala or entrance of the citadel. Beyond the temple of Jupiter Olympian is the bridge of Herodius Atticus across the Ilissus. The bridge had three small arches of which the foundations are distinguishable. The river or rather the bed of it is very narrow. I crossed it in twelve steps. Now there is no water in it. But in the rainy season it

185. The subjects of the sculptured metopes are the labors of Herakles and Theseus. The figures of alto-reliefs are deeply cut.

186. See note 173. The form of the Pnyx was changed substantially in 404–403 B.C., when the democratic constitution of Athens was temporarily in abeyance and the city was ruled by an oligarchical clique of rich men called the Thirty Tyrants.

187. C. Julius Antiochos Epiphanes Philopappos, an exiled prince of Commagene in Asia Minor (the kingdom had become a Roman province in A.D. 72), because he was a great patron of the Athenians, was granted a burial place on the Mouseion hill, where his tomb was built between A.D. 114 and 116.

forms a little torrent. On crossing the bridge you reach a stadium. This is a fine large building 630 feet long; the form however only is seen. None of the seats can be found. Yet it seems so perfectly formed that it waits for people & appears to ask where are the men of Athens. There is a large cavern or covered way thro' which the beasts were brought in, or the magistrates came probably the the former.[188] On one of the hills commanding the stadium are ruins of the temples of Ceres & [..].[189]

Farther on [is] the fountain of Callirhoe so much honored & where Plato has placed the scene of one his dialogues.[190] It is nearly dry, tho' there is still a little stream of the size of a finger. It is very near the place where the Ilissus makes or ought to make a cascade of about 18 or 20 feet. It is singular that in digging here at the depth of 20 feet under the Ilissus they found water. A little church [is] close to the fountain.

The Anchesmus[191] is the handsomest mountain near the city. It commands the citadel on the northeast side. Mr Fauvel[192] says that the same character distinguishes the people of Greece as formerly. The Boeotians are still a heavy, clownish & vicious people (ils aiment les garcons [d'autrui?] & s'en vantent)[193] but the Athenians have not these vices & are comparatively polite & affable. They always salute you as you pass them with a "good morning." They are also very acute, & this acuteness for want of education degenerates into cunning. The Spartans are rude & uncivil. All over this country are scattered Albanese villages of which the people speak no Greek but a peculiar language of their own, a mixture of Sclavonic & other languages. These are very industrious people. Their dress is white consisting

188. As early as the fourth century B.C. the Athenians had constructed a simple stadium on this site. In A.D. 143–144 Herodes Atticus gave the whole site a monumental facelift and made it a typical Roman stadium, building the bridge across the Ilissos at the same time. The bridge survived until 1778, but the stadium was stripped of its marble seats long before.

189. The remains Biddle mentions are probably a temple of Tyche, also built by Herodes as another of his benefactions to the city, and his own tomb.

190. *Phaedrus*.

191. Now Mount Lykavettos.

192. Louis-François-Sebastien Fauvel (1753–1838) was a protégé of the Comte de Choiseul-Gouffier and was his representative in Athens from 1786. From here he dispatched to France many cases of sculptural fragments and plaster casts for his employer, who displayed them in his house. In 1789, Fauvel chose to remain in Greece on his own, where he sold antiquities and acted as a cicerone until the Greek Revolution, when he fled to Smyrna. Biddle happened to be in Athens when both Lusieri and Fauvel were on hand.

193. In this edition Biddle's French is printed just as he wrote it—without correction or modernization of either grammar or accentuation. As was the custom at the time, Biddle resorted to French when a topic might prove embarrassing or salacious.

of a sort of hunting shirt & trousers differing from the Greek costume. It is singular that the people of Megara have the same dress & a different language (being Greek). Mr F says that the people of Athens are much more civilized now than they were 20 years ago. Then the women ran away at the sight of a Franc.[194] The Duke de Choiseul[195] who lodged in the house of the French Consul could not see her[196] until after 12 days of demand & excuse & then only in the presence of a crowd of relations. At present a Greek receives you politely. The commerce is chiefly in oil. A vessel or two of grain in the course of the year. The people of the Morea are depressed more than the Athenians. They have the appearance of being vexed & harrassed. At Athens you may live well but to the south & in the islands you cannot get any meat. Provisions in no part of Turkey so cheap as at Athens. They are however comparatively dear. Athens is not subject to any provincial governor but it is under the protection of the Kislar Aga[197] an officer of the Grand Seignior[198] (who is chief of the black eunuchs) & is like a fief which holds not of a noble but immediately of the Sovereign. The city has a sacred firman which protects it from the jurisdiction & visits of the Bashaws.[199] The city was about one third greater anciently than now.[200] To the north the old walls serve as foundation for the modern. I should observe that altho' Athens formerly releived[201] of the Kislar Aga, it now is subject to a commission at Constantinople. I forget the name but it is a sort of board of commissioners.

194. Applied originally to the French, who conquered large parts of the Aegean after the fall of Constantinople in the Fourth Crusade in 1204, the term was later used of any visitor from western Europe.

195. Comte M. G. F. A. de Choiseul-Gouffier (1752–1817) toured the Levant in 1776, was ambassador to Constantinople in 1785, fled to Russia in 1792, and returned to France in 1802, where he enjoyed his antiquities and wrote his celebrated book: *Voyage Pittoresque de la Grèce*, vol. 1 (1782), vol. 2 (1809), and vol. 3 (1818).

196. That is, the Greek wife of the French consul.

197. The chief of the black eunuchs commanded the guardians of the sultan's harem. He sent a representative to govern Athens and collect the sums that provided his maintenance. The Voivode was his subsidiary in Athens (including Eleusis and Megara) and had to obtain his place yearly. The term *aga* was a title of distinction originally used by military officers in the Ottoman Empire and later also by civil officials.

198. The sultan in Constantinople, who at this time was Selim III (r. 1789–1807).

199. Pashas, or provincial governors.

200. Biddle seems to refer to area rather than population. In his time the population may have been about 8,000; and the Haseki wall, built in 1778, lay everywhere within the limits of the Themistoclean wall built in 479/478 B.C.

201. The spelling of this word, as well as its meaning, is now obsolete. "To relieve of" is to hold a feudal estate from a superior.

Athens Thursday. 29. May

My dear brother,

I have just returned from Aegina for which we started yesterday. We rode to the Piraeus a distance of about five miles. All along we saw the ruins of the famous wall planned by Themistocles & executed by Pericles.[202] It seemed to have been of the breadth of one of our roads & built of large stones. The Piraeus is a large fine harbor subdivided into 3 little ones. Spon & W[heler] say that 45 or 50 of our ships of the line might lie there. Four hundred gallies[203] did anciently. From that all around the Phaleron & Munichia[204] is a wall made by Themistocles. At the entrance of the Piraeus are two foundations one supposed to be Themistocles' tomb.[205] There are also some foundations in the water which seem to have served to shut the port. [Excavations] made by Fauvels predecessor.[206] Munichia is a poor little road, not a port, but Phaleron tho' small is secure & handsome. All over the promontory which connects them are large ruins the remains of warehouses &c. The wall round the port is very fine that is the foundations of it.

We sailed from the Piraeus after night & by the light of the moon reached the port of Aegina about 3 miles distant at 2 o'clock this morning. Having taken some refreshments we set out to walk to a temple on the other side of the island, the chief object of our visit. After about 2 hours walk we came to a little town singularly built in a conical form on a hill.[207] It was in vain that we searched for milk or even water here. It was a long time before we could find the latter after leaving the town and in the whole

202. A walled corridor, called the Long Walls, connected the fortified ring wall of Athens itself with the fortifications built around the harbors at Piraeus by Themistocles, thus making Athens and its port a kind of island. Cimon and Pericles built the Long Walls in the mid-fifth century B.C.

203. That is, warships, or triremes. The Athenians built permanent storage sheds for these ships.

204. Phaleron was and is an open beach where ships could only be drawn up on shore in antiquity. The fortified harbor of Piraeus consisted of three separate bays: the main one, or Kantharos, on the north side of the Akte peninsula; and Zea and Munichya, two small enclosed bays on the south side of the peninsula.

205. This Athenian politician actually died in exile in Asia in 462 B.C., but his bones were supposed to have been brought back and buried in Attica. In Turkish times his tomb, marked by a fallen column, was pointed out on the north shore of the Akte peninsula at the entrance to the Piraeus harbor.

206. This fragment of a sentence is a mystery.

207. Palaiokhora, capital of the island from the ninth century A.D. until 1826, is now abandoned.

island did not find a drop of the former. The people as do indeed most Grecians live upon onions bread olives & sometimes fish. We at last reached the temple. It is situated on the highest part of the island on a commanding situation Attica being on one side & Peloponnesus with its islands on the other. This is perhaps the most ancient building in this part of the world. For want of a better name its foundation is ascribed to Iacus. It is called the temple of Jupiter Panhellenicus.[208] Almost all the columns of the building of about 20 feet high large & of the Doric order show that it must have been a very handsome temple. It is of stone, & the pieces immensely large & evidently of great antiquity. After we had gratified our curiosity & Mr Williams had sketched the temple we returned. The island is rich & well cultivated tho' hilly. We started & after passing Salamis & seeing the field or rather sea of battle between Xerxes & the Athenians[209] got back to the Piraeus in about 5 hours, the wind being fair. From the Piraeus we walked home. Mr Williams & myself lost our way & wandered about in the fields for some time so that I calculate on having walked at least 18 miles. Such a walk is not friendly to writing so good night.   N B.

                                         Athens Monday evg
                                         June 2d

My dear Tom

   Another excursion from which I returned this evg will fill up the interval between my last. On Saturday May 31st at 5 o'clock we left Athens. We took the road between Anchesmus & the citadel, & in about 4 hours reached the little town of Cephissia. This is no way remarkable except as being the birthplace of Menander & as being near the rise of the Cephissus which begins at Mt Pentelicus. The comic poet would find more subject of sorrow than mirth in the present state of his town. We stopped but for a moment, & went towards Marathon[210] which we reached in about 4 hours

---

208. Built in the late sixth or the early fifth century B.C. on the site of earlier temples, the existing structure was dedicated, as we know on the basis of inscriptional evidence, to Aphaia, or Britomartis. Its pedimental sculpture, now in the Glyptothek in Munich, was uncovered in excavations in 1811. Aikos was a legendary king of Aigina.
209. The famous naval battle of 480 B.C., described in Herodotus's Book 8.
210. This is a plain on the northeast coast of Attica, the site of the battle between

more. The country is in general very good, & the plain part well cultivated with olives & grain but towards Marathon you cross the ridge of Penteli which is barren & the road disagreeable. As we descended into the plain we stopped to see two caves in the side of the hill & called I think the cave of Pan. Yet they are wholly unworthy of notice except that Pausanias mentions them & that Wheeler could not find them.[211] Near this is the course of the stream which waters the valley. Descending from Pentelicus this long & fine valley presents itself in nearly a semicircular form being made by a large bay of the sea, one end of the land (the northern) stretching over nearly to Negropont. It is singular that Barthelemy does not give this bay in his map. The valley extends along the sea side about a mile or mile & ½ in breadth & perhaps 5 or 6 in length. It is very rich & well cultivated. As we entered it from the north we left the little village of Marathon on the right. This village still inherits the great name tho' it does not probably occupy the same spot. It is so very small that I passed it unperceived. We rode on & about the middle of the valley on the eastern side of it we saw one of the Tumuli.[212] We of course approached this venerable monument of Greek patriotism. It is a simple mass of earth about 35 feet high & 30 diameter. It was of a conical form but they have dug on two of its sides for antiques. Fauvel did it. He found nothing—thinks it a Persian tomb. In the apertures the bees have taken possession & perforated every part. After seeing this we went on towards the south, & soon came to a little island in the midst of a marsh. The marsh was formerly the lake & on the island are ruins which point it out as the spot where was the tomb of the Athenians.[213] There remain some pieces of marble, one or two prostrate columns, & four or five pedestals. In digging here Mr Fauvel the F. Consul found a bust of

---

Athenian hoplites under the command of Miltiades and the Persians in 490 B.C., described in Herodotus's Book 6.

211. Pausanias 1.32.3ff. If Biddle entered the plain from the north, keeping the big marsh on his left, the caves he mentions must have been on Mount Koraki on his right, because he next mentions the stream (the Kharadra) and the village of Marathon. The cave of Pan is now thought to lie west of the village and just above Oinoe, on the road to Kephissia and the modern Marathon reservoir.

212. The Soros, or burial place of the Athenian infantry slain in the battle against the Persians in 490 B.C., is the largest of the tumuli in the plain. Fauvel was wrong to consider it a Persian tomb, for later excavations confirmed its identity. In another tumulus farther west were buried the Plataians.

213. The Roman ruins in the small marsh on the south edge of the plain were certainly not those of the Athenian dead of 490, but perhaps a temple of Athena Hellotis (so Leake), decorated by Herodes Atticus, whose country estate was in the neighborhood, or else perhaps Herodes' family mausoleum.

Marcus Aurelius & a number of Roman coins, that is Romanized Greek
ones. The bust might have been placed there originally to flatter the emperor & [was] after buried to conceal it from the barbarians. Unfortunately
we did not see Mr F before going there & therefore did not examine the
spot to so much advantage. We rode on the marsh being towards the
southern extremity of the plain, & after leaving it reached the little town of
Cochla which overlooks the whole plain. We here stopped and made a sort
of dinner under a tree. Our dinner would be unworthy of remark were it
not that we got here the best honey that any of us ever tasted the tyme of
Pentelicus being delightful. I omitted to say that in coming from Athens
to Marathon we passed a part of the ancient road on the hill. We left
Cochla & after a ride of three hours of hilly bad road reached the monastery
of Penteli on the mountain of the same name. We roused the slumbering
friars for it was now dark & after eating went to bed, having made 13 hours
of disagreeable road.

    We left the monastery on Sunday June 1st morning, & having rode up
the mountain about half an hour & there walked about a quarter more the
road being too steep for a horse we got to the quarries whence was taken
the famous Pentelic marble. They seemed to have worked in many parts,
but the grand quarry is a most beautiful thing. The marble is cut down
perpendicularly as in our quarries for about 70 or 80 feet in a rectangular
manner. At the angle below is a large cavern from which the marble was
also taken. This grotto is of a stupendous size. On each side on entering are
seen large niches or places for the workmen to live in. By means of light we
advanced about 150 feet inside to the end of the cavern which has been
worked at the very extreme part where are seen the marks of the chisel. The
roof does not seem to have needed support; there are however several columns of the marble left perhaps for that purpose. They are small and
roughly hewn. At two corners are springs of water. They are very low down
& the passage to one of them is long & disagreeable. The water drips thro'
the rock & forms some petrifactions which it is however difficult to get
entire. The marble is in some parts very brilliant & has the appearance of
being christallized. The entrance of the grotto is covered with beautiful
long ivy. The view of the plain & the city of Athens which is about two
hours off is very pretty. The whole quarry with the enormous masses of
stone which are some of them half cut gives a great idea of this people. We
returned to the monastery mounted our horses at 7 & took the road for
Sunium. In doing so we were obliged to cover a part of the land we came,
Penteli being out of the road from Marathon to Sunium. The ride lies

much thro' fields of grain there being no direct path in many parts. After a good deal of heat, & stopping at one or two hamlets, among the rest Vraunia[214] probably ancient Brauron, we reached the village of Cheratia. This is a large village 10 hours distant from the monastery of Penteli. It has almost 3 or 4 hundred people. I here made a purchase of one or two coins partly from curiosity & partly from charity. In the morning we left this town & after three hours & a half of disagreeable country reached the promontory of Sunium now called Capo Colonni. We were recompensed for our fatigue by the sight of its ruins. The port is small & to the westward around it are the remains of docks & things of that sort. On the hill are the ruins of the wall & still further up those of the fortress of which there is a large part of one side still a little above ground. On the top is the famous temple of Minerva.[215] This overlooks the fine bald rocky shore of the point. Of the building which seems to have been small there remain [..] columns towards the sea [..] columns & two pilasters towards the east three to the north & none to the west. A part of the architrave yet remains. The entrance was to the east between the pilasters. The view is delightful. It embraces a part of Negropont, Long Island or Macronisi [&] still nigher the continent, a number of other islands & among which is Idra the whole coast of the Morea Aegina & Salamis. The columns are Doric. We remained here some time to admire & to bathe, & starting about 9 rode along the coast & came on to Athens at night the ride being about 9 hours. Adieu

N B.

The next day Tuesday June 3 I remained at Athens. I was glad to find my Venetian acquaintance Savy who has followed me here. With him I passed the morning & afterwards went to Mr Fauvel's the French consuls where I dined [Fig. 9]. He is a very amiable sensible man & better informed than any other of all that relates to Grecian antiquities &c. From him I got much information. After dining I walked with Savy until night when I returned to my lodgings & slept.

Wednesday June 4 was passed in the same way. Le soir je quittais avec beaucoup de regret mon ami Savy. C'est un des hommes les plus interessants que je connais. C'est un disciple de Rousseau par un pupile duquel il

214. Anc. Brauron, mod. Vraona or Vravrona.
215. This temple, now attributed to Poseidon, was built in the 440s B.C., perhaps by the architect of the Hephaisteion (Temple of Theseus) in Athens.

a été elevé. Les malheurs de son pays l'ont chassé de Venise, mais je le crois toujours aussi honnete et aimable & malheureux. Au point de son depart, il m'a confié ses besoins et je me fis un veritable plaisir de l'assister. C' etoit peu de chose ce que je pouvais lui offrir. Mais c'etoit donne du coeur plutot que de la main. J'éspere un jour d'etendre de meilleures nouvelles de lui. Il va m'envoyer à Paris un de ses ouvrages. Vingt cinq pieces que je lui e donné aujourdui etoient quelque chose pour ma pètite bourse mais je les gagnerai par oeconomie. Au reste je crois d'avoir fait des biens à un honnete homme. Quoique j'ai fait beaucoup de follies il me reste toujours un assez bon coeur à ce qu'il me semble, & il me fait toujours un grande plaisir de pouvoir suppléer aux besoins des malheureux.

The next day Thursday June 5 I spent in examining more minutely the temple of Theseus the Areopagus & Pnix, as well as the Musaeum. I then paid a visit to Mr Fauvel with whom I remained a long time occupied in discourse upon Greek antiquities from which I derived much information. After dinner I went with Mr Palmer & Walpole to look for the situation of the Lyceum Cynosarges & some old walls in which we were about half successful.

Friday June 6th morning Mr Lusieri called upon me & I walked with him first to the Areopagus afterwards to his house where I saw a number of curiosities in his collection.

After dinner I had the pleasure of a visit from Mr Fauvel the French consul with whom I had a very interesting walk to the Academy & Ceramicus.[216] The information I gained today & for a few days past is put into my next notebook.

{On page 187 is a diagram labeled the Pnix, followed by two more smaller, preparatory sketches of the same on succeeding pages.}

{On the back of the last page and written upside down in relation to the journal as a whole are seven words in Greek script in a hand other than Biddle's. They are followed by an address. I transcribe the words exactly as they are written and without correcting them.}

ἠγαπιμενοσου φίλος μεχμετ
σελύμπαοις της γλαρέντζας[217]

---

216. The Kerameikos was the major cemetery of ancient Athens and was located in the valley of the Eridanos stream to the northwest of the Acropolis, outside the city walls on the road to Eleusis.

217. These seven words are a fascinating bit of social history. They are without doubt the actual signature of the customs official whom Biddle met on first entering the Peloponnese

Mr McKenzie
No. 26 Upper Guildford Street, Christ Church[218]
Oxford—Thebes 1806
{On the first unnumbered page of the journal are a few reminders:}
Paid for Mr Savy at Messina nineteen taris & a half.
For Mr Semple one onze nineteen taris & two baioes.
When I see Paris let me get Guise's letters on Greece. Guise was a Marseilles merchant, & he wrote about 1770 two books in Duodecimo, some learning much sense & a good deal of the philosophy of a traveller.
Rousseau lodged at Paris hotel St Quentin. Rue de Cordeliers proche la Sorbonne—*Confessions*, Liv. 7

---

and whom he describes in detail. Translated, they read: "Your devoted friend Mechmet Selim Bey at Glarentza." Though a Turk and a Moslem, the man spoke and wrote Greek. It was common for Turks to be completely ignorant not only of Turkish in its Arabic written form, but even of the spoken language itself. This official may well have been bilingual, but it is worth noting that he could conduct business in Greek. By modern standards his spelling is erratic, especially his problems with itacism.

218. Upper Guildford Street is actually an address in London, presumably that of Mackenzie's father.

The temple (called also the Parthenon) probably
has not certainly lost its statue in the irruption
of Alaric. The Christians made it a church
the Turks a mosque, the Venetians in 1687
threw a bomb which broke the roof & damaged
the building. They then made a new mosque
now standing in the middle of the temple. It
spoils much the effect of the building.

To the north is the temple of Neptune Erechtheus
& Minerva Polias an odd shaped building of
something like this form.

This temple built jointly for Nep. & Min. is
very beautiful — the columns ionic — the capitals finely worked — one entire column
taken by Elgin — the Nep. side was the well
in Minerva's the lamp to be filled annually.
The temples were quite single. The portico is
singularly placed. The Pandrosion where was
preserved the famous olive tree — is a small one
are building annexed to the temple of Min.
around the sides are six female figures supporting the roof with a crown or basket
something on their head. These are the Caryatides, representing the women of Carya.

The present ascent to the citadel differs from the
old one which went up near the grotto of Pan
say Andrechaix's Medal.
This grotto of Pan is a cave just under the citadel
& in the pock of it. There are some rests of brick wall
probably of a Christian chapel.
The Pelasgi had been employed to level the
acropolis. In proportion as population increased
the city extended towards the south & afterwards
all around. The ruins of its old walls are still visible in part, being incrusted in the new, & serving as
a base for them. The acropolis is somewhat of an
oval, most perpendicular to the east.
The Pelasgicon thinks Chandler, was the ground
under the citadel & above the houses, which is
now uninhabited; the long rocks some large single
rocks now fallen near Pan's cave.
Under the acropolis to the south is the situation of the theatre of Bacchus. Here were represented the celebrated works of Euripides Soph. &c
afterwards the contests of gladiators which they
learnt from Rome. The form alone remains,
there being no ruins above ground, but we see
enough to appear how great was the building
It must have been magnificent, the spectators
sitting on the declivity of the hill. The people sat
here sometimes. Over the theatre in the rock
of the citadel is a grotto converted to the church
of Panagia Spiliotissa, the Virgin of the grotto.
The front is adorned with corinthian marble
pilasters, on the entablature of which are 3 inscriptions denoting the names of the victors in
the chorusses who then placed tripods on the
monument. On the top of the cavern is an
ancient sundial moved out of its place. There
was also a statue of Bacchus without a head,
taken away by Elgin. Still higher up are two
unequal columns with triangular capitals
to support tripods. On the base of one is an unintelligible inscription from which however
could collect that the victor has a Roman
name. A little to the east of the theatre is a little church
in false ruins, where was once the temple of Bacchus & an ancient temple here
is an ancient sundial in the wall of the church

Fig. 2.   Bombardment of Tripoli, August 1804, by Currier and Ives. Courtesy of the
Library of Congress

Fig. 3.   The town and harbor of Zante, plate XII of James Cartwright's *Views of the Ionian
Islands* (London, 1821). Courtesy of the British Library

Above: Fig. 4. The Piazza of St. Marc in Zante, plate XI of James Cartwright's *Views of the Ionian Islands* (London, 1821). Courtesy of the British Library

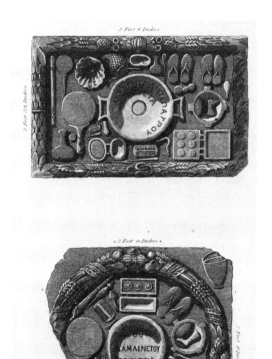

Left: Fig. 5. Aberdeen's marbles from Amyclae, plate facing page 446 of Robert Walpole's *Memoirs Relating to European and Asiatic Turkey* (London, 1818). Courtesy of the Library Company of Philadelphia

Fig. 6. Dinner with the Bishop of Chryso, Edward Dodwell's *Views in Greece* (London, 1821). Courtesy of Archives and Rare Books Department, University of Cincinnati Libraries

Fig. 7. Interior of an Athenian House, Otto Magnus von Stackelberg, *Trachten und Gebraüche der Neugriechen* (Berlin, 1831). Courtesy of the Art and Architecture Collection, Miriam and Ira D. Wallach Division of Art, Prints and Photographs, New York Public Library, Astor, Lenox and Tilden Foundation

Fig. 8. View of Athens from Anchesmus, John Cam Hobhouse's *A Journey through Albania* (2d edition, London, 1813), vol. 1, opposite page 292

Fig. 9. The Athenian Acropolis from Fauvel's House, plate XIX of Louis Dupré's *Voyage à Athènes et à Constantinople* (Paris, 1825). Courtesy of the Philadelphia Museum of Art Library

Fig. 10. Athens seen from the Academy, Otto Magnus von Stackelberg's *La Grèce*, vol. 2 (Paris, 1834). Courtesy of the Library Company of Philadelphia

Fig. 11. The Athenian Acropolis from the Propylaea, Edward Dodwell's *Views in Greece* (London, 1821). Courtesy of Archives and Rare Books Department, University of Cincinnati Libraries

Fig. 12. View of the Erechtheum, Edward Dodwell's *Views in Greece* (London, 1821). Courtesy of Archives and Rare Books Department, University of Cincinnati Libraries

Fig. 13. The "Pantheon" of Hadrian, Otto Magnus von Stackelberg's *La Grèce*, vol. 2 (Paris, 1834). Courtesy of the Library Company of Philadelphia

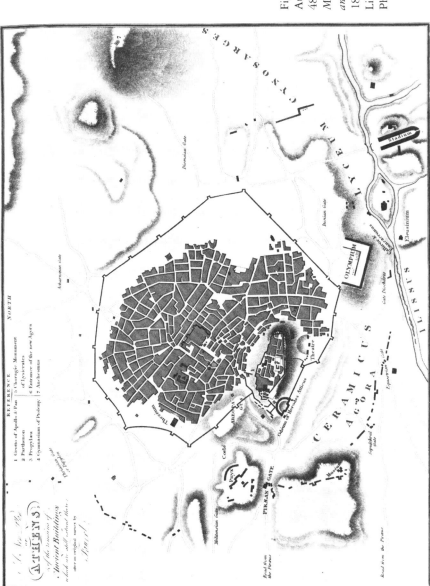

Fig. 14. Fauvel's Plan of Athens, plate facing page 480 of Robert Walpole's *Memoirs Relating to European and Asiatic Turkey* (London, 1818). Courtesy of the Library Company of Philadelphia

Fig. 15. The Capuchin convent in Athens, J. Stuart and N. Revett's *The Antiquities of Athens*, vol. I, chap. IV (London, 1762)

Fig. 16. The ancient agora of Corinth, Otto Magnus von Stackelberg's *La Grèce*, vol. I (Paris, 1834). Courtesy of the Library Company of Philadelphia

Fig. 17. Interior of the Treasury of Atreus at Mycenae, plate 10 of Edward Dodwell's *Views and Descriptions of Cyclopean or Pelasgic Remains in Greece and Italy* (London, 1814). Courtesy of the Library Company of Philadelphia.

Fig. 18. Plain of the Eurotas; View of Mistra, Otto Magnus von Stackelberg's *La Grèce*, vol. 1 (Paris, 1834). Courtesy of the Library Company of Philadelphia

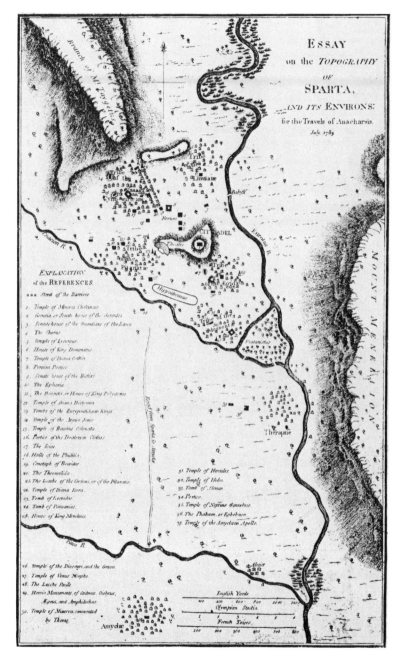

Fig. 19. Topography of Sparta by Barbié du Bocage, *Maps, Plans, Views, and Coins Illustrative of the Travels of Anacharsis the Younger*, No. 25 (Dublin, 1795). Courtesy of Archives and Special Collections, Shadek-Fackenthal Library, Franklin and Marshall College

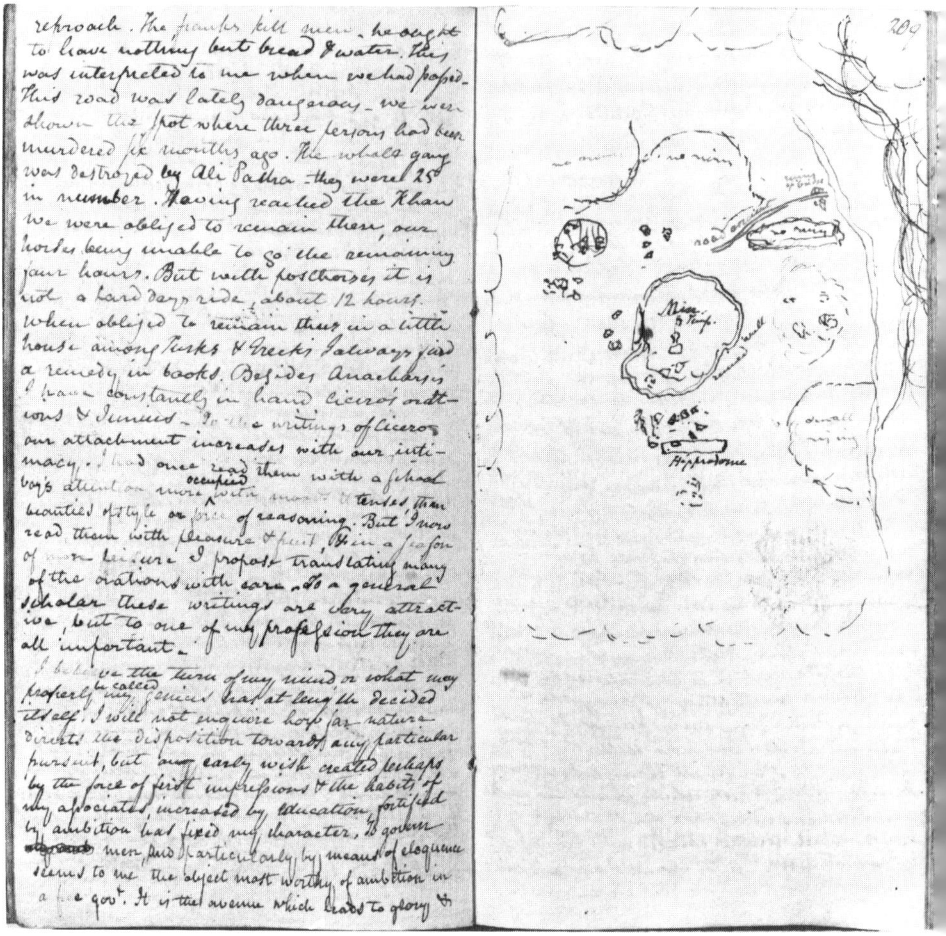

reproach. The Franks kill men, he ought
to have nothing but bread & water. this
was interpreted to me when we had passed.
This road was lately dangerous. we were
shown the spot where three persons had been
murdered six months ago. The whole gang
was destroyed by Ali Pasha. they were 25
in number. Having reached the Khan
we were obliged to remain there, our
horses being unable to go the remaining
four hours. But with posthorses it is
not a hard days ride, about 12 hours.
When obliged to remain thus in a little
house among Turks & Greeks I always find
a remedy in books. Besides Anacharsis
I have constantly in hand Cicero's orations & Junius. To the writings of Cicero
our attachment increases with our intimacy. I had once read them with a school
boy's attention more occupied with moods & tenses than
beauties of style or force of reasoning. But I now
read them with pleasure & profit. If in a season
of more leisure I propose translating many
of the orations with care. To a general
scholar these writings are very attractive, but to one of my profession they are
all important.

I believe the turn of my mind or what may
properly be called my genius has at length decided
itself. I will not inquire how far nature
directs the disposition towards any particular
pursuit, but an early wish created perhaps
by the force of first impressions & the habits of
my associates, increased by education, fortified
by ambition has fixed my character. To govern
men, and particularly by means of eloquence
seems to me the object most worthy of ambition in
a free gov^t. It is the avenue which leads to glory &

Fig. 20. Biddle's Second Greek Journal, Map of Sparta and autograph pages 208–9. Courtesy of the Historical Society of Philadelphia

Second Greek Journal

Athens June 7th 1806
Saturday

I occupied myself today in reading & writing relative to the antiquities &c of this place. In the afternoon I walked over & examined the Lycabettus,[1] the Pnix, the Musaeum, the fountain of Calliroe & the temple of Hadrian.[2] What struck me with regard to these objects I have put together at the end of the book. In the afternoon called at the convent to see Palmer.

Sunday June 8th 1806

I this morning walked out to Colonos [Fig. 10] where Oedipus retired & gave occasion to the tragedy of Sophocles.[3] After dinner I called on the Austrian consul & afterwards on Mr Fauvel who I found on the point of coming to my house. There is to me nothing more agreeable than to converse with a man of sense on a subject which he knows thoroughly. I experienced this pleasure many times with Mr Fauvel [Fig. 9]. An amiable Frenchman of the old school of manners, & perfectly acquainted with this country, which he first saw 25 years ago, & where he has resided 20, he is

1. What Biddle called Lycavettus, a hill to the north of the Pnyx, is now known as the Hill of the Nymphs, where an observatory was built in 1842. The ancient name may have been the Hill of Hyakinthos.

2. The temple of Olympian Zeus, finished by Hadrian.

3. The hill of Kolonos Hippios, which in antiquity lay west of the city, was immortalized by Sophocles' tragedy *Oidipos at Kolonos*, in which the Theban hero Oidipos comes in his old age to take up residence on the hill to be a protecting genius of Athens. He was later buried on the Areopagos.

able & willing to convey all instruction. I walked with him up to the citadel which I now saw well with his explanations. After a walk we stopped at the convent [Fig. 15] where we remained until after night. What I learnt I have put for the sake of order at the end of this little book.

I have sometimes thought that there might be such a thing as honest neutrality that a man in private life might mingle with the bitterest enemies without compromising his integrity or impartiality. In politics it requires much independence & an almost total want of ambition. I smiled in passing from Naples to Messina to find myself transferred from the camp of the French to that of their enemies. The same thing occurred the other day when I walked in the morning with Lusieri & in the afternoon with Fauvel. Both artists & both here on the same object they lost no opportunity of abusing each other grossly. Yet most of our enmities arise from misintelligence & if men would only explain before they quarrel there would certainly be less disputes. I listened to both these gentlemen with gravity & endeavored to extract the knowledge of both without entering into the animosities of either. Fauvel is however much the superior man.

Monday June 9th

I was this morning occupied in asking questions & writing. We had intended starting today, but the delay of an expected courier from Patras prevented us. In the afternoon I was at the convent where were some gentlemen & much talk. The English consul (The Logotheti[1]) is a very stupid & I think a very bad man. The Austrian consul is a French merchant & a gentleman. The French consul a very good man; the Russian I do not know. The information gleaned today put at the end.

Continuation of a Few Notes on Athens

The town began with the citadel [Figs. 8, 11, and 14]. Anchesmus tho' higher was not preferred because its top is pointed. In the infancy of states security from the violence of neighbors is the first object in choosing a

4. The family name was Khromatianos; his title was logothetes. Nikolaos Khromatianos had been appointed vice-consul by Elgin in 1802 and was promoted to consul in 1816. Nikolaos's father, Spyridon, had served in the same capacity.

position. The citadel well calculated—the top extensive, the rock perpendicular, to be taken only by famine or rather want of water. It is now
surrounded by a wall defended by towers & cannon and covered with small
houses most of which are deserted. The two temples which once adorned it
still remain. The temple of Minerva built by Pericles—fine ruins—100
feet broad, 227 long, 69 high. The order Doric, the marble Pentelique, &
its original whiteness has been softened by the yellow tinge perhaps peculiar to this country. The columns fluted & without bases. There are 8
in front & 17 on the side. In the fronton are or rather were a groupe of
statuary representing the birth of Minerva.[5] It has all disappeared except
two statues mutilated of Adrian and his wife. Probably new heads to old
statues not true original statues says F [but] put there by flattery. On the
other fronton was her contest with Neptune for the city. On the northern
side the games of the Panathenea.[6] On the back fronton or eastern side are
little holes in the architrave under the reliefs to which were attached buck-
lers as round some of the holes there are circular marks. There are also a
number of indentures near the holes to which ornaments were perhaps attached. All the reliefs of this temple have been taken away & even the
architrave injured by the agent of Elgin. On the north side 9 columns are
standing & perhaps the same number to the south. The temple runs east &
west. The place of the statue is marked by a square of stone, not marble
but stone, it being unnecessary to make of marble what was covered & by a
little descent in the pavement [was] to receive the water to preserve the
ivory of the statue from shrinking.[7] The temple everyday crumbling into
pieces is a melancholy monument of our littleness & our grandeur. The
temple (called also the Parthenon) probably tho' not certainly lost its statue
in the irruption of Alaric.[8] The Christians made it a church the Turks a

5. The sculpture of the east pediment showed the birth of Athena, that of the west
pediment the contest of Athena and Poseidon. After Elgin's removal of the sculpture from
the east pediment, their was nothing left for Biddle to see there. The two mutilated human
statues he mentions may be "Kekrops and his daughter" from the northwest angle of the *west*
pediment.
     6. Since the metopes on the northern long side of the building, which showed scenes
from the Sack of Troy, were mostly destroyed, Biddle seems to refer to the frieze that ran
around the outside of the top of the cella wall.
     7. Pausanias (5.11.10) says that before the gold and ivory statue of Zeus at Olympia lay
a pool of olive oil to preserve the statue from the marshy air of the place and that the Athena
Parthenos was protected by a pool of water against dryness.
     8. The disappearance of the Phidian gold and ivory colossus of Athena cannot be dated
exactly. The last reference to it is in the middle of the fifth century A.D. Whether the

mosque. The Venetians in 1687 threw a bomb which broke the roof &
damaged the building. They[9] then made a new mosque now standing in
the middle of the temple. It spoils much the effect of the building.
To the north is the temple of Neptune Erechtheus & Minerva Polias an
odd shaped building [Fig. 12]. This temple built jointly for Nep. & Min.
is very beautiful—the columns Ionic the capitals divinely worked. One
entire column taken by Elgin.[10] In Nep.'s side was the well in Minerva's
the lamp to be filled annually.[11] The temples were quite small. The portico
is singularly placed. The Pandrosion where was preserved the famous olive
tree is a small square building annexed to the temple of Min. Around the
sides are six female figures supporting the roof with a crown or basket
of something on their heads. These are the Caryatides, representing the
women of Carya.
   The present ascent to the citadel differs from the old one which went up
near the grotto of Pan says Anacharsis' medal.[12] This grotto of Pan is a cave
just under the citadel & in the rock of it. There are some rests of brick
walls probably of a Christian chapel.
   The Pelasgi had been employed to level the Acropolis or citadel.[13] In

---

original had previously survived fires and the stripping away of its gold plate is anybody's
guess. It may well have fallen a victim to Christian fanaticism. Alaric the Visigoth devas-
tated Greece in A.D. 395.
   9. The Moslem inhabitants of Athens. When this mosque partially collapsed in 1842, it
was decided to clear it away completely as an eyesore.
   10. As well as removing sample architectural fragments from the building, Elgin took
one of the Caryatids, which is now in the British Museum. No one really knows why the
Athenians used the figures of women to support the south porch. They called these figures
simply *korai*, or maidens. (The Roman architectural writer Vitruvius [1.1.4] says that the
Peloponnesian town of Carya sided with the Persians in the Persian war and was afterward
conquered by the Athenians, who killed the men and enslaved the women. To memorialize
the shame of the town, the Athenians made statues of women carrying burdens.) A sketch of
the Erechtheion is in Figure 1. Biddle identified the shrine of Pandrosos, daughter of Kekrops and first priestess of Athena, with the Caryatid Porch. The actual shrine is now
thought to have lain to the west of the building.
   11. In the mythical contest with Athena for possession of Attica, Poseidon struck the
rock of the Acropolis with his trident and produced a salt spring, symbol of the Athenians'
future career as a sea power. Before the cult statue of Athena Polias burned a lamp whose
light was never allowed to go out.
   12. Biddle refers to a coin illustration for chapter XII of Barthélemy. Each edition usually
contained a separate volume of maps, views, and coins. When the Acropolis was fortified in
the Middle Ages, a long, winding ascent from the southwest replaced the older, straightforward climb from the west.
   13. This legendary race of non-Hellenes was employed by the Athenians to fortify the
Acropolis (Herodotus 6.137). The "cyclopean" wall they were supposed to have built was

proportion as population increased the city extended towards the south first, & afterwards all around. The ruins of its old walls are still visible in part, being incrusted in the new, & serving as a base for them. The Acropolis is somewhat of an oval, most perpendicular to the east.

Under the Acropolis to the south is the situation of the theatre of Bacchus [Fig. 14]. Here were represented the celebrated works of Euripides, Sophocles & afterwards the contests of gladiators which they learnt from Rome. The form alone remains; there being no ruins above ground; but we see enough to assure us how great was the building.[14] It must have been magnificent; the spectators sitting on the declivity of the hill. The people meet here sometimes. Over the theatre & in the rock of the citadel is a grotto converted to the Church of Panagia Spiliotissa, the Virgin of the grotto. The front is adorned with Corinthian marble pilasters, on the entablature of which are 3 inscriptions denoting the names of the victors in the choruses who then placed tripods on this monument. On the top of the cavern is an ancient sundial moved out of its place. There was also a statue of Bacchus without a head, taken away by Elgin.[15] Still higher up are two unequal columns with triangular capitals to support tripods. On the base of one is an unintelligible inscription from which however I could collect that the victor has a Roman name. A little to the east of the theatre is a little church where was once the temple of Bacchus called *in paludibus*.[16] Nothing remains of the ancient temple. There is an ancient sundial in the wall of the church. Still more to the south or south west are the ruins of another building which Chandler supposes to have been the Odeum of Pericles of which the masts & yards of Persian ships formed the roof so as to resemble

---

identified with the earliest fortification, stretches of which still exist. Modern archaeologists, who have no use for the legend of the Pelasgians, date this wall to the period 1250–1200 B.C.

14. Here Biddle correctly identifies the position of the Theater of Dionysos.

15. The choregic monument of Thrasyllos, built in 320 B.C., was destroyed in the Turkish siege of the Acropolis in 1827. The Roman statue of Dionysos replaced the earlier Greek tripods. The two columns were Roman additions, which also supported tripods. Thrasyllos had dedicated the small cave, now some thirty-four feet long and twenty feet wide, to Dionysos; but with the arrival of Christianity, the cave was rededicated to the Virgin.

16. An integral part of the Theater of Dionysos Eleuthereos was his shrine. Two small temples were built to him, one in the sixth and one in the fourth century B.C. These lay to the south of the theater and were unknown in Biddle's time. Before the fifth century, theatrical contexts in honor of Dionysos were held in the Athenian marketplace, where there was another shrine of Dionysos, the Lenaion, which has not yet been located. As for the shrine of Dionysos "in the marshes," no one can yet say with certainty where it should be located, whether in some place near the theater, in the marketplace, or in some third place.

Xerxes's pavilion, celebrated as a beautiful building. It was afterwards rebuilt by Herodius Atticus for his wife Regilla.[17] Barthelemy however says that it is indeed the temple of H. Atticus, but not the Odeum of Pericles, which he places at the other corner of the citadel. Pausanias [was] not saying that H. At. *rebuilt* but *made* (εποιησεν) [it]. Between it & the theatre of Bacchus is a row of arches supposed to have supported a portico.[18]

This theatre of Atticus is much smaller than that of Bacchus. The inner wall of the proscenium consisting of a number of arches & serving as part of the castle wall still exists, as do also some of the two wings of the circular part. Near this theatre is now a Turkish burial ground.

The Areopagus is a small hill near the citadel which seems to have been once joined to it, for the rise from the first to the second is gradual & there is [a] very little valley [which] intervened. This is now a barren rock which is crossed in the middle by the city wall.[19] There was formerly a building there as the remain of its roof is mentioned by a writer in Augustus's time. Now utterly ruined on the side towards the city are seen some cuttings on the rock, a small stair case out of it, & a ruin of a church called St Dionysius, built says Lusieri (how does he know?) on the spot where Dionysius the Areopagite lived.[20] The court of judicature old & venerable [which] sat here existed in Pausanias's time, not in Theodosius [the] younger's.[21] Actions for murder [were] tried in open air so that criminal & accuser should not be under the same roof.

Near the Areopagus is the Temple of Theseus built it is not known by whom. It is composed of 6 columns in front & 13 in the side. Of a beautiful Doric, they have been put out of order (the pieces lapping one over the other) by an earthquake. The shape resembles that of the Parthenon. The roof is modern. The old one was plain the present one vaulted. It is now a

17. The Odeion of Herodes Atticus, built for his wife, Regilla, lay on the southwest slope of the Acropolis; Pericles' Odeion lay on the southeast slope. The former was not *rebuilt* by Herodes. Chandler was wrong, and Barthélemy right.

18. The long stoa built by Eumenes II of Pergamon (197–159 B.C.) and anciently connecting the odeia of Pericles and Herodes, was made a part of the lower fortification of the Acropolis by the Turks in 1687. The arches were originally the back wall of the stoa and served as a retaining wall.

19. The Turkish wall of 1778.

20. In A.D. 51 the apostle Paul, preaching on the Areopagus, converted one Dionysios, who became St. Dionysios, the patron saint of Athens. A succession of Christian churches were built on the northern side of the hill in honor of the saint. The remains of the last of them are now visible.

21. The traveler Pausanias flourished around A.D. 150; Theodosius the younger was responsible for the Theodosian law code of 438.

Greek church [of] St George. They have spoilt the pronaos the entrance of the temple to make the Altar. The door is modern & in the side of the building. On the citadel side the earth is as high as the steps but on the others you see the mounting place. In the temple is a circular piece of marble once employed as a baptismal fount. It is covered with names which seem to be those of the persons who had a right to sit at the public tables, or the Prytaneum. On the freize are the combats of the Centaurs & Lapiths & the Athenians & Amazons.[22]

Nearest the temple of Theseus is the hill Lycabettus. There are no remains here, except chambers cut in the rock and steps indicating its having been inhabited. It was out of the town for there are tombs in the rock. There are also a number of traces of ancient wheels over the rock. Two large excavations like wells. Near one a number of marks. Mr F is surprized at seeing traces of wheels on both sides of this. I think it is a sort of reservoir of filth & the traces those of a cart approaching to empty itself.

The Pnix is but a small hill. On the side you see a large wall level with the ground whose shape shows that it must have made a semicircular platform of earth. About the middle of this is the pulpit cut out of the rock which is cut perpendicularly on each side of it for a considerable distance. On the pulpit's right is a niche supposed to have been occupied by Hygaea from the *ex votos* about it.[23] On the pulpit's left is another niche which from its shape says Fauvel must have been a Neptune & still further on small steps. On each side of the pulpit, on a level with it are steps perhaps for magistrates. Going from the pulpit up the mountain there is a second platform cut out of the rock. Here are steps & niches corresponding with those below & on the pavement of the platform certain holes of about half a foot diameter & in the form of a parallelogram intended thinks Chandler for "tablets containing decrees & orders," says Fauvel for stretching tents across in hot weather. It was from this top that the orators must have harangued first, for here they see the water; below they cannot.[24] After

22. The eastern frieze within the peristyle shows Theseus subduing the sons of Pallas; the western frieze, just over the porch, shows Lapiths battling Centaurs.

23. The site of the Pnyx was also an age-old sanctuary of Zeus Hypsistos as a healing god. The many niches cut into the rock face beside the bema, or pulpit, were intended for dedicatory plaques, usually of parts of the human body. As early as 1803 Lord Aberdeen had carried away a number of these plaques, which were acquired by Lord Elgin and are now in the British Museum. Others have since been found.

24. Biddle refers to Plutarch's *Themistocles* (19.4). The earliest bema did "face the sea." Later the Thirty Tyrants turned it to look inland. But Biddle was wrong in his surmise

much looking I cannot think these holes destined either for tablets or tents.
I cannot explain them.[25]

The temple of Jupiter Olympian to the south east of the citadel is composed of sixteen columns, Corinthian & fluted, about 6 feet diameter & 60
high, some simple, some with a piece of architrave on a part of which are
the ruins of the habitation of a hermit [Fig. 13]. These columns form the
part of the building, & of a triple row of columns. The whole number of
columns when the building was entire was 116 or 120; began by Pisis-
tratus, finished by Hadrian. In 1676 there were 17 columns. Their form is
a strait line. Three of the columns are detached from the rest. The others
are arranged in 3 rows.

Behind Anchesmus are some ruins of the aqueduct made by Hadrian.[26]

The Musaeum so called from Musaeus who was buried there.[27] [The?]
ruin of the monument of Philopappus is the part of a semicircle, the convex
side turned to the Piraeus [Fig. 14]. There are now two niches & there was
a third. In the first is a sitting statue with the inscription King Antiochus
son of King Antiochus. In the second another sitting statue inscribed "Philopappus son [of] Antiochus Epiphanes of Bisa." They do not know much
of this man or why the monument was raised. There is a pilaster between
the statues which mentions the name of Caius Julius Antiochus Epiphanes
who lived under Trajan & who was perhaps the subject of the monument &
placed in the third niche. The other two are thought to be his ancestors.[28]

---

about the upper rock, which probably never served as the bema. He did not know that
originally the bema was at the *foot* of a north-facing slope and that though it did face the sea
to the south, neither the speaker nor his listeners could actually *see* the water. The audience
looked north and down over the marketplace to Parnes and Penteli, and the speaker looked
up into the cavea of a natural theater.

25. The cuttings in the rock of the terrace above the bema, if these are what Biddle has in
mind, may be those for an altar or a sundial.

26. One of Hadrian's many public works in Athens was an aqueduct, begun in A.D. 125
and finished in 140. Part of the monumental facade of its reservoir on the southeast slope of
(present) Lykavettos stood until 1778. In Biddle's day, part of the inscription of this facade
was built into one of the gates of the Turkish wall around Athens. Edward Dodwell (*Views
in Greece*) drew a fine picture of it.

27. Mousaios was a mythical singer supposed to have taught cures and oracles.

28. The central figure was Philopappos of Besa, who was buried here; the one on the left
was Antiochos IV of Commagene, Philopappos's grandfather; the missing figure on the
right was King Seleukos Nikator, founder of the Hellenistic Seleucid dynasty, from which
Philopappos claimed descent. Thus Philopappos's ancestors flanked him on either side. It
was Philopappos who lived under the Roman emperor Trajan and was a contemporary of
Plutarch. As late as 1436 the whole facade of the tomb, with its three statues and five

The Academy has no remains [Fig. 10]. The place however where it stood is indicated by the plain among the olive trees. It still bears that name among the peasantry who point immediately to the academy. There is in the neighborhood a large ruin supposed to be the reservoir for the academy. A little to the south of the academy is the Ceramicus that is the place where they made tiles, a sort of Tuilleries. You still see some excavations &c which point out the spot. It is difficult to say where was that part of the city called the Ceramicus. It is natural to think with Mr Fauvel that it was that side next to the Ceramicus out of town, the quarter of the Ceramicus that is, on the side of the Ceramicus. The Academy is a fine piece of ground covered with olive trees & grain. It is watered by little canals which lead the water of the Cephisus. It is therefore unhealthy at certain seasons, just as it was anciently when Plato was obliged to leave it & go to Colonos.

Colonos is a small hill to the north west of the Academy. It is rather a gentle pretty rising ground in the midst of the plain. On the tip is a small house. Besides the story of Oedipus it has celebrity on account of Plato's house & temple near it. Some ruins in the neighborhood are supposed by Mr F to be those of the temple. I did not however see them.

The Greeks have the character of an enslaved people—vile as slaves, cruel, haughty when they can [be] with impunity. They are obliged to exert their talents & are therefore acute whilst the Turks being the masters have no necessity for exercising ingenuity & are therefore dull in comparison. There is a good deal of disorder & immorality among their society, tho' to the eye the exterior has the appearance of simplicity & purity.

I have seen few objects so disgusting as a Greek woman—their dress & manner is enough to shock licentiousness itself. There is only one part of it, the letting the hair hang over the shoulders which is tolerable. This remark applies only to women of a certain rank. The peasantry are very prettily dressed. Whenever the women go out they have their head & face muffled up in a white hood or veil which makes them look like the heroes of the middle age, the face all covered except the eyes. Whenever they see a Franc, for that is the name they give us, they turn & hide their faces with a sort of alarm & I was astonished in looking over the curiosities found by Mr Lusieri among the tombs [at] a little female statue in earth in which altho' the drapery is in the best stile & determines its antiquity, the head & face

---

inscriptions, was still intact. The frieze below the statues depicts Philopappos' inauguration as a Roman consul in A.D. 109.

are veiled in the same way. Yet so it is. Equal degrees of civilization suggest similar usages, similar dresses. The Greek women now are perhaps very nearly in the same state in which they formerly were. It is true they tell us of female philosophers but generally speaking it may be true the women here have no education at all. There are no public women; the present governor having punished some severely, & prohibiting them not from motives of justice, but to share in the penalties of transgression. There are still of course some, but I should not suppose them sufficiently seducing to incur the severe risks of seeing them. Philosophically speaking, the Voivode did wrong to suppress them. All wise states should not encourage but regulate them, as does France & Prussia. En parlant au medecin de Tripolizza j'ai trouvé (see page 177) que les lois sevéres de la Turquie n'ont pas pû eteindre dans la Gréce l'amour de la debauche. Si un homme est pris avec une femme d'une maniere que ne laisse rien à prouver, le Vaivodé a le droit de la faire esclave, ou même de la jetter dans la mer, ou la precipiter d'un bout de quelque rocher. Tout cela empeche qu'il ne soient ouvertes des maisons publiques, mais il n'y a pas moins de femmes Grécques & Turques que pretent a la débauche, à laquelle même elles sont fort dispossées. Au reste elles sont femmes: la nature & la climat a des droits qu'on ne peut pas resister. La maladie vénerienne est commune dans toute la Gréce, mais surtout dans la Romelie.

With regard to society there is in fact none among the Greeks. What is society without females? And what kind of intercourse is that between a set of men without any information, whose only employment is to smoke? There is no such thing as an assembly of the sexes, a danse, a theatre, music. The country is in that respect barbarous.

With regard to language the Athenian thinks Mr F is the softest—it is a little Italicised. For instance, they pronounce their K like our CH, the Italian C. The Moreans [are] more harsh & the Constantinopolitans still more harsh, tho' they laugh at Athenian pronunciation. There is a dispute about the present Greek pronunciation, whether it be the proper standard of the ancient language. Let us see. The principal difference is this. The B (beta) is pronounced like our V. The Δ (delta) like our TH.[29] ε & η (epsilon & eta) the reverse of our way, η being pronounced our I & the epsilon like our A (as in bad).[30] The Z (zeta) like our S.[31] The K like CH (tho' this an

29. That is, a voiced *th*, as in English *they*. The unvoiced equivalent (English *thin*) is represented by Greek theta.
30. The sound of *i* in English machine can be represented graphically in five different

Athenian custom rather); Y (upsilon) like our B or rather F.³² They pronounce EY EF; AI like A simple,³³ EI like E;³⁴ after N, tau is pronounced
like D thus: εντα [=] ενδα. Pay no attention to metre but [be] strict to
accent, so that by accenting whenever we see the mark we cannot err.
Much better than our way.³⁵

Can a foreign people dictate to the descendants of the Greeks how Greek
is to be read? It ought not to be so. It is said that the Greeks themselves
pronounce differently, but the variety of dialects does not affect the substance of the language. None has more than the German yet there is not
the less a standard of pronunciation. The controversy turns upon the Beta.
The moderns pronounce it V, and to make our sound of B they write ΜΠ
(MP). Now they ask whether they had not anciently such a sound of B in
the Greek for MP was never used. They say also that the Romans wrote B
always for the Greek B as in Thebes & surely they would not have done so
if the Greeks had pronounced it V for then they would have put their own
V. But it occurs to me that the old Greeks used B as the moderns because
in all the Greek inscriptions where Roman names are found they write B
for Latin B, for instance Balerianus, φλαβιος &c sometimes with an OY
as Ουαλεριανος. And as to Roman translation from Greek it is to be
remarked that the Romans most probably knew the Greeks first by their
writing [and] the Greeks first [knew the Romans] by intercourse with the
Romans. The Greeks therefore copied from actual hearing, the Romans
from books; and finding in a Greek geographer the name of a town they
put it into Latin by substituting the same letter of their alphabet, & afterwards pronounced them as they chose. In the same way as do the French &
English now. A Frenchman hears an English name. He puts it down in his

---

ways in modern Greek, one of which is the letter eta. A better English equivalent for
epsilon is *bet*.

31. At least in standard modern demotic Greek, zeta is pronounced like English *z*.

32. Upsilon by itself is another graphic representation of the *i* in English machine. As
part of the "diphthong" alpha upsilon, it is indeed pronounced *f* (before voiceless consonants), but *v* (before voiced consonants).

33. AI and E are different graphic symbols for the same sound in modern Greek: English
bed or *met*.

34. EI is another grapheme for the *i* of English machine.

35. Modern Greek has a stress accent. Biddle was taught, when he learned ancient Greek
in school, to pronounce the language metrically—as a succession of long and short sylla-
bles—and to disregard the accent marks appearing in his texts. He was also using the
so-called Erasmian, or restored, pronunciation, which was presumed to be closer to the
actual sound of ancient Greek. Hence his interest in the points of difference between his
own pronunciation and that of the Greeks whom he met.

own spelling & makes the right sound. He sees it written in an English book, he copies it letter for letter, retains the spelling & pronounces it wrong. See Cicero's book entitled "*M. Tul. Cic. Orator ad Mar. Brut.*" page 165. Speaking of pronunciation we say "*tamen & Phryges & Pyrrhum aurium causa dicimus*," that is to conform to the mode of pronouncing it which they must have had from the Greeks; formerly he says they wrote *Purrum & Fruges*, at least Ennius did so. This seems to me a strong argument in favor for the use of modern pronunciation.

Demos[thenes]. Θεμοσθῆνες
Socràtes. Thukythìthes
Aristìthis. Alkiviàthis
Periclès. Alèxanthros. Aristotèles
Pythagòras
ΜΠ makes our B. Anacrèon
I and Y (ipsilon & eota) are pronounced in the same way. Sapfò[36]

Athens is favored in its govt & might do well if the Greeks were not jealous of each other. They count about 8000 or 10000 inhabitants of which 1/5 [are] Turks. The Turks are just numerous enough to keep the Greeks in awe without being dangerous, so that they are both civil, the Turks being much more affable here than elsewhere. Mahomet 2d[37] sent a new colony to Athens, but the Athenians got some privileges. They are now governed by a Voivode, a Cadi, & Archons. The Voivode buys his place for a certain term. I think a year, of the Grand Seigneur.[37a] The Cadi in the same way. The Archons are elected by the people every two years but the thing is so arranged that if a man is once elected there is no way of getting rid of him. The people meet in the court of the Voivode's house, & he then asks them if they will have such a man as Archon. Things are so managed that if any man objects he is sure to attract the vengeance of govt & he is therefore silent. The Cadi is the Judge in all civil & criminal affairs between Greeks & Turks or men of the same nation. His salary is ten pr cent on all cases decided, & the presents of the parties, which are some-times very large. The Greeks of course try to evade this jurisdiction as

36. This list seems to be an attempt by Biddle to reproduce the modern Greek pronunciation of ancient Greek names in Roman script.
37. After capturing Constantinople, Mahomet the Conqueror expelled the last Frankish duke of Athens in 1456.
37a. The Padishah, or sultan, in Constantinople.

much as possible, and submit their causes to the Archons from whom however an appeal always lies to the Cadi.

The Voivode is the executive. He is governor, & the Archons are his counsil. The Archonship does not detach them from business, for the salary is about 2 or 3 hundred piastres. If they had talents they could rule the Voivode who is a sort of Police man to keep order & receive the taxes. But they govern the town, or ought.

There is an appeal to Constantinople from the Cadi's judgments if they exceed a certain amount which is small. He cannot proceed to a sentence of death without a note from the Mufti or archbishop declaring with a passage of the Koran that the crime merits death. This is called a Faitpha, & is also gotten in civil cases when important by suitors who go to the Mufti & get a passage from the Koran in their favor.[38]

The Francs are obliged to give only 3 pr cent in suits against Greeks or Turks; however as the gainer is to pay & the Cadi inclines to the best payer, the Francs have waved this dangerous privilege.

No particular class of advocates or lawyers, but a man may have his cause supported or defended by any friend of better tongue than himself.

The people cannot be called litigious, lawsuits are so short. Are not Turkish forms of justice preferable to ours? The lawsuits of Europe, I am ashamed whilst I add of America too are a disgrace to civilization. We boast of our institutions, & yet in obtaining justice, the branch of policy the most interesting we consume years & lives whilst the meanest Turk gets his cause decided in two minutes. It will be said sometimes unjustly. Be it so. But does no injustice happen in our courts? And is not the monstrous delay of our law more injurious than the occasional injustice of a Cadi? With him at least you have a chance equal with that of your adversary; you may intrigue with the Cadi, & surely it is better to sacrifice a small part at once than to have a great deal sacrificed by delay. With us justice may be bought sometimes, but never bought soon. Here it may be bought immediately. I should really prefer Turkish to Pennsylvania courts. The people of Athens, says Cicelli of Corinth [are] still distinguished as of old for their eternal jealousies & differences among each other.

The Albanese are of doubtful origin, partly Turk partly Christian.[39] The

38. A *fetva* was a kind of order or manifesto, both religious and political, a sacred ordinance consistent with the Koran and obligatory on all Moslems. The Turks, as Moslems, did not recognize a distinction between secular and religious law.

39. The term Albanian is properly linguistic. Many Albanians, including most of the women, spoke only Albanian. Some were bilingual and also spoke Greek. Some Albanian

Turkish part is a very bad race of thieves & assassins. The Christian part forms the agriculturers of Greece, the country being covered with Albanese villages. They are a very good people—a simple people—with the manners of Homer's people: they are in fact more Greek than the Greeks themselves, the features & figure being finer for the Greeks have Lent more than half the year & living on salted fish &c spoils the complexion. The Albanians will perhaps bye & bye swallow up the Greeks who rather diminish than increase & who would do more so if the Albanians did not affect the Greek dress, for the Greeks despise the Albanians. It seems to me that the Greeks love to decry & disparage each other. At Malta I was told sad stories of the savage ferocity of the Greeks who sometimes murdered passengers, particularly the Idriotes & Sclavons. At Zante I was warned against the men of Cephalonia & the Morea. Here I am told that I may trust the Sclavons but those islanders [of] Zante, Cephalonia &c are dangerous fellows. In the Morea [I was] told to be on my guard in Livadia. Arrived at Livadia they say that the country is perfectly safe but they cannot vouch for the south. The Greeks abuse the Spartans, they the Mainotes.

The Ancient Agora or market place is very near the present Bazar or market. Probably on the spot.

The Pecile is along side of the market place.[40] We now see one side (the western) consisting of a long & high wall with Corinthian columns attached to it not as a portico but for ornament. There are also some remains of the other sides which sufficiently indicates its form which has been completely discovered by Fauvel. Between it & the temple of Theseus is a part of a large wall, once belonging to the gymnasium of Ptolemy.[41] Both these objects are badly placed by Barthelemy, being much more directly to the north than they are represented. I should say the Pecile only, the gymnasium not being of Anacharsis's time.

---

speakers were Christian; and some were Moslem, but did not necessarily speak Turkish. Though since Ottoman times the Albanians in Greece have acculturated to the Greeks and become indistinguishable from them in speech, in religion, and even in dress, there are still parts of Greece where the Albanian language is spoken. Contrary to Biddle's expectation, it was the Greeks who swallowed up the Albanians.

40. The site of the Painted Stoa, or Poikile, built in the mid-fifth century B.C. in the Greek marketplace, was in Biddle's time buried under houses. His "Pecile" was actually the Library of Hadrian (A.D. 132), once part of the Roman extension of the old Greek marketplace. Most of the modern Turkish bazaar filled the interior of what remained of the exterior walls of this library. A sketch of the ground plan of these walls has been omitted. On the sketch Biddle remarks that he lived in a house near the wall of Corinthian columns.

41. The Gymnasion of Ptolemy has not been found. The wall said to belong to it was actually part of the Stoa of Attalos, a long, elaborate market hall facing the square of the Greek marketplace and donated to the city by King Attalos of Pergamon (159–138 B.C.).

Mount Hymettus [is] celebrated for honey. [This mountain has] undergone a change of name which Fauvel thus relates. When the Venetians came here, they asked how the mountain was called. The reply was Hymetoros. What means, they asked, *oros?* Mountain. Here then was Mount Hymettus which they italicised into Monte Matto. The Greeks afterwards translated it into Trolovouni which means Foolish mountain.[42]

The same change has produced another modern name. The Venetians asked the name of the island. The Greek thinking they asked the distance, answered εις την Ευριπο (pronounced tenevripo) which is the name of the Channel & now of the town of Chalcis, & which they pronounce evripo. By degrees it became Negripo, & as there is a bridge across the channel, at last, it became Negroponte.

The first is ingenious but I objected that people would not change the names of places to accommodate foreigners. The answer was that Hymettus had probably no name when the Venetians came and that they took home the learned the Grecian name. The last is downright Swiftish.

The Temple of the Winds is an octagon building of marble, now incrusted in a mosque.[43] What can now be seen is about one half. The whole is about 30 feet high without columns. Near the top are carved in relief the figures of the winds, Boreas &c. They are very prettily executed tho' perhaps they might have been lighter.

The lantern of Demosthenes is a small circular building making one of the corners of the Monastery of Capucins [Fig. 15]. It was intended or perhaps raised by Lysicrates who was victor in the games & who the inscription shows to have lived in Demosthenes's time. It is of a very pretty architecture. On the architrave are represented one of Hercules's exploits, his changing some people into fish & other animals by a touch of his club. (What is that story?) On the top is a place for a tripod.[44] This monument was in the street of Tripods which I should suppose extended around to the

42. The anc. and mod. name of the mountain is Hymettos. The medieval name, Trellovouni, arose from the Italian Monte Matto (Mad Mountain). The Venetians had shortened Monte Imetto to Monte Matto. The Greeks merely translated the erroneous name into their own language.

43. Built as an elaborate water clock, with eight sundials and a weathervane, by Andronikos Kyrrhestes in the second half of the second century B.C., the Tower of the Winds was and is well preserved, except for its clock mechanism. In Biddle's time it served a sect of dancing dervishes.

44. This monument was built in 335 B.C. to display a bronze tripod won in a choral contest. Knowledge of the true purpose of the building was forgotten, hence the peculiar name. Demosthenes was thought to have written his speeches here. The frieze depicts Dionysos changing pirates into dolphins.

tripods over the theatre of Bacchus. The inside is now a chamber for a Russian painter.

The Lyceum was opposite to Herodius Atticus stadium. There are no remains except some level ground which may be supposed to have been the spot. Behind it are some ruins which Mr F. conjectures to be those of the Cynosarges, that is of its temple.[45]

Near the port Dipylon on the ruins of which is now a dwelling house is a large pedestal supposed to be that of Thrasybulus.[46]

Beyond the Lyceum among the olive trees is the spot called the gardens of Venus recognized by Fauvel from the name which is still that of garden. He found there the well to which the Canephori came from the temple of Minerva with their jugs. The story is in Pausanias.[47]

Near the gate Aegeus is a ruin [Fig. 14] supposed to be the pedestal on which Anarcharsis sees Praxiteles place his statue (says F.).[48]

45. These gymnasia were outside the city walls on open ground.

46. The grave of Thrasyboulos (d. 388 B.C.), a general and statesman responsible for the restoration of the Athenian democracy in 404 after the Peloponnesian War, lay, with those of many other noted men, on the road to the Academy very near the State Burial Ground and east of the Dipylon gate in the city wall.

47. The shrine of Aphrodite in the Gardens must have been on the banks of the Ilissos in southeast Athens. Another shrine of the same name may have been at the foot of the cliffs on the north slope of the Acropolis (Pausanias 1.27.3). It was perhaps to and from this second shrine that the young girls in the service of Athena carried certain objects.

48. Fauvel seems to have misled a great many tourists! If Biddle had checked his own copy of Barthélemy, he would have found that Fauvel's collocation of the Gate Aegeus and Praxiteles' horseman was dubious. Coming up from the Piraeus to Athens by the road between the Long Walls, Anacharsis says (chapter XII): "Do you see the concourse of spectators near the city gate, the litters stopping there, and that man upon a scaffold surrounded by workmen? That is Praxiteles. He is going to fix upon a base that serves by way of a tomb, a grand equestrian statue which he has just finished" (Pausanias 1.2.3). Pausanias does not specify the gate where this work, which is no longer extant, once was; he says only that it was a warrior standing next to a horse and that it was indeed a grave monument. Barthélemy's map of Athens duly shows the Equestrian Statue at the Gate of the Piraeus, between the Long Walls. In ancient times, burials were not allowed within the walls of Athens, but were made along the roads outside the city's gates. Though graves of the fifth and fourth centuries B.C. have been found all around the walls, the biggest graveyards, including the main one, the Kerameikos, were located on the west and northwest side of the city, where three roads from the Piraeus converged on four or five separate gates. Praxiteles' work, probably a relief, may have been outside any one of these gates, including the gate, the ancient name of which we do not know, between the Long Walls. Scholars usually think that Pausanias entered Athens at the Dipylon Gate, through which passed the main road into the city, and where lay the cemetery of the Kerameikos, and that Praxiteles' work stood here. But a careful comparison of 1.1.2 and 1.2.4 will show that Pausanias need not intend the same road or the same gate in both passages. In any case, Barthélemy might have arrived at the right answer, but quite by accident: he could not have known enough about the

Greece [is] much more civilized since travelers have come into it. About 26 years ago when Fauvel went to Delphos, the old men of the town alarmed at the sight waited on the party to know what they wanted saying that since the Francs had come there they had been unfortunate. They

---

topography of ancient Athens to place Praxiteles' monument definitely between the Long Walls or anywhere else. Since Barthélemy's source leaves the location doubtful, we could accuse the novelist of rushing to an unjustified conclusion.

Fauvel, however, only made matters worse by connecting the "Gate Aegeus" with Praxiteles' pedestal and by equating that pedestal with actual ruins upon the ground. In chapter VIII, Anacharsis, listing no ancient source, does mention such a gate, though not in connection with Praxiteles. On his way to the Lyceum, he passed through it and followed a path along the Ilissos. This gate was in the southeastern part of the city wall, and it appears on Barthélemy's map. Though no ancient source specifically mentions such a gate in the Themistoclean Wall itself, both Barthélemy and Fauvel may have had in mind a passage from Plutarch's *Theseus* (12.3), wherein we are told that Theseus's father, Aigeus, is said to have built the shrine of Apollo Delphinios in this part of Athens. The site of Aigeus's house was later pointed out in the shrine itself, east of which stood "the herm at Aigeus's Gate." (Since Hermes was the god of traffic, ithyphallic statues of him were commonly put up in streets and squares.) Fauvel seems to have assumed that this Gate of Aigeus was one of the actual gates in the *southern* city wall. John Travlos, *Poleodomike Exelixis ton Athenon* (Athens, 1960), 53, assumes, on the strength of the passage from Plutarch and another from Pausanias (1.19.1), which only puts the shrine of Apollo "near the Olympieion," that the Gate of Aigeus fits certain ruins that he found just *north* of the Olympieion itself, that is, some distance to the northeast of Fauvel's preferred site.

In Fauvel's day, on one of the paths leading south from the Acropolis and over the Ilissos (this area then lay outside the built-up part of the Turkish town), there were the remains of what he thought, correctly, were the ancient Themistoclean walls and also, beyond them, of something he called "the pedestal on which were Praxiteles' horses." This "pedestal," now gone, appears as a rectangular structure southeast of the Mouseion Hill on his plan of Athens, originally published in Guillaume Antoine Olivier's *Voyage dans l'Empire Ottoman* (Paris, 1799–1807), Atlas pl. 49. Fauvel's plan, reproduced in this book as plate no. 14 from Robert Walpole's *Memoirs Relating to European and Asiatic Turkey* (London, 1818), was revised (by Hawkins?) to show an "Equestrian Gate"; and the rectangular structure was left unidentified. Fauvel's own plan gave the remains of the gate itself no name, calling it merely "ancienne porte." Beyond this gate, probably the one anciently called the Seaward Gate, stretched the main road to the Bay of Phaleron not only in antiquity but well into the nineteenth century A.D. Since there were certainly ancient tombs along this road, it is quite possible that the ruins of some tomb survived to Fauvel's time. Dodwell's description of these ruins (*A Classical and Topographical Tour*, vol. 1, 391–92) as arched, composed of brick, small stones, and cement, and presumably once veneered with marble, indicates a Roman date. Whoever revised Fauvel's plan also located both the ancient agora and the Ceramicus just north of this gate, in response, probably, to the widespread if mistaken belief that these places lay south of the Acropolis. But Fauvel himself, as we know from his own plan, located the "chemin du Ceramique" to the northwest of the ancient town, where the excavators have shown that it really was. He should have known that Praxiteles' monument ought to be associated with one of the western roads and gates—and probably with the cemetery of the Kerameikos—and that the "Gate Aegeus," whatever it was, had no known connection with Praxiteles either in ancient sources or in Barthélemy.

replied they came to see the antiquities, & producing Spon & Wheeler's book showed them that in such a place was such a stoa, such a fountain, such a cave. If you know all this said they, why do you come here? They kept the travellers in a house three days, when they let them go off to Salona where they came from. One of the party lacking merchandize, asking if he could buy oil &c they were a little softened, & having asked permission of the Papa (whom they consulted to know if it was right to shew the town to strangers) let them see a little of Delphos. But the party was always surrounded by a crowd who would not let them copy anything. They complained to the French consul who had a fine of 7 or 800 piastres imposed upon the Delphians, who became civil since.

In the citadel is still seen a part of the wall of Theseus particularly to the southwest.[49] The former entrance was by a staircase of which the vestiges are still seen near Pan's cave. Pericles made a new noble one the Propylaeum. This beautiful building consisting of six Doric columns at each end was adorned by the Temple of victory[50] on its left & a building or gallery of paintings on its right. At the entrance was a large door intended for chariots beneath the level of the steps which rose on each side. At least this is the discovery Mr Fauvel made when we visited it together. It was always supposed that the steps were all on a level, but the Turks having cleared away some rubbish, it seems that the steps are unequal.[51]

Towards the temple the passage was by 5 doors of different sizes the places of which are still visable. The Propylaeum is towards the southwestern[52] angle of the Temple of Minerva so that they saw two sides of the

49. The reference is to the Pelasgian, or cyclopean, wall of the late Bronze Age, which belongs to the thirteenth century B.C.
50. The temple in which Athena was worshiped as bringer of victory was probably built around 425 B.C. It stood on the bastion on the right of anyone approaching the Propylaia. Torn down in 1686, it was used in the defensive walls of the Acropolis. It has since been rebuilt out of the ruins of the Turkish walls.
51. It was thought, that is, that the steps extended unbroken across the whole front of the building. Originally a broad ramp led steeply up to the five doors of the Propylaia. In the first century A.D. this ramp was converted into a marble stairway. But in both cases a processional way for animals led up through the central passage of the Propylaia, and there was a necessary gap in the four courses of the foundation blocks which supported the Doric colonnade. It is to this gap that Biddle refers. He is not saying that the courses of the foundation, which the architect intended to be visible, were of different dimensions vertically or horizontally, though this is an interpretation that Biddle's sketch, which is omitted, might lead one to expect. Or did the existing condition of the site not allow him to see that there were in fact four courses of finished masonry, above the foundation courses, on both sides of the central gap?
52. Actually *north*western.

temple on coming up to it. A very fine effect. At the temple of victory whence Aegeus[53] threw himself we see only the ruins which serve as materials for a fort near it. The building on the left still shews three columns & the wall but like all the propylaea is incrusted in the walls of a sort of bastion for the fortress.

One sees more of the Turks here than at Constantinople. There they do not mingle with the Christians but here they are on a very good footing with them. They are tolerant. The other day for instance says Mr F, a Turk, an Emir came to see him on some festival in the presence of the elders of the town, kissed his hand, an honor or a ceremony most rare in Turkey.

The Emirs are the descendants of the family of Mahomet. Their distinction is that of wearing a green turban, of not being bastinadoed, but no particular political rank. It is however a species of distinction, for a man is raised for merit to the rank of an Emir. Sometimes however he is bastinadoed. Should that arrive they first take off the turban & kiss it with great respect; then inflict the punishment. A process worth copying in punishing European great men.

The family of Mahomet is now very numerous. The other day at dinner at Fauvel's an Emir waited on table. He was not obliged to do so but chose it. I may rank it among the memorabilia to have been waited on by a descendant of Mahomet.

The old houses of Athens [were] probably built says F, like the smaller houses now, of sunburnt bricks, a sort of dry mud. The houses thus built are thought to resist earthquakes better than the others.

At Athens there are two schools for the ancient language. They may have about 60 scholars but they are little boys who never go beyond a dark comprehension of some easy author, some of them not even so far. The best Greek scholars of Greece says Walpole are about equal to an English school boy. These schools are supported by the public, the richest scholars paying a stipend also. One of the masters, Beninzello, is a good scholar, the best at Athens and has written a history of later Athens. His style like that of all the modern Greek writers borrows much from the ancient. They all say that if these were scholars who wrote in modern Greek & would purify the language, it would be a very elegant one. All the rich phraseology, the

53. When the legendary Attic hero Theseus, on his return voyage from slaying the Cretan Minotaur, failed to hoist a white sail to show that he had been successful, his father, seeing the approach of a black sail, threw himself in despair off the western (later the Nike) bastion of the Acropolis.

refinements of the Hellenic would be at their disposal, & they could liberally borrow from every neighbor both European & Asiatic. At present the Turkish side of Greece adopts many Turkish words, the Italian, Italian words. It is a soft pleasing language in conversation; melodious & not destitute of force.

I think the Turkish language softer than the European languages. There are however many terminations in consonants. It is poor in books there being scarcely anything original except the Koran. Not worth the trouble of studying; the Arabic much better worthy of a man's trouble. Thousands of commentators on the Koran.

A Turkish wedding. The man goes to the Cadi accompanied by his relations, & of those of the woman & declares his intention to marry such a woman. The Cadi sends an Officer to the woman. He finds her seated on a saddle with her feet in the water, a relation on one side knitting, another reading prayers on the other side. The Officer asks three times if she agrees to marry the man. She nods approbation which he conveys to the Cadi who then makes out the writing—the parties sign &c. The husband is brought to the wife's house & shoved into the house as it were by his relations, as if forced in.

Entering he strikes the door with his poignard to denote his mastery & breaks a grenate on the wall. He finds his wife on a sopha, one foot on, the other off the sopha, veiled. He approaches, sits down, gradually puts his foot to her's, lifts the veil & kisses her on the forehead. The relations retire, the couple who now for the first time see each other, occupy themselves as they please; a bed with two tapers is ready on the floor.

A Greek wedding is much meaner in every respect. The ceremony disgusting and ridiculously unmeaning. The Monday before the marriage presents of clothes &c are interchanged by the couple. Saturday following they see company at their respective houses. Those who visit the husband find him sitting upon a chair, with a fellow shaving him, & in this position they make him their congratulations & throw paras or other money on the head of him or his barber. On her side the lady sits with the most unbending stiffness whilst a female relation arranges her tresses & in this way sees her friends. On Sunday comes the husband with his relations to the wife's house. He enters & sits gravely in a chair opposite to hers. Here they sit. The ceremony is performed. They see their friends, & two days after they for the first time make common bed.

The old Greeks placed over the grave of a deceased person a stone smaller than ours & wrote on it only the name of the person, his father & his country. There are still some of them visible in the Turkish burial ground near the Acropolis.

The old Greeks seem to have had the custom of putting into the tomb of the deceased, something symbolical of his profession. This they seem to have taken from the Egyptians if I can believe a drawing taken by Fauvel when in that country (tho' that drawing were rather from the tomb itself). Mr Lusieri has many of these figures. In some tombs he found a looking glass of bronze one or two of which are in good preservation. These were for the ladies, whilst the warriors had spears or heads of spears and swords. These swords seem to be a kind of "cut & thrust." They are a good deal injured. He found a magnificent urn of bronze of a curious tho' I do not think elegant form (being too broad) & a little branch of myrtle in gold. He supposes it to be the tomb of queen [..].

The lacrimary urn which was found near it is of most beautiful alabaster. He has a number of these urns.[54]

But he has also a very curious thing; a little machine like our carriages for children to be drawn by a string. It is a [piece?] of earthern ware about a foot square, with two horses drawing a little wagon of two wheels, open behind in the ancient style. In the carriage two men one a charioteer; the other in armour, helmet casque &c. The wheels to the machine are wanting. Found in the tomb probably of a charioteer or a victor in a race. The household utensils are very prettily made of earthern ware with figures on them. One head of a spear found at Marathon where many have been discovered.

Greek houses generally two story, the upper floor inhabited (i.e. houses of any distinction) the poorer class one—of stone & covered with a sort of convex tile. The meaner houses of sunburnt clay or mud. There is always a piazza & in the towns the market place where the shops are, & [where] the business is done are lined with piazzas. The rooms surrounded with a little bench 9 or 10 inches high, on which are cushions. The room in which you sit serves you as a bed chamber. The Greek & Turkish dress much more elegant than ours which looks very mean. The long robes quite majestic, & being loosely clad they are much more healthy than we are, at least their clothing better calculated to make them so. There is also something very lazy & enticing for a warm climate in their way of sitting or lolling upon cushions.

---

54. A small drawing of an alabastron, or oil jar, has been omitted. Such jars, or unguentaries, were used to dispense perfumed oil. Some travelers refer to the smallest of such jars as lachrymatories. The modern term is *aryballos*.

There are 70 thousand karatsh orders sent to the Morea annually.[55] [They] seem to indicate that there are that number of Greek families there. Morea divided into govts or districts of which the following towns are capitals. Corinth; Argos, Napoli; Tripolizza, Mistra, Corone, Vostizza, Patras, Leondari, Caritina, Calavrita, Mothone, Gastouni, Fanari,[56] Pirgo; Arcadia.

It is droll that in the Greek law (of their church) there is the same rule of hotch pot as in England.[57]

Each of these divisions governed like the rest of Greece by a Voivode, a Cadi & a Yian. This last is the officer of finance, a sort of committee of ways and means how to extort money, the only object say the Greeks of Turkish govt. The Cadi cannot put a man in prison longer than 24 hours without the Voivode's permission.

Between the Turks & Greeks in cases before the Cadi, the Khoran is the law, the Turks believing that in that sacred book they can find a decision of every possible case. But before the Archons & particularly before the Archbishop, the Theodosian code is the rule of justice.[58] These two (the Archons & Archibishop) have only a jurisdiction as arbitrators, no compulsory power.

A Pasha has complete power of life & death over every man in his kingdom. A Voivode too if a strong man, or like the V of Patras a relation of some [of] the great men at Constantinople may exercise the same power

55. Biddle oversimplifies the system of imperial taxes. The poll tax, or capitation, was the karatch, so called by the Greeks themselves, who used the term inappropriately. The real karatch was a land tax, which Moslems and Christians alike had to pay. The poll tax itself, Turkfish cizye, was paid only by non-Moslems. The fixed sum due from each district was apportioned among all who were liable to pay, whatever the population of a district, and whatever the increase or decrease of the population over time, though generally the people were divided into three different income classes for purposes of payment. In addition to the poll tax there was the land tax, which was a tithe on agricultural produce. In general, Turks paid a smaller percentage of tithe than others. A third major tax was the *avarisi*, which was paid by towns where the population was not agricultural. There were also internal and external customs duties, generally about three percent, and certain excise duties, mostly imposed by Selim III, on items like gunpowder, wine, and snuff. These taxes could be increased by all sorts of irregular exactions and forced contributions from Moslems and non-Moslems alike for the needs of local government.

56. I have corrected Biddle's Fanale. Fanari, in the western Peloponnesos near Andritsina, was the seat of a voivode and a capital of a vilayéti and contained five or six mosques and three hundred to four hundred houses, almost all Turks (so Leake).

57. Property was commingled so as to be divided evenly among a man's heirs.

58. The Greeks managed their affairs in accordance with the Roman system of law, which had grown up in late antiquity. The Code is a compilation of laws issued by the Roman emperors from A.D. 313 to 438. Theodosius II decreed the codification in 429, and it was completed in 438. See now Clyde Pharr (trans.), *The Theodosian Code* (Princeton, 1952).

with impunity. There are says Consul Strani of Patras about 450 thousand souls in the Morea.

The Turks have a great veneration for storks which they permit to come about their churches. It is a good omen when one of them takes up his residence near the house of an individual. They migrate in the winter season to the coast of Africa & return in the spring. What is singular is that they return to their habitations which they remember notwithstanding the absence. The origin of the prejudice in their favor is thus related by Greeks. The Grand Seignior saw from his palace window a serpent who entwined itself round the neck of one of the poor creatures. With much humanity he offered a reward to anyone who would kill the snake. An expert bowman (for there were in those days no guns) executed it, & the grateful stork returns its thanks by a noise which expressed tho' somewhat gutterally all that a stork's noise could. The following year in his migration he brought to the Grand Seignor the seeds of melons & garlick with which the Turks were unacquainted. After some surprise, the G Seignor bethought himself of putting the seeds into the ground & his experiment was so successful that the storks were by royal order thence forward deemed sacred. They were also anciently sacred in Thessaly, & there murderers deemed homicides. They had delivered from the large serpents which infested it, the whole country. A[n?]. 5.246.[59]

(There are constant migrations from the Morea to Asia & the islands incited by the oppression of the Turks & the hopes of bettering their fortune.)

There is a branch of a family of Kalemera's at Zante which is anxious to arrogate to itself the honor of a connection with Bonaparte who, they say, sprang from a Kalemera of Sparta, who a long time since migrated with other colonists to Corsica.[60]

On inquiry I learned from Dr Abramioti that these pretensions were unfounded. He however says that in the small town of Vitulo on the sea coast of Laconia, there was a remnant of the family of Comneni, the Emperor of Constantinople. A colony emigrated from Vitulo & went to

---

59. Whatever this reference means, the story of the Thessalian snakes and storks occurs in Aristotle's *de Mirabilibus Auscultationibus* 832a15.

60. About 1650, so the story went, some fifty families migrated from Vitylo in the Maina, the presumed last refuge of the ancient Spartans, to the island of Corsica. One of these families changed its name from Kalomero to its Italian equivalent, Bonaparte. No Kalomeri, however, ever migrated from the Mani, where the name is unknown; and in any case the Bonapartes originated in Treviso and Bologna and were established in Corsica long before the Greeks came.

Otranto. Unsuccessful there, it went to Corsica where it fixed. The Comneni family were among them, & the legitimate heir with his titles to the succession well established went to Paris in the time of Louis 16th & was very well treated by him, married honorably &c. Since the Revolution it is not known what has become of him. Fauvel mentioned the same fact.[61]

The Cujabashe is a Greek officer in the villages.[62] He buys his place of the Grand Seigneur & is the lord of the village. Always Greeks, they are rather a kind of council of the most respectable men for the service of the Vyvuda who consults them & uses them as instruments to squeeze the people.

The Logotheti is a character which occurs often in Greece. It is an office in the Greek church altogether honorary. The business seems to consist in carrying some sacred article of furniture in the public processions on festival days. He is a kind of aid de camp to the Bishop, after whom he ranks.

Such is the terror which the Turks inspire that among the Greeks when a child cries they terrify him by saying that there is a Turk coming, & he is silent immediately. Marlborough in Holland & Richard Coeur de Lion in Syria have inspired the same and a more durable fear. How can a nation rise against its oppressors when their very babies are taught to fear them?

The lower people of Greece, surprized at seeing so many foreigners come among them & spend their money & purchase stones & statuary; and unable to conceive how a man can spend money unless with a hope of making more have now nearly made up their minds with regard to the object of strangers. They think that anciently the Kings & great men of Greece hid their money & that instructed by the ancient books of the places where it is deposited, we came to look for it, & dig it up. They think that there is money in the pieces of statuary which strangers purchase, & under this impression they have often broken handsome things to find gold. Their

61. The Comneni were the last Greek family, or dynasty, to rule at Constantinople before it was captured by the Turks in 1453. The Stephanopouli of Vitylo in the Maina claimed descent from this family. They moved to Corsica in the seventeenth century and were finally settled at Carghese, where they have since amalgamated with the Corsicans. An Italian branch of this family, eager to claim imperial connections, blazed a path through the social life of France in the time of Louis XVI, Napoleon, and the Restoration. It was one of these latter-day Stephanopouli who concocted the theory that the Bonapartes, originally named Kalomeri, had some kind of imperial origin in the Mani. Thus were the Kalomeri and the Stephanopouli families fictionally joined.

62. The terms *cujabashe* and *archon* (plural = *archontes*) meant the same thing: a Christian notable, or primate. In conformity with their policy of letting subject peoples take care of themselves, provided that they paid the required taxes, the Turks turned over the management of local affairs to councils of important men, or elders.

idea is that the English are paid for coming here, & that when they go home they go & tell the King what they have seen & then get their money. Indeed we can scarcely be surprised at their strange ideas about everything that is Palaio or Hellenic as they call it, when they see strangers come 2 or 3 thousand miles to look at an old wall or a hill & write down pages upon the subject. Indeed you gain more respect by making notes in their presence. It has an air of wisdom, & in fact what is wisdom but show.

The oppression of the Turkish govt is altogether exercised by the inferior tyrants. In Greece, there is no other tax for the Grand Seignior except the Karatch, a small tax of 3 or 5 piastres on every male Greek of 15 years & upwards. The duties of the customs are small. But the Vizirs (or Pashas) are the men who do the mischief. Coming hungry from Constantinople they enrich themselves by plundering the people who are absolutely at their mercy & whose complaints can never reach the Grant Seignior. They lay taxes without controul, & take every opportunity of making new exactions. For this reason it is considered as dangerous to have much appearance of wealth because it excites suspicion. It makes part of the Turkish system not to oppress individuals. That office is left to Pashas Agas & even private men, who when they have enriched themselves by plunder are in their turn stripped of their property & sometimes of their heads by a firman from Constantinople whither all the fruit of their exactions at last goes. The brother of the Logotheti of Livadia lost his head in this way, & I have seen at the Logotheti's house creditors wait in vain for sums which he could probably have given them easily, but he assumes an air of distress to avoid suspicion. Tyranny is uniform in its effect. I remember when I was at Lyons, the people there were selling their horses & trying to avoid seeming rich for fear of some new contribution, some requisition for the army &c.

There being no taverns in Greece you are always lodged in the houses of individuals. I have often had occasions to go to the houses of those to whom I was unrecommended. In such cases the priests are the best people to go to. This therefore has the appearance of hospitality, for you pay nothing to the master; but it is always understood that you are to give presents to the servants so that if you remain but a day or two in a man's house you pay as much as you would in a tavern. I have however seen some real hospitality, such as at Chryso & Mistra. I should observe that in places where there is a frequent passage of strangers, the servants of the house have no other wages than the presents of travellers. It would be wise for a man to carry a number of little things such as scissors, knives, combs &c which well applied, gain him friends at little cost.

The general system of Turkish govt is nearly feudal. All Greece releives as it were of its immediate Pasha, but certain places as for instance, the Mainotes, Athens, some of the islands (Tenos of a bishop or ecclesiastical man at Constantinople) are exempted from the Pasha's jurisdiction & depend immediately on their lord at Constantinople. The Pashas do not buy their offices but get them as favors. There are 3 Pashas in Greece at Tripolitza, Negropont & Yanina. This last is the famous Ali Pasha a man from the neighborhood of Yanina who rose by his talents from lowest obscurity & has now been Pasha 23 or 24 years. He is represented by his enemies (the Greeks, Fauvel too) as a cruel, unprincipled tyrant; by his friends the English as a fine fellow. He is a man of vigor & activity & has been serviceable in destroying the robbers who infested the high roads.[63]

These Pashas have their governments subdivided into districts each of which has 3 officers (see page 158) all of which buy their places. The Vyvuda for so it should be written is governor civil and military. The Ian receives the taxes. The Vyvuda has of course influence in the judgment of criminals before the Cadi.

The chief oppression under this govt is from Pashas & Vyvudas. The Karatch or Poll tax is the only one paid to the G. Seignior & is very small. Children at the age of 15 I think pay it (see page 161).

Athens still retains some spirit. Whilst I was their, our friend the Pasha of Negropont sent to make a requisition of a large sum of money. They replied that they owed him no allegiance having a firman which put them out of his power. He got angry & sent another demand. They refused to accede & finding things grow warm the Athenians began to repair the walls, guard the gates, & make every preparation to defend themselves. The Pasha highly offended sent word that unless what he asked for was granted he would come himself with his army & attack them. This was his ultimatum which arrived just as I left Athens. I was curious to learn the consequence but heard nothing. Fauvel I think was of opinion they would pay rather than fight but it argues boldness to oppose a Pasha in anything.

The price of articles in Greece is dearer than in common in Europe. The

63. Ali Pasha (1750–1822) was an Albanian brigand who through murder and intrigue made himself virtually the independent ruler of the Turkish province of Ioannina and much of the surrounding territory. Born into a family of Epirote notables, he was recognized by the Porte in 1784 because of his ability to control the territory and keep it subject, if only nominally, to the sultan, who had to withdraw troops to fight revolts elsewhere. In the War of the Second Coalition (1798–1802) he became governor of Roumelia, and in 1807 his two sons were appointed to govern the Morea and Thessaly. Thus Ali's family came into possession of almost all mainland Greece except Attica, Boeotia, and Negropont.

post horses may be gotten cheap, since if a traveller understands how to manage it, with his firman he gets horses and then pays what he likes merely as a present. So that he may get a horse for 2 piastres a day but the country horses are in some places extremely dear. From Chiarenza for instance to Patros a distance of 36 or 39 miles [or] a days ride I paid 8 piastres a horse.

Suppression of the Baratrairs. Every foreign ambassador on his arrival at Constantinople was presented by the Porte with one or two or three hundred firmans, exempting any one the ambassador pleased from the Turkish government, & placing them under his own. A singular privilege. The Porte has lately taken them all away. It is supposed that this step was made under French influence as there [were] a vast many Russian Baratrairs.[64]

The money used in Greece is that of Turkey & as follows. A Para is the smallest coin—it is a very small piece of silver & copper mixed together, not so large as a French six liard piece. Of these Paras forty make a piastre or Crush as it is called in Turkish & adopted in Greek. This is the only division of money. Simple & convenient. There are pieces of 50 paras, 100 paras & five crush; and pieces of 8 crush. The three first are like the Paras adultered silver; the last is the Turkish sequin of gold adultered with copper. The Turks buy up Spanish silver & gold in order to adulterate it for their own coin. Let me enquire if the Chinese do not make the same use of our Dollars. On these pieces of money is written [..].

Their comparative value with our coin of course varies with the course of exchange. A Venetian sequin is worth from 8 and a half to 9 1/2 piastres in Greece & further up in Turkey still more. Our dollar (Spanish) was worth when I was there about 3 1/2 crush or piastres.

I have not heard anything which gives me more satisfaction than what some men from Scutari told me in the Lazzaretto at Trieste.[65] In their

64. The system of barats, or letters of naturalization, began in the sixteenth century, when the sultan granted certain rights to foreign merchants that allowed them to trade in the Ottoman Empire. As time passed, the various foreign embassies in Constantinople used the barats, which were supposed to be issued by them only to Turks in their direct employ, as a means of interfering in the affairs of Turkey. These letters were issued by thousands to the Christian subjects of the Porte and exempted their bearers from Turkish taxes and laws. Thus certain Turkish subjects and their families acquired European protection by false diplomatic appointments. The foreign consuls profited from selling these appointments; and the lucky recipients, especially Greek traders, put themselves and their activities outside the reach of the Turks. Not only were Turkish merchants put at a severe disadvantage, but the baratrairs posed a standing threat to Turkish sovereignty. Selim III tried to stop this abuse, but the foreign missions resisted this threat to their profits and prerogatives.

65. Some parts at least of this section "Continuation of a Few Notes on Athens" were clearly written after Biddle's departure from the Athens.

neighborhood is the nation of Morlachs,[66] a tribe composed of Turks & Catholic Christians very poor & miserable constantly fighting—great robbers &c. The merchants & others of Scutari who are obliged to go into their country secure themselves in this way. In going nigh a town they call for someone of its inhabitants whom they know or even without knowing. They pronounce his name saying John Peter as the case may be "I come upon your faith." As soon as the name is pronounced, you are under the protection of that man, & your person & property is sacred in the sight of men who without this ceremony would have robbed or murdered you. Should anything happen to you, the misfortune becomes that of the family on whom you had called. They defend or revenge you at the expense of their lives. Such is the good faith of savage society. A fact like this gleams thro' the darkness of their vices. They are also a hospitable people. Yet hospitality & good faith are the virtues of barbarous people. Yet how unwise to judge of a nation from insulated facts. Such anecdotes have made the idle affection of talking (I will not say thinking) that savages are better & happier than civilized people, a talk fit for novel writers & [which] should not circulate beyond a young ladies boarding school. What! shall we shut up our books, and putting our heads within our shells lie torpid without advancing in knowledge? Why one of these days, we shall all die, and then we shall be quiet enough. But whilst we do live it is better to go forward. Burke was ironical & Rousseau avowedly insincere. After a long dream about the matter, I have reasoned myself into a perfect contentment with civilization. I have no idea of being an Indian. Let us take refined society as it is with its vices & its amusements. They [seem?] always in its favor. Yet one of course prefers the middle state of society. Switzerland, above all Geneva, has the most comfortable society I have seen. If I am not biassed by affection, the growing society, the coming people of Pennsylvania will be as good as any in this part of the world. They resemble much Geneva. Tolerable fortunes easy good manners & particularly cultivated minds. Pennsylvania is infinitely superior to the rest of America in that respect. They have got some faults which partiality itself cannot conceal, but in every picture there must be light & shade.

After seeing France & Italy we can form a better comparison of ancient man & things with those of today. The sneer of satire the illusions of poetry, & that miserable cant which induces us to decry everything around

66. Biddle refers to one-time Murlakia, that part of modern Croatia directly southeast of the Istrian peninsula. The Morlacchi, or Black Vlachs, spoke a Slavic language, not the Romanian of the Vlachs of Greece.

[us] & to bewail the degeneracy of men deceive us. We read of great actions, heroic sentiments done by [the] individuals of a nation & communicate them to all the men without considering that they would never have been known to us were they not exceptions. In fact strip any of the great things of which we read, of the glare which renders them dazzling & we find that instead of increasing they rather diminish our admiration for antiquity. When we see the bridge where Cocles[67] showed his valor, we admire his bravery but we forget that he had been descried by his countrymen. One man stood, but how many ran away? The deserters should be despised, but not forgotten. Socrates was a great man. One good man was then put to death by some thousands of bad men. Admire the pyramids of Egypt & the ancient monuments of architecture &c. They are certainly fine, but let us not forget the misery which accompanied their construction. Such a work was made by so many thousand slaves. This, by a tyrant who ruined his people to show his magnificence. Let us not mistake. The present generation of men is more civilized, more moral, more enlightened, better than any of those whose exploits are transmitted by history. There is but one thing which hinders me from believing so implicitly. It is their wonderful genius in sculpture & architecture, which shows an astonishing degree of refinement. Yet I still give infinitely the preference to our state of society. It is not unamusing to see how men mutually despise & decry each other (see page 150). National prejudices are very idle things. I think I love my country as well as any man & would go as far as any man to support its honor. But I do not feel this sentiment at all weakened by my indifference about the birthplace of other souls. I do not think I would ask a stranger any question except whether he were an American or not. Where he was born I should not care, if he was a worthy man. I have lost all that since honor & baseness, good & bad men have no particular residence. But one may smile at the prejudices of others. In religion it is particularly amusing. The Turks put us all outside of the railing; at the beard of Mahomet, the black-eyed damsels and the crowd of joys that await the Mussulman we must gaze with dry admiration. Their adversaries revenge themselves for the exclusion by shutting out wholly & utterly the barbarous infidels from all manner of comfort in future. This is done by their neighbors the Greeks. But the poor dogs are paid in turn for the intolerance since the good Catholics laugh at the Patriarch of Constantinople & his crew, &

67. Horatius Cocles was a Roman soldier who, in the traditional story, held up an Etruscan army at the wooden Sulpician Bridge over the Tiber until it could be demolished and who then leaped into the river and swam to safety (Livy 2.10).

think that no soul of them will ever reach the *sanctum sanctorum*. Yet even these do not enjoy their triumph, for the Protestants use their endeavors to exclude from heaven any man that believes transubstantiation, or thinks the Pope infallible. What is worse some of them think that there is no hope not only for those who interpret wrongly the text, but even [for] those who have never heard of it; & that the savages & the Eastern people who know nothing of Christianity are to be punished not for offending against [it] but for their ignorance. The same fallacious way of reasoning would make us punish them for not believing any other truth in morals metaphysics & science. The Protestants themselves quarrel at once with their mother church & with each other. The Church of England looks with disdain on the rabble of Methodists & Quakers & Baptists & Presbyterians & Anabaptists. Not content with chusing his own path, & going along quietly, each sect jostles its neighbor & if it cannot make him fall, at least throws dust in his face.

Any man but a republican would perhaps be offended at the sad degeneracy of the names of nobility. A Baron is a title which tho' common is still respectable in Germany. The Italians, to call a man a rascal make use of the indecent expression *Barone fottuto*. The Greeks as do indeed some of the Italians leave out this last adjective & designate scoundrel by the name of Barone; so that a Baron & a scoundrel have become synonimous.

Note made on my map of Anacharsis, June 6 1806. Good map, but the walls much too large; on the east & south not very incorrect; but to the west quite wrong. The old wall crossed the Museum exactly behind Philopappus's monument, for close by are tombs which could not be within the city. To the north & north east the actual wall is on the old foundation. Fauvel has made a very good map of modern Athens.[68]

ὑπὲρ πατριδος καὶ τιμης[69]

I took a Greek master at Athens & afterwards at Trieste. The first was an Athenian, the second a Macedonian. They gave me ideas of modern pronunciation. With the first I read Lucian, with the second Demosthenes, Homer & Anacreon.[70] The language of the ancient Greeks assumes in the

68. See plate no. 14 and note 48 above. A diagram of three hills (Biddle's Lycavettus, Pnix, and Musaeum) and of the run of the ancient walls across them has been omitted. On the sketch, Biddle criticizes Barthélemy's map of the city walls.
69. "For fatherland and honor."
70. Lucian was a rhetorician and satirist of the second century A.D.; Anacreon was an Ionian poet (born c. 570 B.C.) noted for his symposiac and erotic lyrics.

mouth of their descendants quite a different shape from what we give it. Accustomed to revere & admire it we have given it a thousand imaginary beauties. So that at first I was disappointed on finding it stripped of so many elegancies until I found that it still possessed a great many. It is a much smoother language as pronounced by the Greeks; the οι's the ου's &c which we pronounce so roundly, are much less noisy when changed into ees (as in geese) and oos (as in goose). Homer they read like our blank verse which I think the right way, without halting at the end of the line. It is thus that the Italians read their poetry. There is very little of our "sound echoing sense" as we call it. Thus that famous line which our schoolboys roar, as if they smelt salt water is quite different, tho' the master remarked it as a very fine passage. The πολυφλοσβοιο θαλασσης becoming quiet: poliphlesvio thalássis.[71] They say θὰλασσις in the nominative, θαλὰσσις in the genitive.[72] Homer is still very musical, tho' they follow the accent without regarding much the metre. Anacréon as they call him is I think less musical than in the Italian translation; tho' the Greek master thought otherwise & was very enthusiastic in his praise of the original.

Corinth June 13, 1806
Friday

My dear Tom.

It was a proverb of antiquity allusive to the luxury of this part of Greece, that it was not every man who could go to Corinth. The remark for a different reason is now equally true, for I find myself the second of my countrymen who has been here.[73] Your classic recollections will be revived by the name & will make you willingly accompany me from Athens. On Tuesday morning June 10th I left that interesting spot for which I felt a great deal of attachment. No man of letters can approach it without veneration, nor leave it without regret. My arrangements would permit me to give to it but two weeks, but they were spent in research & enquiry, & as I was aided by Mr Fauvel I cannot reproach myself with having made a superficial visit to Athens. On Tuesday morning then I left it, & taking the "sacred way" the road on which the processions for the Eleusinian mysteries

71. Homer's "loud-resounding sea."
72. Biddle indicates the correct demotic pronunciation of the genitive of *thalassa*, but the nominative is simply *thálassa*.
73. Biddle again refers to Joseph Allen Smith.

passed crossed the plain. In coming out we passed the spot of the gate
Dipylon. The sacred way is still seen in many places. The richness of the
plain covered with grain & olive trees is very pleasing. We ascended the
mountain & I remembered that I left Athens for ever. At 1½ hours from
Athens on the mountain is a monastery called Daphne, as is I believe the
mountain itself. The monastery is now ruined. We descended to the plain
& after crossing the Cephissus & one or two little springs running out of a
lake walled in between the hill & the sea shore got to Eleusis. This famous
place is situated near the sea side partly in a plain & partly on a small
rising. This is now a miserable little village of a few houses. It retains
however the name of the ancient town corrupted into Lepsina. It was here
says mythology where was first planted grain taught by Ceres.[74] You know
the story. Near one of the mountains in the vicinity is a fountain where
Ceres sat down for repose, says Wheeler. All that I saw was a number of
ruins scattered about the plain. We could distinguish on the decline of the
plain large masses probably of the famous temple of Ceres; among the ruins
lies a bust of a Roman emperor without a head & set as it were in a round
cave of marble the only example I know. On entering the town is a square
marble ruin arched underneath, not known what. There are also ruins of an
aqueduct which is low, & not so majestic as those of Italy, tho' I believe it
built by Hadrian. For mysteries read Warburton, Pluche's "Histoire du
Ciel" &c.[75] The port seems good being covered by Salamis. Left Eleusis &
in about 3 hours (crossing a ridge of mountain) reached Megara & found
Palmer, Williams, Walpole, who had arrived 1/4 hour before. Begin to see
the town. [It] is beautifully situated on a hill descending into the plain. In
the neighborhood are several small hills now uninhabited. The port Nisea
is about an hour distant: anciently famous, now a single ship there bound
for Trieste. There are no monuments remaining. We saw what Wheeler
did—some ruins of the wall & a large stone with inscriptions in honor of
some man who had gained prizes. This was probably nigh a gymnasium.
The view is delightful of the sea Salamis, Morea &c. Remarkable that these
people at Megara speak Greek but are dressed like Albanians, & their
houses unlike those of the other towns are flat-roofed. They however under-

74. As modern excavations have shown, the sanctuary of Demeter and Persephone, site of
the Eleusinian mysteries, the substance of which was never revealed to the uninitiated and
has since remained a secret, has an architectural history reaching back to the Bronze Age.
The Homeric *Hymn to Demeter* records the mythological story of the cult's foundation.
75. William Warburton, bishop of Gloucester (1689–1779), *The Works of the Right Rever-
end William Warburton* (London, 1788). Noël Antoine Pluche (1688–1761), *Histoire du Ciel*
(Paris, 1738–39, and subsequent editions).

stood Albanian. They may [be] a wandering tribe of that nation who have lost their language, (at least in part) sooner than their dress. This is however contrary to the natural order of chance. The next day, Wednesday June 11th we left Megara for Corinth. The ancient road by the sea famous for the rocks & the robberies of Sciron[76] is not now used, not I believe so much on account of the danger of the road as for the convenience of having one passage into the Morea, & thus securing custom house duties, the police having placed a guard there. The other road is across the Mount Gerania. This country is sadly depopulated, a rich soil being useless. We made a pause at the narrowest part of the trail, at a place where there is a guard. Here the strait is 6 or 7 miles broad tho' wider than it is near Corinth. Our baggage was unexamined. We gave 15 paras to the soldiers, the usual gift. No traveller can pass from the Morea into Attica without a firman, but may come into the Morea without it. Here is a fine view of the two seas. We continued & at evening reached Corinth [..] hours from Megara. We went to the house of a sort of English consul, who was at Patras. We however occupied his house tho' without a letter for him. As soon as we had sat down to a little yhourt, a person came in who they said was the master of the house. I began to tell him that we had taken the liberty to come there, knowing his hospitality & made many excuses. I then asked if he had seen Dr Cicelli to whom I had a letter & who I was told was absent. He was the very Doctor himself & a very polite man. We now saw the town & retired to bed.

The next morning Thursday June 12th Mr Palmer & I rode to the port Cenchraeus at the other end of this isthmus,[77] & afterwards to see other things (see below). About one o'clock the gentlemen set out for Patras & I accompanied them as far as Sicyon where we parted. I abandoned after much deliberation my plan of going to Constantinople thence over land to Paris, the more so as Palmer makes the same route as far as Vienna. He is an English clergyman. The name conveys the idea of much honesty & stability. He is a good man but not very much conversant with the world. The same may be said of Walpole, a young man who is a good Greek scholar, but not much else. These Englishmen are strangely deficient in politeness. I have seen these two men sit down & talk to a gentleman who

76. The legendary Attic hero Theseus killed the brigand Sciron (originally a local Megarian cult hero), who had a habit of throwing travelers off the cliffs into the sea, where they were eaten by a gigantic turtle. The main road from Athens to Corinth now skirts the bottom of these cliffs. In antiquity it was a narrow ledge high up the cliff face.
77. Anc. and mod. Kenkhreai on the Saronic Gulf.

stood up & to whom they did not offer a chair, & this to a stranger who came to see them. The Painter Williams having lived longer out of Engd has more manners than either of them. I returned in the evg to Corinth.

This morning Friday I remained in the house of Dr Cicelli where I came last night. The weather being disagreeable & I fatigued joined to the prospect of information from Cicelli induced me to stay another day in Corinth. I shall now add what has occurred since my last.

Corinth like the other Greek cities finely placed at the foot of a hill, its Acropolis [Fig. 16]. To see the Acropolis that is to go up, it is necessary to have an order from the Bey given on a firman for that purpose expressly or by a present to the Bey. There are no antiquities on the Acropolis. It is a high steep rock surrounded by a castle wall—it is strong. Towards the north it is a perpendicular rock, tho' towards the north west the ascent is less difficult. The present town occupies the ground of the ancient town of which it still bears the name. The port Lechaeus formerly joined to the town by a wall of 1-¼ miles is now without a name, or a boat. It is indeed rather a road than a harbor. The country in the neighborhood is beautiful. The plain begins after crossing the hills which shut up the eastern side of the isthmus. It begins to be well cultivated near Corinth. The strait may be 8 or 10 miles long, & 5 or 6 miles broad, 5 in the narrowest part. About halfway you see a long sort of ditch which extends nearly ½ a mile, & about 25 feet broad. It is the commencement of the canal of Nero.[78] The port of Cenchraeus preserves its name a little modernized. It is small & about 6 or 7 miles from Corinth. You see the ruins of the old wall of the port, but [I] asked in vain for Helen's baths mentioned by Pausanias tho' McKenzie saw them.[79] Near a little village called Exemilia about 1 hour from C are a number of ruins which look like those of a stadium & theatre. Perhaps here the Isthmic games were celebrated.[80] In the city are seven Doric columns of stone & of a singular proportion the diameters being large for the height. Said to be the temple of Venus or rather of Neptune, that of V being much nearer the Acropolis says Pausanias.[81] Cicelli says Gropius[82]

78. The idea of cutting a canal across the isthmus goes back to the sixth-century B.C. Corinthian tyrant Periander at least, but was actually taken in hand by Nero in A.D. 67. The modern canal, built in 1882–93, removed all traces of the earlier attempt. In antiquity ships were hauled across the isthmus on a special stone road, the Diolkos.

79. The Bath of Helen, mentioned by Pausanias (2.2.3), is a hot sea spring still in use.

80. The sanctuary of Poseidon at Isthmia was the site of one of the four Panhellenic games.

81. The temple to which Biddle refers is actually the archaic temple of Apollo, one of the earliest extant stone temples.

82. Georg Christian Gropius, a German painter and originally an agent for Lord Aberdeen in Athens in the early years of the nineteenth century, became Austrian vice-consul in

has discovered the theatre much farther down in the plain. Near the Acropolis I saw a number of unintelligible ruins hewn out of the rock. In the garden of Nozari a Greek we saw a fine round piece of marble now serving as the upper part of a well with some very fine bas reliefs representing a number of Deities. The owner has some ancient spirit about him—declares it disgraceful to rob Greece of its masterpieces & will not part with it— odd for a Greek. Corinth has about 4000 inhabitants, very poor & oppressed.[83] No commerce except a little cheese & grain, the Bey of Corinth having obtained, as a favor from the G Seignior, permission to export, but all the rest of the Morea is subject to the prohibition. The reason of which is, says Cicelli, that the grain may be sent to Constantinople. The view from the Acropolis famous. You know the old history of Corinth—famous sailors—Syracuse one of their colonies. The town was under the protection of Venus their tutelary goddess.[84] She still ought to be so for allowing for circumstances they have still the same attachments says Cicelli tho' without the means. Story of the postboy illustrative of manners. The air of Corinth very bad in summer. I do not know whether it is owing to fatigue or air but I had a little fever & headache & sick stomach of which a little cream of tartar rid me. There are now 3 or 4 persons ill of putrid fevers.[85] Yet there is nothing stagnant about here—but the city lies low & the isthmus is badly cultivated. The postmaster has a particular firman authorizing him to take money from everybody—there is no exception. He avails himself of it to charge immoderately. From here to Vostizza he asked 12 piastres a horse & Palmer & Walpole gave 10 after great scolding. To Argos he asked five, but I got country horses for 3—paying 13 for four horses.

The ride to Sicyon is across a beautiful plain divided about half way by a wood of olive trees. The distance is called three hours. We made it in about 2, but rode fast. There are two or three little villages on the way. The Asopus a little blue stream is near Sicyon which is on a fine commanding eminence—nothing more beautiful. The ridges of Parnassus & Helicon on the other side of the gulf. The island of Aegina & its sea, the rich plain below form a fine picture. It is now called Vasilicon & is a village of about 50 houses. The antiquities are the situation of a theatre, ruins of a building

---

1811 and consul in 1816 and was well known to travelers both for his topographical knowledge and for his trade in antiquities.

83. Leake agreed with Wheler that the population of Corinth was about 1,500, two-thirds Greek and one-third Turkish.

84. Ancient Corinth was renowned for its temple of Aphrodite, for Aphrodite's temple prostitutes, and for a general profligacy.

85. Typhus fever.

in brick (Roman) near it. A ruin also of brick called the Palace of the King, the ruins of a modernised church, i.e., a church made out of old materials. There is also a large sort of ravine with some ruins in it. What it was is unknown. All the ruins poor & unsatisfactory. Its only beauty its position, its only happiness that it has no Turks here. They have all left it. I had in the course of the day much talk with Cicelli which I may afterwards repeat to you. At present good night.   N.B.

Argos Saturday June 14

My dear brother,

The descendants of Inachus[86] who sit crosslegged around me may stare as they please whilst I continue my story. This morning about 5 I left Corinth & after traversing part of the large plain went into the mountainous or rather hilly parts. After some bad road I reached in 3 hours (about) a Khan & nearly an hour & a half more brought one into a large plain which I believe was once occupied by the Nemean city—the famous games.[87] The trees have disappeared & given place to grain. There are two ruins, one on the roadside, small & from the part of the wall yet remaining seems to have been in modern times remade into a church. Of the other which is 100 yards distant three columns remain. They are large & Doric, & two of them support an architrave. They are of stone & seem to be part of the vestibule. There are all around mutilated fragments of the building which (according to McKenzie's notes) is the temple of Jupiter. Leaving this place where there is no house (the village of Cutsomathi being about ½ an hour to the right) we rode on 3 hours more to the town of Kharvati.[88] This is to the left of the road to Argos & Napoli but this compensated for by the ruins of ancient Mycenae![89] These are about a mile or a mile & ½ to the northwest

86. In Greek mythology, the river god Inakhos was the ancestor of the Argive kings. He introduced into Argos the worship of Hera instead of that of Poseidon, who in retaliation dried up his waters.

87. The sanctuary of Zeus at Nemea was the site of another of the four major Panhellenic games. The Doric columns are the remains of a temple of the fourth century B.C.

88. Biddle thrice mistakes Calavrita (an important town in the north central Peloponnesos) for the village of Kharvati, or anc. and mod. Mykenai. I have therefore changed his text.

89. Though there was a small classical and Hellenistic town on this site, the extant ruins belong to the so-called heroic age described by Homer and currently equated with the period 1500–1100 B.C. Biddle saw only walls and tombs. The excavation of the even earlier

of Kharvati. All that is now seen are the ruins of the wall round the Citadel, of which two of the gates still remain. Over one of them are the two bas reliefs of tygers or lions of which Pausanias speaks & which are ascribed to the Cyclops. They are carved out of a single stone, of a triangular form. It is to be hoped that the gentlemen understood forging thunderbolts better than making tygers, for the workmanship of these is in rather a blacksmith style tho' better than my draft of them.[90] The citadel is small & I observed that this eminence is very small & the access easy unlike the strong & high citadels which some of the other towns have. There is however a very high hill which overlooks the place. On the top of the citadel are some loose stones & a sort of well. At some distance from the citadel towards Kharvati are the famous subterranean caverns.[91] They are on the slope of a hill & you descend to the entrance by some steps which have not yet been all cleared of the earth [Fig. 17]. The door is of large stones & of a handsome architecture. Near it is a well worked pilaster which most probably belonged to it. You enter, 8 or 10 steps from the door into a large circular room, terminating pyramidally. This is all of large stone & very prettily built. There are two apertures by which the light enters—one near the top, one in the side. To the right is a door leading into several chambers now in part filled with earth. This circular room is called the tomb of Agamemnon. This circumstance & the beauty of its structure render it a very interesting monument. It is more so from the degradation it has suffered from the brutal violence of the Scotch vandal Elgin who has dug up the floor without returning the earth to its place. The ashes of the hero are uncovered by the profane hand of this man & his monk Hunt.[92] He is about adding to his disgrace by selling his pillage. Erostratus[93] burnt for glory, Elgin robbed for gold.

Descending to the village which consists of 30 or 40 houses, I eat a little yourt with the Aga, & then set off for Argos. The road lies across the plain.

Grave Circles was begun by Schliemann in the 1870s, and later the remains of a palace were also found.

90. A small drawing has been omitted.

91. Known in antiquity as treasuries, or depositories of wealth, these constructions were tombs built in the late Bronze Age (fourteenth century B.C.). Biddle describes the so-called Tomb of Agamemnon, the best preserved of the lot.

92. Parts of the ornamental semicolumns framing the exterior of the doorway were carried off by Philip Hunt, Elgin's chaplin and the director of his operations on the Acropolis in Athens.

93. The Ephesian Herostratos set fire to the temple of Artemis at Ephesos in 356 B.C. to make a name for himself.

Near the town we crossed the bed of the Inachus which is wider than that of most Greek rivers. I say bed for there is not a drop of water on it. Arrived in the town we looked about for 4 persons to whom I had addresses. Like the men of scripture they had all some occupation which took them away so that I did not see a soul of them. I went to the Aga in this dilemma. He received me with politeness & gave me a room in his house. He is a native of Napoli.[94] It is fatiguing to be obliged to answer the thousand enquiries which these fellows make. I mean the Greeks & Turks in general—they beseige you—your watch your clothes your books—all is to be examined & wondered at. The Greeks seem greater news mongers, for they are more interested; they constantly hope for the coming of foreign troops here & are very inquisitive about politics. I answered as well as I could & sometimes am obliged to make news to answer at random in order to satisfy them.   N.B.

Monday June 16, 1806

Dear Tom,

I continue my talk from a Kahn situated on a fine hill about 4 hours from Argos where my last left me. Yesterday morning I left the house of the Aga. The town of Argos is beautifully placed. The Acropolis or Citadel is very high & strong & overlooking the houses which are all on the southern side of it & in the plain. I should imagine Ancient Argos to have [lain] more on the side of the mountain & to the southwest rather of the present town. The modern Argos is a large village, scattered about but some parts thickly built. It may contain [..] inhabitants.[95] There is nothing in it distinguishing [it] from other Greek towns. The antiquities are besides a number of scattered pieces of walls &c, a portion of the wall of the citadel not far from the root of the mountain; the form of a theatre on the declivity of the hill. The steps hewn out of the rock are in quite good preservation. Near it is a large ruin which I could not explain. It is of brick & seems originally to have been square. Two sides only remain—most probably undergone some change to accommodate it to Christian purposes. To the north of this is a ruin of a small temple on the side of the hill & built on the rock. Three sides remain & I think excavation might be rewarded with some discovery in the interior. In the rock is the niche for the Deity &

94. Napoli, Anapli, or Napoli di Romania is the modern Nauplion.
95. Leake estimated the population at 1,200 families, of which 60 to 80 were Turkish.

behind is an aperture leading out of the temple. It was probably here that the priest entered to dictate & to direct the motions of the God. However I looked in vain for some building near the temple, for now the aperture ends in the open air. It is a thing I remarked also at Pompeia & Nisanes[96] that the place where the priest is said to have entered is exposed to everyone's view, so that the mischief would carry its own remedy. Must enquire about this. The errors of ancient priestcraft are now proverbial, its vices exposed to shame—but our priestcrafts still want to be understood. I perceive that these buildings are all brick, as were the earliest temples of Rome.[97] Singular that man should make a new material rather than use the ready made stone; but want of instruments to cut it [must be the explanation]. Argos, as you know, [is] one of the oldest towns of Greece, &c. In two hours time [we] reached Napoli de Romania. Here a new difficulty. Two of the men who had escaped me at Argos I hoped to see here. They were not [here]. The Doctor whom I thought settled here, is not. The English Consul who appears to be a shabby fellow denied himself & his rascally dragoman Jew whom we found at his door said that the people were sick in the town & a great many dying. This uncomfortable news made me resolve to leave the place without stopping when we were told of a house where Englishmen were received. We went there, & found a woman—I think like Ledyard['s]—he ought to have said young women, for in general old women are morose, young & middle aged amiable.[98] This was a very good lady who tho' she does not take strangers into her house consented to let me have a place seeing my embarrassment. Her brother arriving was very serviceable to me in showing me the town. His name

96. Pompeia is of course Pompeii, which Biddle apparently visited when he was in the vicinity of Naples. What he means by "Nisanes" (the reading is perfectly clear), I have been unable to determine.

97. Biddle was looking at the scattered remains of Roman Argos. Hence the nature of the building materials. The Romans preferred to build in brick and concrete rather than in quarried stone, which was usually used only for the exterior facing of brick. Only in late antiquity and the Middle Ages were Greek buildings torn down and their quarried stone reused for new construction.

98. John Ledyard (1751–88), an American adventurer, sailed on Cook's third voyage in 1776–79 and published an account of it: *A Journal of Captain Cook's Last Voyage to the Pacific Ocean* (Chicago, 1963 [Hartford, Connecticut, 1783]). I have punctuated Biddle's sentence exactly as he wrote it, adding only a letter. Biddle seems to refer to an incident described by Ledyard in the course of his solo exploration of an island off the coast of Alaska in 1778 (90ff.). Arriving at the house of an Indian chief, Ledyard was much impressed by the women who greeted him and by one woman in particular, who was eager to please him and to whom he gave presents. If Biddle alludes to this story only from memory, his memory was very good indeed, because Ledyard does not in fact mention the age of the women!

Antonio. Naples is situated on the southeastern side of a large bay which extends in towards the land until it forms a long sheet of low water almost like a marsh. This circumstance & the bad state of culture in which the adjacent country is, makes Naples somewhat unhealthy in the hot season— the town is on a little sort of promontory which is commanded by a high fortress built by the Venetians (I believe) and strong.[99] The town is sur- rounded by walls & at present there is a commander who has the rank of a Pashaw. I should say that the part of the town along the port is outside of the walls & inhabited by Greeks, whilst the interior is occupied principally by Turks who form the strength of the town. They count about 2000 souls. Not much commerce now. The smuggling of grain abroad is the principal [activity]. From Candia now called Cani[100] [Napoli] is about 2 days sail. No antiquity except a fountain where says my informer the opinion was that drinkers grew young. What does he mean? One large stone all that re- mains. The port good; vessels of war may lie at a little distance from the town on the western side of the bay. Near the town small vessels only. In fact no fort. I do not think there was any old town here.[101] About an hours ride to the north are the ruins of an old wall on a small rising. Here was perhaps the town of Nauplia, or possibly Lyrinthus. Nothing but the large walls to see.

I slept at Naples this night, & in the morning left it on mules accom- panied by a Tartar of the Pasha whom I take for greater surety. We passed by old Nauplia & after a short stay at Argos set out for Tripolizza. I am thus far on my road. This place overlooks Naples. The plain in which this town & Argos & Mycenae are placed is very extensive & good but in many parts uncultivated. I had intended to have gone to Epidaurus from which Naples if about 7 hours & Argos nearly the same. But from what I learnt there is nothing but some walls to see which are not worth the trouble, & I gave it up. It is still called Pidavra. It is close to Egina. In going to it from Naples you may pass by Ligurio[102] where is a theatre, that is the situation of one. These objects were not sufficient to attract me there the city itself being uninteresting.   NB

99. The Palamidi was first fortified by the Venetians in 1686, and they built the present fortress in 1711–14. A small sketch-map of the area has been omitted.

100. On the island of Crete.

101. In antiquity Nauplion was probably the port town of Argos. The town may have been small, but the site was inhabited in the Stone and Bronze Ages.

102. Med. Lessa. The famous theater was actually in the sanctuary of the healing god Asklepios at Epidauros. Even in Biddle's time the ruins were more extensive than he indi- cates; and, in missing the theater, he bypassed one of the most curious remains of Greek antiquity.

Tripolizza[103] Tuesday June 17

I left the Khan in the morning. The road is rocky & mountainous. You enjoy the pleasure of passing over the ancient road in many parts perfectly preserved. In three hours we reached a Khan opposite to the town of Agios Georgios, a small village on the side of a hill. It is near here that begins the large plain which contains this place & which is celebrated in the history of Greece. From Agios Georgios direct to Tripolizza is about 2 hours, but I turned aside to visit the town of Tegea.[104] Of this ancient place nothing now remains except a circular wall in the midst of the plain, & a single church called Palaio Episcopo. The wall is much ruined. There was no citadel & the part inclosed must have formed a small town. The church is of modern times & built on the spot & of the ruins of some other building. On the outside wall are some remains of capitals cornishes &c. and a piece of stone with a small unintelligible inscription. Inside of the church is a large piece of marble, with a number of names of μετοιχοι[105] upon it. The church is ruined and disused there being no houses near. It is nearly south of Tripolitzza where we arrived in about an hour. I went to the house of Ianetachi, the English agent. A good man—found there a young Cephalonia Docter just come to settle, & also Dr Abramioti of Argos for whom I have a letter & from whom I got much information. Tripolitizza is on the north side of the large plain. It is among the largest towns of the Morea & is the residence of the Pashaw or governor general of it.[106] Pleasant situation & the air is esteemed more healthy than any of the Morea. It has no monument whatsoever of antiquity being I think composed of the wrecks of the people of Tegea, Mantinea & another place called if I don't mistake Thana.[107] In the plain is seen the bed of the Ifis a little waterless stream.

Wednesday 18th I went early in the morning to Palaeopolis the ancient Mantinea[108] about 6 miles to the northeast of this place. The road first goes

103. Mod. Tripolis. The city was founded probably in the fourteenth or perhaps the fifteenth century A.D.
104. This was the site of the temple of Athena Alea and of a famous city of ancient Arcadia.
105. Resident aliens.
106. At the time of Biddle's visit this person was one Osman, whom Chateaubriand visited on August 14, 1806, and whom he describes at some length. Veli, younger son of Ali Pasha of Ioannina, became pasha of the Morea in 1807.
107. Perhaps anc. Pallantion, though Leake preferred to locate Pallantion on the site of Tripolizza.
108. Mantinea was an ancient rival of the city-state of Tegea and the site of two famous battles, in 418 and 362 B.C. In the second of these the Theban leader Epaminondas was killed, and his death marked the end of Thebes' brief hegemony in the Greek world. The fourth-century walls (c. 370 B.C.), the circuit of which is almost complete, are a fine example of Greek fortification.

thro' the large plain; then turns aside into the northeast corner of it where it is less wide. Near the extremity is Palaeopolis. It is in the plain without any rising or citadel; tho' there is an eminence in the neighborhood now occupied by a small village & which might once have served as citadel to Mantinea. There is now no person living at Palaeopolis; the whole surface of the ancient town being sown with grain. Nothing now remains but the old walls a little above ground with the bastions or castles at regular & small distances. From the size of the walls the city was much larger than Tegea. Indeed its greatness & opulence is mentioned. To the town's right is a village called Kapso which has taken or communicated its name to the mountain near which it is placed. Mantinea is famous for the battle which saw the death of the Theban hero. You know the history. Returned home, I was unable to get horses to leave Tripolizza & was obliged to remain the day. I tried to occupy it by talk with Abramioti & a young physician about settling here & whom I found in the house where I stay; by reading Cicero's oration for Plancius; and by seeing the people. This place being the residence of the court, things are more plentiful & cheap than elsewhere. In the evening I had much talk with two brothers, vagrant charlatans of Cephalonia looking out for employ. The elder had lived much in Asia. The Turks much more humane than the Christians to animals.

Friday following Thursday 19th unwilling to wait for posthorses I took others & set out for Mistra about 8 o'clock. The large plain in which Tripolitizza [lies] is first to be passed. In 3½ hours we reached a Khan. Nothing was here to be procured but some saltfish & eggs, the day being one of the fast days so numerous & so foolish in the Greek religion. Four hours more brought us to another Khan almost the only building on the road. The road is all the way thro' narrow passes of the mountain with very little plain and vegetation to enliven it. We passed some flocks of sheep & goats watched by moustachoed shepherds whose savage looks would have alarmed a reader of pastorals. One of them an old man was not quite so civil as any of Jemmy Thompson's heroes.[109] As we passed him, the postillion enquired if we could get any milk. The fellow asked who I was, & being told I was a Frank, what does he want with milk said he using some term of vulgar reproach. The Franks kill men. He ought to have nothing but bread & water. This was interpreted to me when we had passed. This road was lately dangerous. We were shown the spot where three persons had been murdered six months ago. The whole gang was destroyed by Ali

---

109. James Thomson (1700–1748), Scottish writer of pastoral poetry and drama.

Pasha—they were 25 in number.[110] Having reached the Khan we were obliged to remain there, our horses being unable to go the remaining four hours. But with posthorses it is not a hard days ride, about 12 hours. When obliged to remain there in a little house among Turks & Greeks I always found a remedy in books. Besides Anacharsis I have constantly in hand Cicero's orations & Junius. To the writings of Cicero, our attachment increases with our intimacy. I had once read them with a school boy's attention more occupied with moods & tenses than beauties of style or force of reasoning. But I now read them with pleasure & fruit & in a season of more leisure. I propose translating many of the orations with care. To a general scholar these writings are very attractive, but to one of my profession they are all important.

I believe the turn of my mind, or what may properly be called my genius, has at length decided itself. I will not enquire how far nature directs the disposition towards any particular pursuit, but an early wish created perhaps by the force of first impressions & the habits of my associates, increased by education, fortified by ambition has fixed my character. To govern men, and particularly by means of eloquence seems to me the object most worthy of ambition in a free govt. It is the avenue which leads to glory & which while shut against the rest of the world is wide & easy to Americans. In Europe there is no eloquence. Language is everywhere prostituted to adulation, & even in England oratory is paralyzed by venality, or trammeled by royal privilege, or chilled by the cold immoveable habits of the people. In America every motive invites to the cultivation of eloquence—at once the engine of power the road to fame and the means of fortune. My dispositions for oratory have been encouraged since I left my country. I remember that whenever in Switzerland the aspect of nature was peculiarly grand, it always obtained from me an harangue. I have trodden the Roman forum & breathed the air of Grecian eloquence. Whilst standing on the lonely spot once crowded with freemen who listened to the eloquence of the greatest of men, I seemed to devote myself to a study which roused the slumbering liberties of Greece & rendered immortal those who pursued it. Yet much, very much is to be done in order to acquire glory. The routine of [an] attorney, pleading, is beneath imitation. To be

110. Dodwell has much to say about the bands of thieves who infested Messenia and Arkadia in the winter of 1806, before Biddle's arrival. Biddle, unlike Dodwell, was untroubled by these brigands precisely because a concerted effort by the Turkish authorities had just caused most of them to depart for the Ionian Islands, where they entered British service.

an orator demands unwearied study. The judgment is to be matured by slow & tedious investigation & fancy must pluck a flower from every science to illustrate and adorn. I can more willingly allow the humility of ignorance than of superstition. The groan of affected piety which counts the multitude of its sins in despair offends the ear of reason which is better pleased with the acknowledgement of the limited bounds of our understanding. When I consider how much must be done before I can reach what I desire, when I examine how very few advances I have as yet made towards it, I feel not the debasing sentiment of despair, but a mingled sensation of the dignity of my pursuit & the labors thro' which it must lead me. We will see perhaps one day. Junius seems to me much the best political writer in our language. I speak merely with regard to style. I should suppose that a mode of writing at once brilliant & unaffected might be found by mingling the style of Junius with that of Gibbon.

Friday morning I started early from the Khan. The road is at first over a hilly and disagreeable country the ancient mountain Mainalon.[111] The old road is in many parts perfectly preserved. It is wide & resembling our turnpikes. The stones unequal, well beaten & at every four or five feet a range of stones traverses the road. It is wide enough for a carriage, but the road going constantly up & down would not permit an ancient carriage to pass. The Greeks were not so good roadmakers as the Romans who built of large flat stones making a smooth surface. The Romans indeed went more I believe in carriages than the Greeks. It was with great delight that on descending the last chain of the Mainalon I beheld the plain of Sparta [Fig. 18]. We soon passed a large ruin which looks like the remains of an aqueduct & crossed the Eurotas. A part of the plain was then to be crossed before we reached the village of Mistra & the house of Dr Talpo to whom Abramioti had given me a letter. I occupied the day in looking at the town. I went up to the ruined castle which overlooks it.[112] The Bishop who had seen me pass, sent to desire that I would stop on my return. I did so & found a very clever, decent old man who received me kindly, & was sorry I

---

111. Biddle's repeatedly writes Menelaion, which actually means a sanctuary in honor of the Spartan king Menelaus; but he must mean Mainalon. The Mainalon mountains close the plain of Tripolis to the west, and their axis is continued in the Parnon mountains, which lie directly east of the plain of the Eurotas River. The main road from Tripolis to Sparta runs through the Kleisoura Pass.

112. The fortress, built in 1249 by William de Villehardouin, attracted the nearby population. The site became the medieval and early-modern Sparta. The present city of Sparta was refounded on the ancient site in 1834, and Mistra was then gradually abandoned.

would not remain in his house during my stay here. I returned to hold converse with my Doctor & to sleep.

I employed Saturday 21st morning first in a visit of ceremony to the Aga.[112a] He is a man of Crete, a respectable looking man. There is indeed something in the exterior of Turkish govt, quite patriarchal. On visiting the Aga you pass upstairs thro' a crowd of inferior domestics. You find a chamber with a number of armed Turks standing in one corner, himself sitting upon the cushions in another. You make your best bows to him. A Turk or Greek takes off his shoes as he enters on what may be called the quarterdeck of the room, the elevated part where are the cushions. The shoes or even boots of a Franc are pardoned considering his being a barbarian. The Aga is richly dressed an old man with a long white beard, unarmed; his natural gravity increased by a hooker or pipe. As soon as you are seated, the pipe is presented to you; then coffee in a little cup with a silver or plated saucer of the same form with the cup. The old gentleman is in general very civil; they know that Francs come only to amuse themselves, & spend their money, & they like the English. The coffee I should observe is without any mixture of milk or sugar & the grounds swallowed without the slightest distinction. One is glad to escape from such a potion & take refuge in the pipe, but a new difficulty embarrasses you. A Turk is so accustomed to smoke that it excites no saliva. Therefore whatever temptation you may have, you must by no means spit, as it would be a higher offence against decorum, than to defile the carpet of an European housekeeper. I obtained from the Aga an order for posthorses which I could not have got without such an order. The post is exclusively for the public service & with the firman you are entitled to take them gratis—of this tho' there seems to be some doubt. I am convinced Foreigners however in general pay. I having no firman might be refused, as indeed every tartar was at the posthouse.

From the Aga's I went to the bath. I do not know whether a Turkish bath is not more agreeable than ours. In the common room, among the Turks, you undress. A coloured sort of callicoat is put round your waist, a towel round your head; another over your shoulders. In this style you are conducted to the bathing room which is of a high temperature & excites much perspiration. Around the room are fountains of water with little reservoirs. A piece of long board the size of a bed is placed on the floor; on this you sit or lie and a little boy with a sort of flesh brush first rubs you all

112a. Is this man the Ibrahim Bey whose "court" Chateaubriand describes at length in much the same terms as Biddle's?

over. This, assisted by the perspiration, is very pleasant. He then throws water over you. This done he takes a basin of soap & water & gives you a thorough rubbing down. The ceremony finishes by his pouring water upon you until you are satisfied. You are then covered with dry linen & conducted to a bed, where if you can forget how many Turks have been there before you you may sleep. It certainly looks clean. Whilst you are there the boy rubs you dry. You rise & go off leaving 30 or 40 paras, somewhat cheaper than those of Paris. After dinner I rode to ancient Sparta where I occupied the rest of the day.

Sunday 22nd in the morning I visited my good friend the Bishop. He was not at home & I looked at his church & also at an ancient sarcophagus. The heat of the day was cooly & tranquilly passed in reading and in the afternoon I paid a second visit to old Sparta & returned to my lodgings. I omitted to mention my being waited on, Thursday evening by the two head men of Mistra to pay me a visit of compliment.

                                                      Monday 23d June 1806
My dear Thomas,

I am at Sparta. Let me respect the venerable style of conciseness which became its greatness, whilst I describe its calamities. Sparta is no more. Its freedom has fled; the monuments of its glory have all returned to the earth which covers its children; the very spot which it occupied is deserted by an unworthy posterity. Athens still boasts of some sad monuments of its greatness & its arts, but the ruins of Sparta offer nothing to arrest the emotions of melancholy & despair. Of its former history you know every thing interesting; let me now convey to you all that I know of its present state. Sparta, in its infant freedom, had no defense but its institutions & its arms. Unlike most Greek cities which began by a fortress on a hill & gradually ventured onto the plain, Sparta unprotected by walls boldly began in the plain itself [Fig. 19]. But a regard for health would of course induce them to chuse the little risings which interrupt the level. The highest of these is now covered by some masses of ruins which ought to represent the ancient temple of Minerva.[113] The ruins are of brick, & without much shape. This hill is surrounded by a wall partly brick partly stone ruined in many places

113. The Greek temple of Athena Khalkioikos (Athena of the Brazen House) was located in 1907 but was not visible to Biddle. What he saw were the ruins of Roman Sparta, including its walls, theater, and circus. His sketch of the acropolis of Sparta is reproduced in Figure 20.

& was constructed in later times apparently of some older ruins. The ruins of the temple are on the highest part of the hill which gradually sinks to a lower & plain rising covered also with ruins once forming part of the sacred buildings which were once found here. [This is] the house in which King Pausanias died. No! It was on the highest part near [the] temple of Minerva.[114] The theatre cut out of the hill still preserves the form, tho' nothing else. The marble steps (if such they were) being taken away. It has served as a central part to fix the other parts of the city. At the end of the rising ground is the hippodrome. This still preserves its form, the level for the races being so perfect that if the stones were taken away a race might be run tomorrow. One side is a plain brick wall with steps on the inside for spectators to mount, on the other the ruins of 15 arches. Opposite the theatre to the west stand three large ruins which may perhaps be reconciled with the spots [near?] which are placed the tombs of Leonidas & Pausanias & the cenotaph of Brasidas (or more probably the house of Menelaus).[115] Farther on are a number of ruins answering to the tribe of the Pitanati. These are the most numerous of the neighborhood. These are on the west. On the north immediately below the citadel are some large ruins apparently of a wall; farther on two little elevations where ought to be the Cynosurae; but I do not see a single ruin there. The same may be said of the Limnati which I believe wrongly placed by Barthelemy, there being no ruin on the little hill & the valley between it & the other hill being too small for habitation. In this valley passes the ancient road to the Eurotas. To the east of the temple of Minerva is a hill which indeed is almost a continuation tho' lower of the great one; here are a quantity of ruins. This place might probably have formed a tribe, tho' Barthelemy does not give it one. It is connected by a ruined wall with a hill to the south east which contains also some ruins, perhaps of the tribe of Egis. To the south east of this hill, is a building in the plain. It is circular, of brick, with a number of avenues or divisions in the wall. I cannot explain it. Must enquire. To the south of the hill is another rising which contains one ruin, & still more south a hill which does not seem to have been inhabited, there being no ruin. To the

114. Thucydides (1.134) tells the story of the Spartan king Pausanias, a hero of the battle of Plataia, whom the Spartan magistrates later suspected of treachery. He fled to an annex of the temple of Athena, where he was walled in and starved to death. I have rearranged several garbled lines in Biddle's text to make it say what I think Biddle had in mind.

115. These are sites mentioned by Pausanias in his tour of Sparta (3.1ff.). Leonidas and Pausanias were Spartan kings; Brasidas was a general in the Peloponnesian war (d. 422 B.C.); Menelaus was a legendary king, the capture of whose wife Helen started the Trojan War.

south west of the Hippodrome is a small village called Mangula, a general name for the whole neighborhood. To the south or southwest about 2 miles off is a little village called Sclavo Horio, which seems to answer to the ancient Amiclae. Following the ancient road towards the Eurotas you find the old bridge which has 4 piers. The middle arch was large—the bridge of brick. The river has deserted its bed, & gone nearly 50 yards to the east-ward. Under the bridge grain is planted. The Eurotas now Eri is the most respectable river in Greece & has a singular property for a Greek river, being always full of water. The Inachus near Argos has I think a wider but a dry bed. The river does not supply a sufficient depth for a bath; where I crossed near the old bridge it was not knee deep & about 30 or 35 feet wide. There is no modern bridge; the river in winter is much wider. The plain between Sparta & the river is very good & pleasant. The river about ½ miles distant. On the other side of the Eurotas another plain of some extent which ends with Mount Menelaion.[115a] On the western side of Sparta is a ridge of mountains called Gula.[116] The large mountain is separated from the plain by a smaller ridge of hills detached from it. On the highest hill is a quantity of snow which is collected & carried by hand to Constantinople for the Grand Seignior's table.

At the foot of these mountains is placed Mistra, the modern Sparta. It is built on the slope of the hill which here breaks off from the large mountain in a singular form.[117]

Like of old, the surly republicans of Sparta have built their houses di-vided into little sections on the hill, unlike the social Athenians. The town has nearly 6 thousand Greek inhabitants. There are not more than 5 or 600 Turks. Things are dearer here than in Tripolizza. The town beautifully situated. On the top of the hill are two castles; one above the other, the highest nearly an hour's walk, the mountain being very steep. These castles as well as the part of the town under them were destroyed by the Turks & are now melancholy walls.[118] The houses are in general small like those of most Greek towns, but there are some very pleasant situations. That of the

115a. In this case I have let Biddle's text stand. He and others recalled their Polybius (5.22.3), who says merely that the Menelaion, the shrine in honor of Menelaus, lay on the hills southeast of Sparta on the left bank of the Eurotas. These hills, a continuation of Mainalon/Parnon, are repeatedly called "the Menelaion hills" by early nineteenth-century travelers. The shrine has since been found and excavated.

116. Presumably the Taygetos mountain range.

117. A sketch-map of Mistra has been omitted.

118. In the Greek rebellion of 1770, which had been incited by the Russians, the town was burned by the sultan's Albanian troops.

Bishop for instance. There being no ancient town here, there are no ruins. The only antiquity are two sarcophages, one of which is near a Mosque & is well executed. It is a representation of a feast of Bacchus or something of that kind. At the two corners of the front are two figures of Pan sitting. Then two Bacchantes with cymbals, then two figures apparently of Hercules armed with clubs who seem contending for a female between them. Her drapery is attached to the vines which cover the surface of the Sarcophage. These figures are in very spirited relief, the drapery of the middle female & the Bacchantes being very well executed tho' a good deal injured. The other sides of the Sarcophage are occupied with figures of a sort of griffin or animal of that sort. It is now a fountain or rather reservoir of one. The other Sarcophage is a fountain; one side alone is visible & represents two or 3 figures carrying a band of flowers & fruit on their shoulders, with two figures, I believe of dogs underneath. Much less beautiful than the others, the faces rubbed off. In the Bishop's church are a number of inscriptions but one I think antique. In the wall of his house is a stone with a figure sitting before a lamp, ancient & perhaps Egyptian. Near this is a stone in a wall with a small ancient unintelligible inscription. These are all the antiquities.

The people of Sparta are accused of being clannish & barbarous. On the contrary I have found them among the most polite & affable Greeks. The country people decent. Seeing few strangers they stare a good deal but nothing more. Whilst I [was] sitting in my room a man came in, whose object was to see me. For this purpose he had come from the country, wanting to see what sort of being I was, not having seen any Franc except Russians. On further enquiry I found that it was a man of Gurania a place about 4 or 5 [miles] distant, a hypochondriac who thought he had an animal gnawing him inside. Supposing him a beggar I offered him money. He declined, saying he came only to see me, not for money. He however took it. He came the next day bringing oranges and a present for me, was much pleased with me & wanted to kiss my feet. Interesting fact with regard to the people of Gurania, & another [?]. A great many crazy people when the Turks & Russians were fighting here. Fear made the peasants go crazy. The people are certainly civil & having few Turks are not so much afraid. I have seen some females, young of fine complexion, as have in general Greek children before exposure has spoilt it.

There are no Albanese in this country [they] having all been sent away by the Grand Seignior's order, being intolerant towards the Greeks in matters of religion.

In going from Mistra to old Sparta you cross a plain of olive & mulberry trees & then a little stream called Mangulitsa, a little further on a bridge across a stream called Mangula, a general name for all the neighborhood, as well as the old mountain Mainalon. A little further on is Palaiocastro, the name of old Sparta.[119]

There are two schools in Mistra, one vulgar, the other Hellenic, the last having 20 or 30 scholars. They do not however pursue their studies far, for there are not more than 3 or 4 men in Mistra who understand Hellenic. Sparta 8 or 12 hours from sea. The Mainotes occupy the country between Sparta & the sea, & along the coast.[120] Their neighbors give them the character of bad people, robber pirates &c. I believe this false. They are free. They have no Turkish govr but one of their own choice; they are subject only to the Captain Pasha, the great admiral; they are the Greeks of Homer's time, always fighting with each other. They have just finished a bloody war (civil). Marathonisi is their capital. They are traders. They do not suffer Turks to come there. At least they lay aside their arms when they do come.

Over the ruins of Sparta a republican has a melancholy pleasure. My own country offers an interesting analogy of which I have thought much. The Mainotes pay a karatch, or poll tax to the Grand Seignior.

There are no manufactures at Mistra.

This day I have been occupied with seeing & writing. I might have started this morning but wished to see Palmer & Walpole who I was told were on the road. They arrived in the evening. Williams mentioned a thing worth remembering. Just after I left Tripolizza there was a man found stealing out of a shop. The Pasha had him brought before him, at the same time two carpenters whom he ordered to make a sort of scaffold or bed with iron nails, in ten minutes. It was made in the time specified, & the unfortunate wretch [was] first suspended & then thrown down upon the nails. This took place whilst the people were asleep & the next day he was exhibited in this miserable state to the people. He languished thus two days & they then finished his pain by cutting his throat. This is a Turkish mode of doing justice. My English acquaintances move rapidly. They have the fault which I observe of almost all English travellers; assiduous hunters of curiosities, riding night & day to see an old wall or column, on purpose to be

119. A sketch-map of the plain of Sparta, "put down on the spot," says Biddle, has been omitted. He comments: "Barthélemy places these hills too far apart. I do not think there was room enough for this tribe of Limnatai. The bridge badly put. Also hippodrome."
120. Biddle means the central peninsula of the Peloponnesos, which ends in Cape Tainaron, or Matapan, which lies southwest of Sparta in the direction of the Messenian Gulf.

able to say I have seen it, but careless about any enquiry with regard to the people their character, their usages, laws, &c. There is a sort of brutal coldness about them which forbids them from mingling with, or deriving information from foreigners. Every man is estimated by the distance of his birthplace from Hyde Park.

These gentlemen arrived here tonight. There project is to get up in the morning early & go down on foot to Palaio Sparta, thence to Amyclae making a circuit of about 8 or 9 miles & returning to Mistra by 9 o'clock, yet off for Tripolizza & arrive in the evg. They could not possibly do more than be able to say without lying that they had been at Sparta. Their example was however so little worthy of imitation that I could not cease my regret at being able to give only four days to Sparta. I prefer in travelling a sight of men than of stone & [am] much more pleased with any new remark on, or new shade of difference among men than the finest old wall imaginable.

Mistra is not unhealthy. Abramioti says the position of old Sparta is not very salubrious but the modern town is very well placed. Rarely putrid fevers. In August the worst time. 30 thousand karatches in the district of Mistra. The country of the Mainotes would fall naturally under the district of Mistra, were it enslaved.

Tuesday 24. I left the house of my good Doctor & the town of Mistra. The road follows at first the route to Tripolizza from which it diverges in about an hour & ½ & follows the course of the little Eri or Eurotas. The old road is still travelled. The Eri gradually sinks in magnitude. A respectable tho' rather small creek at Sparta, it soon becomes a run. Five hours of hilly road with an occasional plain brought us to a fountain of water & some shade where we refreshed. We had passed the village of Perivollia at the bottom of a hill without perceiving it. It is on the right & may perhaps represent Pellana. Three hours more brought us to Leondari.[121] Some call the route 8 hours, some 12. It may be gone conveniently in 6. As soon as I arrived & lodged I waited on the Voivode to whom I had a letter from the yhan of Mistra. He received me with great decency & politeness, & his brother afterwards enlivened my visit. My interest with the Voivode could not however get me horses & I was obliged to remain at Leondari the rest of the day. It is a small place perched on a hill forming a part of the entrance

121. The medieval town of Leondari, or Londari, replaced the Greek town of Kromnos, or Cromi (so Leake), about a mile distant. In the vicinity of ancient and modern Megalopolis and primarily a Turkish town in Biddle's day (Leake estimated 250 Turkish houses and only 40 Greek), the place is now quite unimportant. Leake presumed ancient Leuctra to lie south of Londari.

of a large & beautiful plain. The scenery is indeed charming & answers almost all our idea of Arcadian scenery. There may be about 3 or 400 inhabitants. It is supposed to be the ancient Leuctra, tho' Abramioti supported by Gale[122] seems to think that a little town to the south west, now called Luttra may be the spot. At Leondari (and Leondari ancient Belmina) at the top of the hill are the ruins of something like a castle. They are imperfect, & I do not know if they are really ancient. Leondari is a sad place.

I read and thought until night & in the morning Wednesday 25 set off. The road is across the large plain which is rich and cultivated tho' we look in vain for the ancient population of Arcadia which counted 30,000 slaves. We left on the north side of the place, the little town of Sinano (about 5 miles from Leondari) near which are the ruins of Megalopolis built at the instigation of Epaminondas. There is now nothing, they tell me, but the spot indicated by stones on each side of the Alpheus. This river runs across the plain & is now called Davias. It has a bed as large as any of the Greek rivers, larger I think than the Eurotas, but would want much of Procrustes's aid to fill it for there is a very small quantity of water.[123] After 4 hours ride we reached the town of Caritina.[124] This place larger than Leondari is on the side of a very steep hill. In coming to it the ancient road is followed, & at the foot of the hill we passed a bridge which seems ancient tho' I could not assign of what epoch. It crosses a little stream called (I don't remember)[125] which runs along the plain (coming down from the hill) & I suppose [goes?] on to the Alpheus. On the top of the hill are some ancient ruins. On visiting them I found a modern aged castle & a single old brick building which may be Hellenic. It is below the castle. They talked of a large cave somewhere which I had not courage enough to visit. This hill must be the ancient Mount Licaeus. The Doctor, a Zantiote to whom I paid a visit says that the town is healthy. And it ought to be so from its position. This man has lived much in Asia which is much less barbarous

122. Presumably Thomas Gale (?1635–1702), English cleric and classical scholar.

123. Procrustes was a legendary brigand who, when he caught his victims, put them on a bed, stretching their limbs or cutting them off as need be to make them fit the bed. The Attic hero Theseus forced Procrustes to undergo the same treatment.

124. Med. Karitaina, anc. Brenthe, was, in 1209, made the capital of a Frankish barony. Its castle was built in 1254 and is a fine example of medieval fortification. The bridge Biddle mentions is in fact medieval. In 1806 the town, much depopulated, contained about two hundred families, twenty of them Turkish (Leake). The remains Biddle saw were all medieval.

125. At this point the Alpheios is called the Karitaina.

than the Morea, that is Asia Minor. He likes this place because there are few Turks & they are therefore more free & tranquil, tho' very barbarous. There is one school for reading & writing with about 60 boys but no old Greek school. There are two or three persons in town who understood Hellenic. I should give the town 1000 or 1200 souls. On my arrival I want to see the Vivodi. He was absent but his Deputy sent me to the house of a priest where I lodged.

Cicero's oration for Quintus good; he had not learnt to talk so much of himself, as afterwards. From the position I should judge Caritina to be Lycosura.[126]

I left it on the morning of Thursday 26. The road crosses the mountain on the way to Andritzina (I quitted Andritzina without going to Sclero about two hours off in the mountains to the south east. This is the ancient Phigalea & there are still the columns of the temple of Apollo.[127] There are upwards of 30 remaining (built by [the] same artist who built [the] temple of Minerva at Athens.) This town of Andritzina is 5 hours from Caritina. The road villainously bad across the hills. This part of Arcadia is very hilly and rugged, & on the road we saw no houses or peasants but the scenery is occasionally very pretty. We overtook two Turkish gentlemen who were travelling and, as the Turks generally are, were very civil. Their appearance gave no favorable idea of Arcadian simplicity & rusticity. They were armed with guns, pistols and swords. In fact Arcadia is perhaps the most barbarous part of Greece. The mountain life naturally inspires courage & a love of freedom; & want misdirects; & they have no education to purify these sentiments. They soon degenerate, & having no Turks to keep them in awe the Arcadians have become a bad race. Andritzina is a small town as usual on the side of a steep hill. Like all Greek towns nothing to distinguish it. There is but one Turk in the town. It required all his influence & that of my Tartar to arrange the ceremony of my departing. Having paid for the horses I was obliged to remain 3 or 4 hours before they came. They dropped in one after the other & at last were all assembled when a fierce dispute arose about our saddles which they refused to take for they wanted to take their own saddles because with them they might load their horses on returning. The wretches made as much noise as if their lives depended

126. Ancient Lycosura actually lay on the south flank of Mount Lykaion.
127. The temple of Apollo Epikourios at Phigaleia, or Bassai, designed perhaps by Phidias, was built between 450 and 425 B.C. The slabs of the frieze in the cella, which show battles between Greeks and Amazons and between Lapiths and Centaurs, are now in the British Museum. Biddle missed another major site.

on it. It was at last arranged & we started accompanied by 4 men each of whom had a share in one horse & would not trust their horses to each others care. The Greeks seem very distrustful of themselves & strangers. Both at the post house & with private horses, you always pay before you start, and in general whenever you want anything, a chicken, an egg you give your money before you see its equivalent. It is true that the conduct of the Turks who take in general without paying at all contributes to this want of confidence.

On leaving Andritzina, the road descends into the plain & then winds about among the hills. The country really beautiful, not very well cultivated, indeed a pasture country. We passed a number of flocks of sheep & goats; but the Arcadian swains!! If to be simply clad & simpleminded, dirty & moustachoed be recommendations, Arcadian shepherds may be looked at even now by a poet. A young lady would run away from one of them. Men are much more characterised by their occupation than their country. Mountain feeders of sheep are mostly the same people everywhere. If Arcadians are distinguished it is by superior barbarity. Yet Arcadia is certainly a beautiful country, poetically so, finely diversified, handsome plains contrasted with mountains, mostly handsome sometimes grand. You see no scattered huts. All villages, tho' sometimes the shepherds are contented with a tree & a sort of blanket or coverlet stretched across poles.

In about 6 hours, after a ride across a mountain which gave frequent opportunities of passing to the other world, so bad was the road, so crowded with trees, whose branches sometimes threatened to knock off our heads we arrived by a short cut across the country at a little town called Graico. This place, out of the road from Andritzina to Pirgo is placed in a little hill which contributes to form a beautiful valley. It is rather a sort of hamlet. I was so fortunate as to get some milk of which I made my supper. It is singular that all over Greece tho' a pastoral country, it is very difficult to get milk—you must bespeak it overnight. It is always three or four miles off—the people make cheese of it & youart. After an hour or two of ride thro' a very pretty country on Friday 27 we reached the plain & the sea side. We passed a village & of which I do not know the name. We then reached the Alpheus which we crossed in a ferry boat, the only one in Greece, I believe. There were a number of Greeks bathing. The water was a little above the middle. They are fine muscular men; hardened by their occupation & not confined by their dress. I wish the American peasantry would adopt it.

In about 7 or 6 hours from Graico we reached Pirgo. The distance from

Pirgo to Caritina is about 12 or 13 hours; a days good journey. Walpole & Palmer made it.

Elis Saturday 28, 1806

My dear Tom,

I have to relate the events of yesterday & today, & hope that as the subject of this will be Elis & Olympia, it may not be unproductive of pleasure & information. Having reached Pirgo, I went to the house of the Aga where I got the address of the gentleman who usually receives Englishmen. Being too late to visit Olympia I remained at Pirgo. This is a town of about 2000 souls, placed on a little rising ground about 2 miles from the sea. There is no port, but a good road which might easily be converted to one. There are here no Turks except the suite of the Aga. The country about well cultivated; chiefly grain which is exported to Zante &c. There seems not to be a rigorous prohibition against exportation, for whenever an Aga is a proprietor he lets his district export. Here at Pirgo, at Corinth, &c, but at Salona for instance they cannot export. No manufactures. The sick season beginning now; there are some putrid fevers.

The next morning early (today) I left Pirgo, & was obliged to recross the plain. There are two roads from Pirgo to Caritina, one of which leads by Olympia, but my horses having brought me by the other which is a little shorter, I was obliged to return. We first pass the large valley of Pirgo in a south west direction; then another valley on one side of which is the town of Miraca where the Aga of Pirgo has a country seat. At the farthest extremity of the valley is the town of Floka.[128] Crossing the hill near it you arrive at the valley of Olympia. This valley, less than either of the others just passed is more beautiful. It runs east & west, but where the city stood the valley made an angle to accommodate the hill of [Kronion].[129] The scenery of it very handsome. The Alpheus now Rofea is a decent stream, tho' weak in summer. The valley well cultivated, covered with reapers of grain. Near the angle of the mountain are the ruins of some buildings; one a square brick chamber. All indeed are brick—but unintelligible masses. Fauvel however thinks he discovered a stadium; this however I did not see. This plain interesting from its history—sad reverse its present solitude presents. There are no buildings near it in the plain. I should suppose it 1½ miles wide. It is about 5 or 6 from the sea. It is 3 hours from Pirgo.

128. A sketch-map of the area of Olympia has been omitted.
129. The sanctuary of Olympian Zeus was the site of the quadrennial Olympic games. The river Alpheios had inundated much of the site and covered it with a deep layer of silt.

Walpole & Williams spoke in raptures of its beauty. It is certainly handsome but I don't think very extraordinarily so, there being some more
beautiful country near it; e.g. the plain of Graico. There is in fact nothing
to see but the plain over which a moralizer loves to speculate. Yet how
many sad recollections does this unhappy country everywhere present?
Greece was free. I returned to Pirgo. The little stream which flows through
the plain of Olympia to [swell?] the Alpheus is now called Langathia.[130]
The spot itself where are the ruins having attracted strangers has acquired a
name; it is called Andilalo. There is also a town near called Miraca a name
which is often applied to Olympia itself. In the neighborhood of Pirgo
many of the peasants wear straw hats, broad like our Quaker hats.

This part of Greece seems the most rich & happy. Less immediately
under the Turkish host, they are less oppressed & the free islands of the
neighborhood offer them a good market [which] stimulates because it rewards industry.

Everything is very dear in this part of the country. They are now bringing in the harvest, & horses to be procured pretty dearly. I gave 9 piastres a
horse to go from Pirgo to Patras, 18 hours. Nine piastres are two & a half
dollars; 18 hours are 54 miles.

In coming from Graico to Pirgo we passed some saltworks along the
seaside about 3 hours from P.[131]

I left Pirgo & began my ride towards Palaeopolis the modern name of
Elis where I have just arrived after about 5 hours ride, across a plain country with some mountains, or rather hills, depopulated, but rich & smiling
wherever the hand of industry is applied to it. Arrived here I rode out to
see the ruins of Elis. They stand in a plain about 6 or 7 hundred yards from
Palaeopolis & near a hill which must have served as citadel. All that is now
seen are three or four misshapen brick ruins to which it is difficult to give
or to ascribe form. They stand in the midst of weeds & grain. They are on
the [eastern?] side of the city & look towards the sea. Walpole & Palmer
having told me that they rode round the hill to look for a stadium in vain,
I spared myself the trouble from which the approach of the night dissuaded
me. They told of some old ruins which they called Palaeocastro on the
other side of the hill, but I know that all I could see was the position of the
old city & contented myself with it. That was pleasant. About 24 miles
from Olympia, the road to which is indeed still passible in many parts.

130. Anc. and mod. Kladeos.
131. A sketch-map of Pirgo and Palaeopolis has been omitted.

From Gastouni it is about 1 hour or 1½ to the eastward. From Chiarenza, its ancient port Cyllene, it is 5 hours or 15 miles, the longest from a port except Sparta of any of the great Greek towns. The little river of [..] now [..]¹³² is to the northward & near the town. Much smaller than the Alpheus. Palaeopolis a little town of 2 or 3 hundred houses. I am lodged in the house of a priest & His sanctity has not saved me from a passion with my postillion. He had the impudence to cut a piece off my pipe which I gave him to carry, finding it of an inconvenient length, so that my Spartan purchase is useless until mended. I scolded him soundly & should have struck him were he not a slave.

The little hamlets of this part of the Morea are very pretty; made of straw, circular & exactly like our beehives.

Adieu NB

On Sunday June 29, I left Palaeopolis & soon got into the road which I passed the first day of my arrival in the Morea. In 6 hours time I reached a Khan near which is a monastery. Here I stopt & eat, & afterwards continuing my ride thro' a scorching sun, reached Patras, which is 12 or 13 hours from Palaeopolis. Not finding Mr Strani at home, I went immediately to the bath, the most refreshing of the recreations. Returned I found Strani & also learnt that there was a vessel going tonight for Trieste. I regretted much the sudden departure, for I had many things to learn & some to buy before leaving Greece. But the opportunity was excellent (I might [wait] long before finding another) & the vessel could not stay till tomorrow because she would lose the windy land breeze to take her out. I therefore asked as many questions as I decently could & in the evening went on board the vessel & left Greece.

I shall always remember with pleasure my little tour in Greece. I have remained in it only about two months, but they have been deployed in eager curiosity & ardent enquiry. In this time I have seen all that is interesting to the south of Thermopylae. Beyond that, as I learnt from the travellers, there is nothing to reward fatigue, expense & perhaps danger. I was tempted to go farther. I had determined on visiting Constantinople, & had dreamed of a still longer journey in Asia. I had many temptations to visit Smyrna, among which the principal was the hope of collecting information in order to extend our commercial relations in the Levant & in this

132. Anc. and mod. Peneios, med. Potami.

way being useful to my country.[133] But on the other hand my journey must
have an end somewhere & unless I soon prescribe its limits I may wander
until I am lost. Of Turks & Turkish govt more is seen in Greece than even
in Constantinople itself, & I have now acquired sufficient lights to conduct
me to a perfect knowledge of them. The season is unpropitious for travelling over the parched & burning countries of Asia, & a prudent man should
not neglect his health as much for his family as himself. Besides another
reason deterred me. By living among a barbarous people much information
is not to be acquired. To waste time in such countries may be pardoned in
Europeans whose lives are to be spent in the centre of information & sciences. But a young American leaves his country not to diffuse but to acquire information, & he should therefore remain near the sources of them. I
have now gone much beyond my original hopes or expectations. It is time
to return. I have many duties to perform to my family, my profession & my
country; and I feel myself an example of the visionary expectations of improvement from foreign travel. The age of selfishness & ignorance which
confined to a single country the knowledge of its children is past, & when
we wish to learn, we must retire to our closet with our books around us,
rather than ramble.

Every expectation which I had formed with regard to Greece is gratified.
I have not consumed too much time, and have seen the manners & con-
versed with the men of two nations wholly different from our own, & the
bitter, implacable enemies of each other. To myself who love to look at
man, this is perhaps as pleasing as the idea of having visited the most
celebrated spots of antiquity of which I had read much tho' with indistinct
ideas. The History of antiquity will now become infinitely interesting from
the vividness of its most remarkable situations which I have acquired. I
have had much fatigue & abstinence & inconvenience, but I consider it all
more than compensated by the pleasure & even improvement it has brought
me. I think I learnt more during these last two months than in any other of

133. It was not until 1830 that the United States concluded a commercial and diplomatic
treaty with the Ottoman Turks. But American ships had been active in the Levant trade
long before, having visited Smyrna, the major port of the Empire, as early as 1804. In 1811
the Philadelphia firm of Woodmas and Offley opened an office there, and by 1827 three
more American houses were in operation. In exchange for cotton, tobacco, gunpowder,
breadstuffs, and especially rum, which the Turks did not use themselves but transshipped to
Russia and Persia, the Americans bought opium, which was a staple of their own trade with
China. Thus in an oddly symmetrical way, both Turks and Americans were middlemen in
their respective traffic in narcotics. Ironically, it was Nicholas's brother James who visited
Smyrna and Constantinople in 1830, and who was partly responsible for the commercial
treaty between the United States and the Porte.

my life. Falling at once among a people so totally different from Europeans one receives a fund of new ideas. Among the pleasant impressions which I have felt I have not been indifferent to that of bringing the veneration & the sympathy of the new & only republic to the ruins of the old & thinking with a melancholy satisfaction that we may one day be as great & as miserable as they.

In the morning Monday 30 June we still continued near the mouth of the Gulph of Lepanto. There are here some Turkish ships of war. The Turks bad sailors. These ships crowded with landsmen; and the men who do the duty of the ships generally from Idra Spescia & the other islands. There are some French officers on board. We were obliged to tack constantly until Tuesday 1st July when a fair wind brought us near Ithaca. It was part of our agreement that we should stop here, I having been unable to get my provisions at Patras, & wishing to see the island. The crew murmured much at my compelling them to comply with this condition; the wind being good, & they feeling no sort of interest in the affairs of Ulysses. We however went to the bay & town. The island is formed like a bow, the port being in the middle of it.[134] The port is amazingly fine resembling that of Malta, one side being formed by a very steep mountain, the other indented by, I think three ports, of which the best, our sailors say is the third. The vessel in order not to pay entrance money, lay to at a distance whilst we entered the town. It is placed at the bottom of the second indenture which forms a noble port capable of containing ships of the line which have in fact been there. Most of the houses are new, the people having come down about 30 years since from the old town which is about 4 or 5 miles off (for convenience only). The town is called like the island itself Thiaki which nearly resembles its ancient name. The island has one or two little villages & on the north side of the port is a monastery. The whole population is about 8 or 10 thousand souls. There are now some Russian troops—the island defenseless, tho' there are some fine spots for fortification, particularly the port itself. The produce is some grain (enough for 6 months of its own consumption) & currants which go to England. The people of Ithaca & Cephalonia are active on the water, those of Zante on land; those of Corfu in nothing says the governor of Ithaca. Indeed I have seen nowhere in Greece such apparent industry as here. Several little vessels upon the stocks. Having reached the town we were taken to the health office where we were examined in due form, who we were where we came from, for what purpose we came &c; the people around looking at us

134. A sketch of the ports of Ithaca has been omitted.

with wonder & avoiding us with fear. Having gone thro' the ceremonies I wished to go & see the antiquities, but I was told that this could not be done, on account of the quarantine. However the English consul, whom I sent for, got permission from the Governor (who is called the Prytani)[135] & who desired I would call on him. I did so & found him a clever young man from Venice whose father having married a seven island woman became *ipso facto* a citizen & made his son so. He dispensed with the quarantine but gave me a guard by way of preserving the form.

I now, after taking some refreshments & talking much politics with the governor set off in the boat for the farthest part of the port. Here I found the guard & the Consul's man who served as my guide. From the town to this part is about ½ an hour or ¾ rowing. I began to ascend the hill which overlooks the port & on which are the ruins of the fort of Ulysses.[136] About ½ way up & about ½ an hours walk from the shore thro' currant & vine fields you come to an ancient well in perfect preservation, every stone of the inside remaining. This is called the well of Ulysses & justly for he no doubt made use of its water. It is excellent water & my pleasure in drinking it was heightened by considering that my countryman Smith of Carolina had discovered it for the benefit of the Ithacans. His discovery looks like a miracle of earlier times. According to the story of the people, "a Milordi" came to visit the mountain & after looking about declared to the astonishment of the people that there must be water in such a place. In spite of incredulity he brought workmen & made them remove stones & dirt, until lo! the water appeared. The man who lives near the well said it was an Englishman, an error which I very patriotically removed. I had heard before another Ithacan say it was a Prussian who had the merit of it. This is perhaps the most useful discovery that has been made in Greece for it is of great service to the neighborhood who were before obliged to get their water from a distance.[137]

135. This word is a variant of the form *pritano* or *prytano*, which Biddle used in his account of the constitution of the Septinsular Republic.

136. Though identified since Schliemann's time (1878) as Homer's capital, the remains of the Hellenic town (at Aeto at the very head of the Gulf of Molo on the isthmus connecting the two parts of the island), particularly its polygonal, or Cyclopean, masonry, belong to the eighth and seventh centuries B.C. The remains of another ancient town lie on the northwest coast of the northern section of Ithaca. Leake presumed this latter site to be Homeric Ithaca.

137. Smith's "well" is something of a puzzle. Leake, arriving in Ithaca just after Biddle, in September 1806, described the site of Aeto and its two springs. One was the source of a torrent flowing into the Gulf of Molo, in the direction from which Biddle says that he approached the town. The other was "a well lined with large blocks of stone of ancient workmanship, situated a little on the descent towards Exo-Aeto" [that is, to the west]. It is

Near the well the ascent begins to be very steep & continues so until in about half an hour you reach the top. The whole mountain is strewed with large masses of a greyish sort of stone which composed the walls. These are in many parts distinctly seen, & are made of large unequal stones placed on each other without cement & forming a secure barrier for these times. The people of here say that the cannon used to be placed upon them. On the top is a large hold or chamber sunk in the rock. It is about 10 or 12 feet deep but is evidently filled up. What strikes me as singular is that it is smoothly plastered with a sort of mortar. I took a piece of it. I do not know where my guide gets his idea that it was a prison for the victims of the old Pirates ravages.[138] It is presumable that the area within the walls was covered with houses. The position of his fort admirable. It embraces a view of all sides of the island. No boat could escape him. A little valley at the bottom of the hill separating it from another nearly as high. This valley about two miles wide, but on the north side of the hill the island is kept together by a little ridge scarcely half a mile wide. The island about 2 or 3 miles from Cephalonia. Strip poetry of its finery & Ulysses will probably be an island Pirate. In walking up towards the mountain I met a damsel spinning with a distaff. As she had the employment I was charitable enough to presume that she had the virtue, & to hope that she had not the beauty of Penelope. Having seen all that was visible I descended to the water side, where having bathed in the sea I got into the boat; the sailors stopped a moment to pay their devotions to St Nicholas & to drink a glass of rum. I soon got on board & set sail having made a very pleasant excursion of 6 or 7 hours.

We [gradually?] followed the coast of Ithaca passing by the little town of Kioni[139] near the northern extremity of it. The next morning Wednesday 2 we were off the western coast of St Mauro. This island (pronounced Santo Mavro) is but a little way from the continent, but extends itself far into the sea. This island was anciently called Leucade, & was for nothing more famous than for its promontory which, like many of our modern remedies was sure to kill or to cure the sick, the sighing, the despairing, or the expiring lover.[140] It was under this promontory exactly that we now passed.

---

this second water source that Biddle seems to describe, but he did not climb up to Aeto from this direction.

138. These are the remains of a cistern. A small sketch has been omitted.

139. Biddle actually wrote "Selioni." He seems to be referring to the one considerable village on the northeastern coast of Ithaca, at the base of the promontory of Akrotiri.

140. The southern promontory of the island, once the site of a temple of Apollo, was known as Lovers' Leap. The Greek poet Sappho is supposed to have leaped to her death here

The whole coast is bold & rocky, & very well calculated in any part of it for a leap. There is no particular part which for its elevation or its abruptness I could designate as the fatal spot, for the sea washes all the coast, & at any point would receive a swain or a damsel. We are told by the poets of the force of love to which we all must submit, against which there is neither shield nor resistance. Its impressions it seems are durable, as they are melancholy. All the island has changed is name into that of a saint, but the promontory with the fidelity of a Philander or a Damon[141] has preserved its name, & is still called Lefcathe, the modern pronunciation of Λευκαδε. At one part there is a little island called Sessla. Sessla is the name of the little scupper, the instrument with which they lighten or scoop out the water from the boat; & on being told this, I began philosophically to conjecture that this little island might probably have gained its name, by scooping up as it were, or giving refuge to the dripping lovers, but my speculations were put out of order when they proceeded to say that the island had in fact the shape of one of their scuppers. I told the sailors of the ancient use to which Leucade had been applied. They grinned.

The crew are from Galaxithi a little town near Salona in the gulph.[142] They are ten in number, and like I think the Greeks in generally gay lively almost babyish. They are very religious. Near the head of my bed I observed a lamp which annoyed me sadly by keeping me from sleeping. I changed its place often but always found it got back again; & upon my remonstrating they said the lamp was before the saint, a little dirty figure on the wall, & that they did not like to remove it. To accommodate the saint I let it stand. In the course of the same day we reached the port of Corfu where we were to stop for news of the blockade of Trieste.[143] We remained but a very little time, for the Captain going ashore & learning

---

because of unrequited love. The story arose because of the practice of diving into the sea as a form of trial or sacrifice.

141. Is Biddle referring to the famous story of the Pythagoreans Phintias and Damon (Cicero, *de Officiis* 3.45)?

142. The Gulf of Corinth.

143. By the Treaty of Pressburg in December 1805, France gained control of Dalmatia from Austria, though Istria and Fiume (including Trieste) were allowed to remain in Austrian hands. But France demanded the right of passage for its troops on their way to Dalmatia. A contingent of the Russian navy, arriving in the Adriatic, occupied many of the islands along the Dalmatian coast and was blockading French shipping. The Russian objectives were to aid the Serbians, or Montenegrins, in their revolt from the Turks and to prevent consolidation of the French position in Dalmatia and a consequent French advance on the Ottoman Empire. The Serbs were Slavic speakers who shared the Greeks' Orthodox Christianity, but they were not otherwise Greek.

that his consul was abed, would not wait, but came off & we sailed. I therefore saw only the port of Corfu, lately become of some importance in politics. It is a fine large road rather than port. Men of war are lying close by the town for the road is very good. The town small & well defended there being two hills which overhang & command it. There is also a fort made by the French on a little island in the harbour. On the whole a strong place. Seat of the govt of the Republic. Their constitution changes sadly. They have no longer a Prince, the office being exercised in rotation by the Senators. Governed wholly by Russia. They have not got a ship of war of any degree. Yet they have just begun a war with France.[144]

In the course of the day the wind came directly ahead & obliged us to put in the next morning Thursday 3 into the port of Cassiope, a small place on the north extremity of Corfu. This is a little promontory on which are the remains of a Venetian castle. At the bottom of the small port is a church & store, the only two houses. The sailors first go to the church then to the store; first pray then drink. We remained here this day which I occupied with walking about & talking to a sensible young Greek [from] near Yanina. Like other Greeks he complains of the cruel tyranny of Ali Pasha the Vizir of Romelia. He has been governor 20 years, a native of Romelia, a man of strong mind but an inexorable tyrant & a most rapacious plunderer. My man says that it is the curse of the Greeks not to be united to be jealous of each other. Could they unite, they could easily be free. A small town resisted for 18 years the whole Turkish power in Romelia.[145] The Greeks certainly would be capable of much exertion, had they hope of freedom; but they think that they were once betrayed by the Russians & are distrustful of foreign help.

The unfavorable wind obliged us to remain in the same place during Friday July 4th. I read much, walked & enquired. This country naturally rich but the people lazy—grain, oil & currants their productions. The mode of making oil simple. The ripe olives put into a heap & mashed with a millstone turned by a horse. Thus mashed, they are put into circular flat

144. The Russian fleet arrived in Corfu in January 1806 to prevent a French attack on the Ionian Islands from Dalmatia. As a Russian protectorate, the Ionian Islands could be said to be in a war with the French, though the Russians were doing the actual fighting.

145. The reference is to the Suliote Christians, who lived in a number of villages to the southeast of Parga, a town on the coast of Albania, and who were finally subdued by Ali in 1803. Before Ali's time they had been independent of the Turks, though recognizing the sovereignty of the sultan. These people commonly spoke Albanian at home, but many could speak Greek as well. Their rebellion, which had begun in 1790, ended with the flight of the survivors to Parga and Corfu.

sort of baskets made of straw; and these being placed one on the other are pressed by means of a screw. The oil oozes out of the straw & is received pure & ready made in a tub &c.

My Greek acquaintance says that in the seven islands the people pay more than in the Morea, for they have the dime[146] from which the Greeks under the Turks are exempt. I doubt whether they are more burdened than the Turkish Greeks.

The next morning Saturday 5th we left the port which I should observe is like the rest of the island very nigh Albania. The wind soon failing we were rocked about in all the luxury of a calm. I read among other things Cicero's contention to be named the accusor of Verres, & Barthelemy's abstract of Plato's *Republic*, a system which I think neither good in theory, or possible to be practised. Why does he leave the class of artizans in such neglect? Why does he reserve his important instructions in science for his few legislators? If false why encourage them, if good, why not diffuse them? His body of warriors always in arms may do well in a state of barbarism, but [it] is not accommodated to a refined age.

Saturday night which among our sailors is devoted to gay thoughts of friends & sweethearts is occupied among the Greeks by sad recollections of the friends & relations whom death has taken from them.

Sunday 6 was spent in the same disagreeable way. The coast of Albania always in sight. We passed the city of Durazzo but at such a distance that we saw its position only. The Greek compass is like their navigation simple & imperfect.[147]

Monday 7th the wind became fresh & favorable & we passed quickly Bocca de Cattaro. This is a sort of bay about a mile wide and perhaps 20 long, running in toward the mountains where it receives the river Cattaro. All along the Bocca are towns of which the principal is Castle Novo. This place is important as being the only passage to the south of Dalmatia. It has been accordingly seized by the Austrians.[148] About 15 or 20 miles to the northward we saw old & new Ragusa. But we saw them indistinctly. All that one can say is that they are on the seaside. They are now interesting because a body of French troops is now besieged there by the Mon-

146. A tithe.
147. A sketch of a wind rose has been omitted.
148. By the Treaty of Pressburg, the Austrians were supposed to turn over Cattaro as well to the French; but before the French could arrive, the Russian fleet seized the place on March 5, 1806. The islands of Lissa and Curzola fell to the Russians in late March and early April.

tenegrins.[149] These are a band of savage, ferocious Greeks who have been stirred up by Russia. They come from the interior of the Bocca. The wind freshened towards night, and in the morning [the] 8th I was surprised to find myself in company of a number of German transports in a sort of port between the island of Gorzola & Dalmatia. It seems that during the night there had been a high wind, & these miserable Greeks had run into port immediately. I had lost in sleep all the terrors of the gale, but my servant tells me that the animals had passed the night in crying and calling upon their saints. The wind was still favorable, but they complained of being tired not having slept during the night, & I saw for the first time in my life a vessel come into port & loose a favorable wind that the sailors might have the pleasure of sleeping quietly. They therefore spent the day in sleeping upon the deck & selling a little cheese & tobacco. The transports are conveying troops to occupy the mouth of the Cattaro. But the people of that country being unwilling to receive them, they wait here for further orders, & amuse themselves, with smoking & washing dirty clothes. I read Cicero—my only consolation.

Pleased with a gain of 4 hundred pr cent on their tobacco & cheese, my Greeks ventured to get under way on Wednesday 9 morning. We were employed nearly all the day in tacking in order to clear the island of Gorzola, & had just reached the mouth of it, when the wind being fresh, & the vessel going a little on one side, the wretches took the alarm, & in the course of changing the sails having broken an old rope, they cried out that their mast was broken & turning about went back to a little village near the place we had left in the morning. I did not fail to laugh heartily & to abuse them for their fears. My servant afterwards told me, that the Captain had expressed great surprise at my wishing to get on to Trieste, & *that as I had nothing to sell or to buy there* it ought to be indifferent to me if we staid a month or two on the passage. Such are the ideas of these barbarians who think nothing worth anxiety or care that is not immediately concerned with money; & who consider time as no kind of value. They are themselves accustomed during summer to make little voyages to Corfu & Zante, then returning to Galaxithi spend the winter like snakes in sleep & torpidity. Were it not useless, a man might think with pain on the small part of the world which is civilized. I wish one of these Greeks had one of Franklin's

149. Though an independent republic, Ragusa was pressured by the French and the Russians alike. When it was occupied by the French on May 26, 1806, it was promptly blockaded by the Russians and the Montenegrins, or Serbians, with whom the Russians were allied.

books in which he insists that "time is money," an idea which they never entertained.

I read Cicero; & in the afternoon, spite of quarantine laws, went to a little village which is near the larger one of Jobbincello. I was delighted on entering it to find a sort of hamlet of 12 families who seemed to enjoy a peace & tranquility consolatory even to a stranger. The man who received me was a venerable old sailor of 87 years of age who, after his long voyages in Spain, Africa Asia &c had spent the last ten years of his life in a retirement unembittered but by his infirmities. He had survived 7 children, one of whom had died in the common tomb of Europe & America, the West India islands. The hamlet contained a number of young people among whom I remarked a girl the image of my old & amiable acquaintance, A. Jones.[150] This circumstance might have contributed to make me think that the female costume of this country is prettier than any peasant dress I have seen even in Switzerland. It consists of a blue petticoat adorned at the bottom & at the waist by a stripe of yellow & one of red. This petticoat is supported by two strips of cloth or other stuff resembling our suspenders, & covering the chemise which is open at the neck; a large straw hat covers the head, & when to this is added the stick & basket which some of them carried, they were really handsome.[151]

This country is subject to the Ragusan govt. At Ragusa they elect a Prince every month, for being on the confines of three powers, they are afraid of treachery. The language is the Illyric, a language common to the people of Ragusa, Bosnia, & Wallachia. (In Istria, Italian.) It is intelligible to Russians to whose language it has much affinity. I understood a little of it, as they have of course interwoven many Italian words in it. In this country, they are all sailors. In Gorzola there are a few villages which may contain about 2000 souls. At present after having often changed masters, it & the adjacent highlands are subject to no govt, tho' I believe it is due to France now.

The people here are alarmed at the approach of the war on their borders; and the old man has seen so much war & dispute during the last half century that he seems to think men have no other object but to destroy each other. I quitted very involuntarily the quiet and decency of this place for my Greeks & a dirty cabin.

On Thursday 10 morning we left the village and tried by tacking to get

150. Is this a reference to Anne, one of the young ladies whom Biddle knew in his years at Princeton?
151. A sketch has been omitted.

on our course. In the course of the day an incident took place which gave me an opportunity of seeing what sort of character the Greeks possess, & also of seeing a new nation.

During the morning we had seen several small vessels near us which the men thought were French privateers. It was laughable to observe the alarm which it occasioned. They all went below & hid their money and papers, & observing that I was very cool & did not partake their fright, they came to me to show me their papers, and to ask me if I thought there was any danger. All this in a way that showed the wretches possessed neither courage nor sense. We came nigh one of the vessels which proved to be Russian & which ordered us on board. The Captn & his men went with their patent & my bill of health. Whilst they were on their way, the schooners boat came off to us, & a man coming upon deck asked for the key of my trunk in a way which appeared much too peremptory & [he] wanted to see my papers. I told him that the Captn had taken my passport on board & that I did not feel inclined to let my trunk be searched. He seemed willing to insist on it, & I asked him if he was an Officer. He said No (I found that he was a Neapolitan pilot) but that if I wished an officer they would send one. I desired he would, & at the same time shewed an old Passport which I had in my pocket, & which indeed I had taken out in the morning in case we should have met the French privateers. It was a Passport countersigned by the French Commander at Naples which I had taken on leaving the place. The sight of a French passport set him on fire. He went & returned with a midshipman & whilst he was gone my servant took from my trunk two letters of Fauvel for France which I had forgotten. The Midshipman, a modest decent young man spoke only Russian, but I understood he wanted to search my trunk. Whilst we were trying to come to an explanation, the Captn of the schooner ordered him on board & me too. I went, & he asked me in English why I had refused to come on board. I told him I had not refused that no one had asked me to come on board before then. I told him that as a neutral officer going from one neutral country to another I thought myself entitled to pass without examination, that I had hitherto done so, & should be sorry if Russian officers should be the first to violate it. He said I should be treated with all possible respect, but it was necessary to examine. I told him that the person he had sent was not an officer, but that he himself if he chose might send for my trunk & examine it. He seemed a reasonable young man but being accustomed to order he appeared more disposed to direct than to reason, and seeing my French passport & hearing me say that I intended going to Paris, & withal a good deal agitated at thinking his orders disobeyed, said he wanted to represent it to the commodore, ordered the vessel back to Gorzola. As soon as the Greeks found that they were free & that it was on my account alone they were ordered back, from the most abject fear they changed to insolence. Among a good deal of talk in their language of which I could understand only that it was insolent, I learnt that they immediately concluded that I was a Frenchman, declared I should pay for the detention, & that if it was indeed necessary to take me to Ragusa where was the Russian Admiral, they would make me pay my passage money then put my things ashore or overboard & go on to Trieste without waiting for me. This trait illustrates the character of their countrymen. For myself I felt a malicious wish to mortify the Greeks, & also a desire to see Russian ships & Russian officers with whom I had never yet an opportunity of meeting, & I was perfectly inapprehensive of anything.

We soon reached Gorzola. I went on board of the schooner with the midshipman; thence with the Captn on board of the Commodores ship, and thence searched for him on board of a neighboring ship. I had thus an opportunity of seeing three Russian vessels. The ships appear good for I am no judge. I do not know if we ought to compare ships on a cruise with those in port, but what a difference between these ships & ours at Malta. The men dirty, the deck dirty, no neatness, no elegance. We found the Commodore who spoke no language but his own, but the Captn of the ship on which he was spoke English well as did also another Captn. To them I explained my being at Paris, shewed them the Passport with which I left it; that being at Naples I should not leave it without the permission of the French commander, that I had since been at Malta, and shewed them a letter of recommendation from Govr Ball to the British Consul in Greece, that as a Neutral I thought I had a right to pass unexamined but that if they chose I would send for my trunks & they might search them. They were extremely polite; said that being on a coast where they expected the enemy every moment it was necessary to be vigilant; that it was useless to examine anything; but that the circumstances of my refusing my trunks had rendered it at first suspicious; that they were perfectly satisfied; very sorry for the trouble they had given me and that I was at liberty to sail when I chose. I remained some time to drink a glass of wine & to talk with them. One of the Captns named Bergman but being in America, knew Nicholson, had seen Truxtun & asked me to come on board to see him if I remained. I took my leave & went on board my vessel. The Captn of the schooner with whom I had a good deal of conversation was quite a clever fellow & at parting asked my pardon for the trouble he had occasioned but which he begged me to impute to a sample of his duty. His name was Captn Nasica.

I was perhaps wrong in refusing to let them examine my papers particularly as I did not shew at first to Nasica my American passport, only the French one but the fact was that the abruptness or impudence of the Neapolitan put me out of humor.

I wanted much to see Russian officers. I have been extremely pleased with those I saw on board these ships; nothing could be more polite than the conduct of the superior officers towards me, and the junior officers seemed quite clever young men.

The next morning Friday 11th we left Gorzola with a fair wind and went on well. The more I see of the Greeks the more I feel inclined to despise them. Their superstition is abject. A case of conscience occurred today which might have puzzled an abler casuist than a sailor. I was eating an egg & the cabin boy brought me the salt sellar which the crew used. I put my spoon in for the salt, when a sailor cried out alarmed to take away the salt sellar & give me salt in something else. I seems that it is their fast & the egg being forbidden communicated the infection to the salt which would afterwards make everything it touched unfit for the fast. A lawyer would have argued that the spoon being wet, carried away all the salt nigh it, & therefore could do no harm to what remained. Their stupidity reminds me of a story which they cited to prove that of the Sclavons. One of their vessels passing by St Mauro in a gale of wind, the son of the captain told his father that there was a port close by where they could take shelter. They accordingly went towards it when the Captn seeing no port, in a rage killed his son & threw him overboard. He had scarcely done so when the vessel turned a point & found itself safe in port. "There," says the Captain with German calmness, "I have lost my son." The place which we saw in passing has acquired a name which means son lost. On Saturday 12 we still went on with a good wind passing the islands of Lesina, Lissa & Brazza. Of these places we saw only the exterior not going to any of them; their form seems well designated in the map, except that Lissa is more to the north than Lesina. I this day offended the Saint of my sailors in a way that had nigh brought upon [us] the terrible vengeance of superstition. It was on my part perfectly innocent & unintentional, yet the savages really talked of putting me ashore upon one of the islands and leaving me.

I shall make tolerance the basis of all virtue, civil, political and religious.

I occupied myself with Cicero whom I relish more & more every day. These transient, slight notes are only observations on what I see; but it would be an endless labor to add what I think on all that occurs to me in my reading. I reserve for another time & place my ideas on the writings of the great master of eloquence.

Sunday 13 was spent in sleep & reading. We were again becalmed; and the same want of wind obliged us to move very slowly on Monday 14 past Brazza over which we saw the situation of Spalatro. Continuing on we were constantly among small islands of which the Greeks did not know the names, applying that of Zaraco to the whole ridge on the coast. On Tuesday 15 the wind became favorable & we gradually approached the coast of Istria. We spoke a vessel from Galaxithi which put our men in good spirits at the hope of selling their cargo well at Trieste, tho' they grieved sadly at having sold their cheese at Gorzola since they might have got more at Trieste. From this time they had no other thought but that of making money, & I took occasion to remark that as soon as this idea possessed them they exhibited new traces of meanness & baseness. I am very well [inclined] to agree with my great Junius that avarice is of all the vices the most apt to taint & corrupt the heart. I have sometimes thought that the greatest blessing or rather the only excuse for standing armies is that they formed a body of men whose pursuit was honor in preference to riches. The only argument I ever felt in favor of nobility is of the same kind, its giving to the state citizens who were not always bent upon making money. In the morning of Wednesday 16 the wind became very fair & we had a charming sail along the coast of Istria. It differs from that of Dalmatia; the latter being rocky & desert, whereas Istria is a fine plain covered with villages of which Borgo & Capo d'Istria are the most worthy of note. In the course of the afternoon we reached the port of Trieste. We had now been just 17 days on our route from Patras. The passage has been long because today is the only one when we have had the wind behind us; north only winds & calms being prevalent at this season. The passage with decent luck is of 8 or 10 days.

The next morning, Thursday 17 we went thro' the formalities of the Health office. On my landing I received a visit from Holland, the partner of Riggin the Consul.[152] Mr R being absent, Mr H acts as Vice Consul. He was extremely civil & attentive. It was not until about the evening that I was able to go to the Lazzaretto & to leave the vessel. I never took my leave of any set of men with more pleasure than of the crew of the dirty little vessel in which I arrived. I have rarely passed 18 days more disagreeably.

152. William Riggin, U.S. consul at Trieste, 1802–15?

They are much the most barbarous Greeks I have ever seen. Indeed I think that neighborhood, Corinth, Thessaly, Livadia the most brutal of Greece. I offended their religion inadvertently, & that augmented my sins in their eyes. Calculating on a passage of 8 or 10 days I had made provision accordingly. My provisions gave out & it was with difficulty I could procure a little something to support life, & not then until I had promised to pay for it. As it was their fast I could get only bread, olives & cheese & wine on which I lived several days. My patience was put to a severe trial. But I reasoned in this way. These men are impudent & beastly. If I resent it, I cannot confine myself to words, for they do not understand me & what credit could I get even if they knew what I said from abusing them. I must therefore strike. Now if I did anything less than kill them, it would be unworthy of revenge, & I myself might be the sufferer for they are much stronger than I am. If I kill them I will [be] punished myself. So that it is better to say nothing than to show an impotent anger, a maxim applicable to all disputes with our inferiors. When we arrived they refused to come to the Lazzaretto to be paid but would not let my things leave the vessel until they saw the money. I came to the Lazzaretto Vecchio where I slept.

Friday 18th I passed in looking round me & getting fixed in my new habitation which I found less uncomfortable than I expected. It is a large building with decent chambers & things can be procured to eat & drink. Quarantines seem really if not wholly useless at least badly regulated, our whole conduct here being a constant struggle between common sense & law. You have a guard to watch over you whom you pay but who takes no manner of pains to watch you, for he relaxes his duty on purpose that he may be paid for his compliance. Every man avoids his neighbor. Two great fat fellows in passing each other shrink up against the opposite walls for fear of infection. The whole scene would delight a misanthrope. Yet there is a comfortable yard to walk in, & I may pass my time comfortably.

During Saturday 19th I was a good deal indisposed owing to something I eat having disagreed with me, & from my resuming my habits of eating after my fasts during the voyage. I amused myself with reading & talking to some people. The women of the island of Tino, says a man of that country (confirmed by others) are the most beautiful of Greece; almost Francs in their habits & manners. They traffic with their beauty all over the Levant & supply wives even to the Francs of Smyrna &c. Indeed I suspect that the handsomest Greek, indeed one of the most beautiful women I ever saw was from that island. She was at Paris & from the similarity between Athénes & Tine I think I erred in believing her an Athenian.

On Sunday 20th the bad weather & the remains of my indisposition kept me in the house. I read & wrote & among other things amused myself with translating part of Cicero's fine oration for Marcellus; an elegant specimen of courtly adulation.

Monday 21 was passed in the same way. A Greek who knows Tripoli says that the Turks of that country are good people, which I believe to be the fact. I got some newspapers from Mr Holland who came down to see me.

Tuesday 22 brought no change. I look from my window so cooly on the noise of Trieste that I seem like one of Plato's wise men who sees the vanity of the shadows which deceive the people in the hole.

Wednesday 23. It would be difficult to say more than that today as well as Thursday 24 and Friday 25 and Saturday 26 and Sunday 27 and Monday 28, and Tuesday 29 I read & wrote. How ought we to appreciate retirement. I seem like a comet stopt short in my course. I anticipated a great deal of irksome time here. Yet it passes tranquilly & agreeably. What situation cannot be made agreeable when peace & books & retirement are present. Wednesday 30 I passed in the same way. Thursday 31 and Friday Augt 1st were the last days I spent in the Lazzaretto.

[*This series of reminders preceded the start of the second journal.*]

At Paris let me find a work of Count D'Osson, a history of Constantinople or Turkey, good thing, the best says Fauvel. Also Cantemir's history.[153]

Athens June 1806

Cadri Trashta is the name of a Turk very officiously good at Tripolitza. The Theodosian Code, edited by Romanopoli or Stephanopoli, to be procured with other Greek books at Trieste.

Let me enquire much about the govt of Ragusa, ancient & interesting. Verify the story of Wilkes at Paris.[154]

Remember Lee of Bordeaux.[155]

153. Ignatius Mouradja d'Ohsson (1740–1807): *Tableau Géneral de l'Empire Othman* (Paris, 1788–1824); Antiokh Dmitrievitch Kantemir (1708–44): *Histoire de l'Empire Othoman* (Paris, 1743).

154. Presumably John Wilkes (1725–97), English journalist and popular politician, noted for his radicalism and his support of liberty of the press. Biddle refers not to some incident in the course of Wilkes's stay in Paris from 1764 to 1768, but to his own wish to learn about Wilkes when he himself returned to Paris.

155. William Lee of Boston (1772–1840), friend of Madison and Monroe and American commercial agent at Bordeaux from 1801 to 1816, was a man well acquainted with Napoleon and especially with the Empress Josephine. He was an auditor in the Treasury Department from 1817 to 1829.

Il faut trouver à Paris un ouvrage sur la revolution en Naples, bien ecrit & juste dit on.

Don't forget old Choiseul's book on Greece. Good at first says Fauvel his protégé, but he is going to spoil it by making it over again. Ask too about the Duke himself.

Letters

I

Patras Monday May 12th 1806

My Dear Thomas

I have at length reached the shores of Greece, the object of so many wishes & the end of my wanderings. With my movements since my sailing for this country my letters will already have acquainted you. I am now about to enter on a new scene of the human drama, which I have long ardently wished to examine. The forms under which man appears in the civilized nations of Europe are very nearly similar. Equal degrees of refinement, almost equal advances in the arts, political systems differing but little in substance have given to him an uniformity of character which defies curiosity. Civilized man is indeed every where the same. The imaginary equality of nations is much more true of their societies which are all on a level because they differ only in some little shades of form sometimes scarcely perceptible & often unreal. But in a country of a different government different laws religion & usages, a soil interesting from its former history & its present ruin, it was natural to hope for a fairer view of mankind. I am now about to see how far my expectations were founded. You are too well versed in the history of the nations whose descendants are now before me not to feel interested in their present condition; but even without this rational curiosity I know my dear brother that your affection will willingly follow me. I have therefore begun a few observations on what may occur to me for your own amusement and instruction. I am not qualified nor disposed to be a writer of travel & therefore shall send you my ideas sometimes at length, sometimes briefly, gaily or seriously, as whim or leisure may suggest. The hasty notes of a traveller will not bear criticism, so you must always have in view that it is your brother who writes.

After the noise and tumult of Malta, I was rejoiced at my arrival on Tuesday last in the island of Zante. I here remained three days which were spent in seeing the island, & making enquiries among the people. Mr. Strani a Greek gentleman to whom I was recommended, the British consul & some other acquaintances enabled me to learn everything to advantage and rendered me perfectly satisfied with my stay there. It is indeed a delightful spot. Your map will indicate its position. It is about 60 miles in circumference & contains a number of villages & nearly 40 thousand inhabitants. The chief town which bears the name of the island is situated on the eastern side of it at the foot of a ridge of hills, & around a fine bay, there being no port. It is long and narrow; the houses generally of two stories with a shaded portico before them. The whole has however a dirty and mean appearance except the triangular square of St Marc. The town contains 18 thousand inhabitants and is defended by a fortress on the neighboring hills. The people occupy themselves with trade and a few manufactories of coton works. Zante has but few attractions; almost unobserved by the ancients, it might have been equally obscure now were it not for its currants which are the basis of its commerce & its fame. This production with some oil of an inferior quality, a little corn & cotton & wine are the sources of its riches. They grow in an extensive plain almost the whole length of the island & forming one of the richest and best cultivated countries I have seen. They were sent to England & all along the European side of the Mediterranean; but the war has nearly ruined the trade. Though rich in products the island does not produce enough of the necessaries of life for its consumption, & a two months blockade would reduce the people to currant pies without even a crust. The soil is not however remarkably good but has been brought to its present state by the industry of the inhabitants. They are indeed an active & an honest race of men; the lower class are very much at their ease labor being high, & the few beggars that are seen are foreigners. The language is of course Greek, but their intercourse with Italy has made almost all of them acquainted with its language whose idioms & many of whose terms they have mingled with their own. The Italian dress and appearance is even found here with the addition of the mustachoes & the loose pantaloons neither of which are however worn by the gentlemen. Their manners are not therefore purely Greek. The women are rarely seen; they appear in the streets but seldom & then with a black mask on; they are all day seated at the windows behind a sort of wicket, where without being seen they can observe & criticise what passes. From the few I have seen I judge them to be handsome & as the insular situation often corrects climate, they seem fairer than the Italians. The civility shown to a foreigner does not at all comprehend an introduction to the family of a Zantiote. This politeness is generally confined to visits to you, but the female part of his family lives in great retirement. There is nothing very singular in their usages. You would be pleased at the little ceremony of sprinkling rose leaves over the breakfast table. At a little village called Volines the people have a custom of putting a piece of money into the mouths of their dead at the funeral They can give no reason for it nor can they say more than that it has been always handed down from their ancestors. Another village is the only spot in this island where the same usage prevails; it is probably a remnant left by some straggling settlement of the custom of providing the deceased with his passage money for Charon. It shows however the force which long established trifles possess over the mind. Their gardens are delightful. Their mode of measuring land is something like Dido's. Instead of selling it by the cow skin it is here dealt out by the bushel. When you purchase a bushel of land you get just as much as you can sow a bushel of grain in. There are a great many families descendants of old English settlers, & it is a sad degeneracy from the Purity of Protestantism, that the greater part of them are Greek priests.

It is much more important to know that Zante is among the largest of those islands which have lately become independent under the name of the Seven island republic; and you may not be displeased to receive some information of our republican sister. These islands were long the object of jealousy between the European powers. Belonging formerly to Venice, it was discovered that no nation could possess them without offending the rest, & it was thought best that all should relinquish what all could not enjoy. A govt was therefore formed in the year 1800 composed of all the islands on the coast of Albania & the Morea which had been owned by Venice, & of which Corfu, Cefalonia, St Maura, Ithaca, Zante, Cerigo & Paxo are the principal. They fixed the seat of govt at Corfu and gave it a written constitution. My Zante acquaintances swear much at the length of this said constitution which they said was longer than the whole territory of the republic, & admired my patience in wading thro' a quarto pamphlet in Italian, of legislative provisions & institutional checks & weights & balances which not one of them had ever read. Do not however be alarmed as I shall mention just enough of it to give you an idea of it. It is one of those productions which has many of the liberal principles of the modern schools but which like too many of these works is badly fortified against attack & innovation. The govt is aristocratical. A body of nobles or Sincliti elect

every two years a Legislative body & a Senate. The first consists of 110
members, the second of 17 and is the executive. The Senate is always
sitting & its President is chosen for two years by the legislative body & is
called Prince. The judicial power is vested in a tribunal of the first instance
in each island, four tribunals of appeal & one of Cassation, the highest of
all consisting of seven members chosen by the Legislative body. The criminal tribunals are divided into two branches, the correctional & and criminal
of which the names explain the object & which are committed to different
hands. Each island is governed by a Pritano or Governor chosen by the Leg
body on the nomination of the nobles of the island. He must not however
be a resident of the island which he governs & he is assisted by a council of
two Regents. The Greek is the established religion, but the general tolera-
tion of all religions has been wisely permitted. Another good part of the
code is the facility of naturalization given to foreigners. After ten years
residence any service rendered to the state, the introduction of any mechanical art, or any industrious or commercial establishment confers citizenship.
This noviciate may be abridged if after five years a man possesses large
landed property any extraordinary skill in science or the arts or if he will
marry a seven islandress. Such is the outline. But constitutions are made of
paper & paper has not yet been able to defend or secure the freedom of a
nation. It would seem that these Greeks have purchased sovereignty too
dearly. They have been forced & inflated into Greatness & may perhaps
soon burst. The forms of govt eat up the produce of their labor, & tho' the
neutrality of their flag is at this moment serviceable yet it will not last
long. Indeed they are now independent only in name as the Russian govt
has its troops in all the islands, & notoriously directs all the public measures. On the whole this little republic promises to sink very shortly under
its own weakness, or to be swallowed up as soon as its neighbors have time
to rest from their campaigns. They have long since begun to alter their
constitution; the Prince will soon lose not his head but probably his title;
and by a sad forgetfulness, at the end of the last two years the Senate
absolutely did not remember that the nobles were to re-elect them, but
persuaded with the jurists that selfpreservation is the basis of all politics
they re-elected themselves. You see me at the end of my paper before I have
begun my letter. However indolently inclined, it is difficult to stop when
we are writing to those we love; and my modest note of Zante has now
swelled to a monster. Yet I must find place for my arrival here & my time
will now oblige me to be concise. I therefore omit a description of the
tarpits at Zante, uninteresting tho' celebrated, and proceed.

On Friday morning I left Zante in a boat bound to Chiarenza the nearest point of the Morea. The distance is about 18 miles & generally the passage is about three hours. We remained however on the water nearly eight, & I was anxious to catch the manner in which Greece would first present itself. A long chain of irregular coast broken by bays & diversified by mountains whose tops were covered with snow gradually opened before the eye. As we advanced we distinguished a hilly country covered with shrubs & enlivened occasionally by little fields of grain. On the height was Castel Tornese an old Venetian Fortress now deserted. The whole aspect was indeed somewhat unpromising, but on passing the little island of Caucalida we soon reached our place of destination, a spot much more agreeable. The ideas of ruin which the name of Greece inspires, recurred to me forcibly as I saw that a wretched custom house & two huts were all that remained to represent the ancient city of Cyllene. As we came nigh the shore a Dozen Greeks & Turks sitting crosslegged on the beach rose to recieve us. I touched the soil of Greece. My letter for the custom house officer was I found useless as he had been just superceded; his successor was not however the less civil. I walked about 50 yards to the custom house, of which the upper story only was inhabited, the lower part being mere walls, and having mounted a staircase outside I passed over a drawbridge into the little castle. It did indeed resemble one when upon going into a room we find the Officer a Turk sitting in a corner smoking a pipe. His appearance as he rose from the carpet was not the most prepossessing. He was dressed in the stile of his country with his turban his jacket loose trousers & red slippers; and his mustachoes vied in fierceness with his pistols & dirk which he carried in his girdle. One of the company was his particular friend & he treated me with great kindness. After some little conversation he asked me to eat, and immediately sent for a sheep and had it killed for supper in a patriarchal stile of hospitality. Whilst it was preparing I walked about a quarter of a mile to see some ruins. They were on a little eminence & I enjoyed a sight of a most perfect picture. The sun was just going down over the ruins of a fortress where vegetation was contending with the fragments; a groupe of cows and sheep were feeding. The shepherd leaning upon his staff stood wondering at the curiosity of this stranger. At a little distance the sea was calm, & the numerous islands which covered its surface gave it a beautiful variety. The eye rested upon Ithaca the little spot which is immortalized by the song of the first of Poets & by the residence of the man who like myself was a wanderer. I now felt that I was in Greece. I felt that I was alone in a foreign country distant from all that was dear to me & surrounded by barbarians who yet occupied a soil interesting from its former virtues & its present ruin. I thought of my country my friends & my family. On my

return to the house I sat down with the Turk, & succeeded so well with
him that before we separated he was delighted, expressed his sorrow at not
being able to receive me better but hoped that I would soon return & stay a
week with him, begging me to let him know of my safe arrival at Patras.
The supper was soon introduced on a table of *six inches* high round which
we were to sit on a carpet. A cosmopolite would have smiled at the proud
disdain of chairs & ceremonies with which we sat & eat & smoked. My
honest Musselman had something of the character of our Indian in him. He
said he had often received at his house & treated kindly the men of Zante,
but when he went there himself no one either took him to his house or said
good day to him. He was pious too. Just before dark, as we were talking,
he got up & having washed himself went to the window & spreading on the
floor his mantle stood upon it & began his devotion. He sighed & seemed
moved, went upon his knees, kissed the floor, rose & repeated several times
the same ceremony, then returned & resumed the conversation. After a
good night's rest we rose in the morning & after bidding farewell to the
Turk, & kissing at him thro' the moustachoes left Chiarenza. At first the
road which runs along the coast to Patras passes thro' a barren country. It
however soon changes. Ancient Elis was celebrated for the excellence of its
soil. It retains its character & altho' part of it is uncultivated for want of
population, yet in general it has the appearance of great abundance being
covered with grain, & the land not being divided by any barrier. The whole
plain begins at Patras & extends nearly all along the western side of the
Morea forming the richest part of it. In about two hours we reached a little
town called Le Kena where we stopped to breakfast. This was the first
Greek town I had seen & I was much pleased at finding that instead of
building their houses in nasty streets one on top of the other, almost every
house is insulated & with a little garden or tree which has a charming effect
particularly after the filthy villages of France & Italy. On going into the
house I looked round as usual for the books & smiled upon taking down a
dusty dog eared little book from the shelf & finding it a Greek collection of
Aesop Musaeus & some other classic pieces. What would our learned ped-
ants think of this sad prostitution of the works on which they build their
fame or how would they be ashamed to find a ragged school boy read Greek
better than themselves. I confess my pride as a Hellenist shrunk at the
idea. I was here strongly tempted to turn aside to the ancient town of Elis
only two hours ride. I reserved it however for another opportunity & continued my ride. We passed thro' several villages of which the largest is
Chaminizza. They are all pretty and rural. I was particularly struck with

the dress of the peasants which resembles much the antique & is infinitely preferable to the clumsy tho' boasted dresses of Switzerland. Every man that I met seemed to be a Nestor. They are a fine stout race of men, & the only regret is that there should be so few of them, the country being sadly depopulated. We reached this place about 8 in the evening after a ride of twelve hours, that being the only mode of computation in this country. The hour may be calculated at three of our miles. Of Patras I will say nothing at this moment, but will close this long and dreadful letter for which I can excuse myself only by saying that it has grown to such a size in spite of my efforts to relieve you. I send this letter to Constantinople [and] thence to the care of Genl Armstrong at Paris. Should it after its travels reach you, I trust it will find you all in health & happiness & convey to you the expression of the sincere love with which I am

Yr Son & Brother
Nicholas Biddle

Mr Thomas Biddle.

Recieved February 14th 1807[1]

II

Athens June [1806]

Dear brother

My heart beats as I date my letter from the venerable presence of the mistress of the world. I seize the first moment of leisure since my arrival to collect & communicate the sentiments it has inspired.

Having now seen many of the objects which distance & fiction have exaggerated into greatness I am able to appreciate the value of Athens. The European cities have generally, in themselves, but few motives to interest us. Some memorable story of oppression, some sanguinary act which stains their soil are almost all they can offer to recollection, whilst the eye is amused or offended by some pompous glare in which the mind is unconcerned. Even Rome itself can present only the image of a half ruined people. To the magnificent remains of her temples no man can indeed deny his admiration & his sorrow. But there is still around them a crowd of beings,

---

1. This note was added by a hand other than Biddle's.

sadly degenerate but Roman, who strive to hide by a luxurious profusion the loss of the primitive virtues of their country; unblushing beggary assails us in the midst of them, & the herd of strangers whose curiosity obtrudes upon your own abstracts the mind. There is even something consolatory amongst these ruins. The destruction of marble is infinitely less afflicting than that of mind, & the Italian nation in spite of oppression is still the first of the world. The ground on which Brutus stabbed a tyrant is indeed disgraced by many a sycophant who trembles before a master whom he dares not punish. But there is still a lambent flame of genius round the Capitol. The forum is still trodden by many a Roman capable of redeeming & regenerating his country, & the arts still hover over the spot which contains their brightest productions. Whilst therefore we feel at Rome a mingled sentiment of melancholy & admiration, Athens reflects the perfect picture of desolation & despair. The Roman ruins are possessed by a polished people who estimate & revere them, but the barbarians of Athens despise whilst they mutilate the fairest remains of antiquity. At Rome let us reverence the manhood & revival of the arts, at Athens let us bend over their cradle, their tomb. Roman genius is obscured by clouds but lightens with the purest flame; the genius of Athens is hidden in the sullen darkness of the storm. Rome is the twilight, Athens the black night of ruin. There is a sanctity around the monuments of her glory which inspires us at once with awe & wonder; nor can we approach without veneration the soil of a people whose religion amused our infancy, whose history has furnished the brightest models of virtue & heroism, whose writings have led us to science & whose works tho' mutilated we have not dared to rival. The recollection of her greatness becomes doubly distressing amidst the traces of her misfortunes, & the mind sickens over the melancholy contrast between the glory of ancient Athens & the misery of her present condition. It is indeed sad & awful & may give to philosophy the fairest lessons of the humility which becomes the transient grandeur of man. The religion of Athens is lost forever. Her temples which have resisted not only the barbarous rage of conquest, but the frenzy of the elements, now moulder under the hand of ignorance or idle curiosity, and on the noblest structures of Paganism a Turkish mosque has raised its solitary spire (shapeless column) to mock the elegance of Grecian arts & to proclaim the victory of a new religion. Her crowded theatres are deserted. The voice of the Muses is silent, & instead of saddening over the recital of fictitious sorrow, they now weep over the real misery of their country. To the Areopagus time has left scarcely a ruin, & the decisions of the people which it once witnessed, are now superceded by the arbitrary judgments of a foreign Cadi. The Lyceum the Prytaneum the

Academy have given place to a little school of elements which has never heard of Plato. But it is on the holy spot where this great people assembled to hear their orators, to frame laws for themselves to indulge in all the licence of freedom, it is here that the fall of Athens is most acutely felt. Where are her orators? Gone forth to enlighten distant nations without a solitary ray for their country. Whilst foreign erudition has lighted its lamp at the flame of their genius, their works are unknown to their posterity. Where are her people? Are these few wretches, scarcely superior to the beasts whom they drive heedlessly over the ruins, are these men Athenians? Where is her freedom? Alas! this is the keenest stab of all. Bowed down by a foul oppression, the spirit of Athens has bent under its slavery. The deliberations of her assemblies were once their laws; they now obey the orders of a distant master, and on the citadel itself, the protectress & the asylum of Grecian freedom, now sits a little Turkish despot to terrify & to command. It was towards the ocean that their great men directed their fellow citizens for empire & freedom. One melancholy sail in the Piraeus tells the sad story of Athenian misery. It is thus by collecting the scattered images of greatness & decay, we become interested in the misfortunes of a nation, & are instructed by the melancholy but pleasing philosophy of ruins.

In the early history of Athens you are too well versed to need any explanation; and I shall therefore confine myself to an account of its present state both local and political.

(Olive [*one word illegible*] Cecrops[1] &e) Elgin superstition & avarice more harm than Attila[2] [&e?][3]

In the infancy of states, security from the violence of neighbors, is the first precaution of settlers. Hence we find that most cities began by a citadel on a mountain & gradually ventured into the plain as they acquired strength & confidence. The first establishments of Athens were of this sort. Yet there is something peculiarly endearing in its origin. It was not a band of vagrant robbers who began by conquest & war [and] established [it] by rapine, but the mild & amiable superiority of civilization over an infant & ignorant people. The ungrateful soil of Attica yielded its fruits to the industry of Cecrops whose dominion was announced rather by the blooming

---

1. A mythical Pelasgian king of Athens and the reputed founder of the city, Cecrops was supposed to have introduced the elements of civilized life, including the worship of the gods.
2. Attila the Hun ravaged the Balkans and Greece in the 440s A.D.
3. This line seems to be a list of subjects about which Biddle intended to say more in some other context. It is introduced between paragraphs but does not seem to be an afterthought. That is, it is not an interlinear addition.

vineyards than by the sword. Its future history partook of the same spirit. Always amiable polite & learned its talents gave it the ascendency over its neighbors. The same superiority is still visible not only in the number & elegance of its monuments but in the comparative politeness of its people, which even time itself seems to have respected. The ruins of Athens are more interesting & in a better state of preservation than those of any other Greek city. This is however but a slender encomium, since almost all that I am about to describe is in a melancholy state of decay & disorder.

On the southern coast of Attica, surrounded on the north by the ridge of Citheron, on the east by the Pentelicus, on the west by the sea, is a plain of considerable extent. Its appearance independently on the pleasures of recollection is peculiarly interesting, nor shall I ever forget the mingled emotions which I felt when on descending the last hill of the Citheron I saw for the first time the eternal city. The general culture of the plain is not good, since a large unproductive portion contrasts sensibly with the grain & the olives of the rest. This last still continues to be the favorite produce of Athens, and indicates rather an unfriendly soil. At the southern part of the plain are two little hills, with several smaller eminences around them. The highest of these, the ancient Anchesmus, was never inhabited & contains no ruins, since its top is too pointed for a city. To the south of Anchesmus is the Acropolis or citadel, the most distinguished part of ancient as well as modern Athens. That its top was levelled by the vagrant Pelasgi, that it was first surrounded with walls by Theseus, and that it has been successively the home of most of the revolutions of Athens is known from its history & [a] more endearing claim to our attention is that it was the spot where stood one. . . .[4]

III

You will be surprised, my dear Watts,[1] at receiving a letter from your friend Biddle with such a date. Yet such is the fact, that after a long & circuitous route I have at last reached the soil of Athens. At the end of my

---

4. This letter is a fragment, the rest of which appears to have been lost.
1. Edward Watts had been a close friend of Biddle's at Princeton, and the two of them had been valedictorians of the class of 1801.

course it is salutary to look back on the objects I have left, & it will be unnecessary to add that among those which recollection presents most agreeably you are in the foremost place. I have many reproaches to make, for not having received a line from you since I left America, and I should feel this neglect the more severely did not my own example prove how very distinct are correspondence & friendship. You will believe me when I tell you that our acquaintance has been the source of many a pleasing remembrance since I have been in Europe, that I have very often meditated & once even begun a letter to you which indolence and occupation prevented me from completing. I am inclined but afraid to believe that you cannot so well excuse yourself.

It would be an endless task to write you any detail of what has occurred to me since I left my country. Nearly two years have been occupied in seeing what are esteemed the most interesting objects of Europe and being initiated in some degree into the affairs of government. From this last, tho' uninteresting and & sometimes irksome, our views & our knowledge may often be enlarged, & we may become more qualified to be useful to the state. With regard to other pursuits, I have been much directed by this consideration, that all which concerns real solid useful knowledge may be learned from books, since the social period which confined to a single soil the knowledge of its people is past; and therefore altho' there is a portion of minor information which rarely [insulates?] beyond the object of it,[2] yet in general our studies may be prosecuted as advantageously in America as elsewhere. But there is something which tho' it may not aspire to the house of knowledge is not without its use, & is peculiar to Europe. An enlarged intercourse with the men & the institutions of refined people differing from ourselves & from each other sometimes corrects our errors & improves the understanding. An actual observation of the common lot of the world renders us contented with our own; & by approaching we destroy the illusions with which distance had surrounded the greatness of Europe. We retire at last sometimes with a heart ameliorated, [and] the judgment, & learn to fix our estimate of man between the sanguine brilliant hopes of his grandeur, & the miserable cant the whining hypocrisy of his vanity. If it be more than poetically true that the object of our existence is to look for a moment at what is passing in the world and then leave it, & if *man* be after all the fairest object of inquiry, there may be something more than a temporary gratification to see & know those who share with us the empire of the

---

2. This concessive clause is perhaps beyond explanation.

world; & to enlarge the horizon of the transient scene which we are so soon
to leave. Under these impressions I have preferred the society of men to
whom I shall never have an opportunity [of returning] to that of books
which will always be at my command, & have [been] anxious to occupy my
short stay in Europe, seeing as far as possible the varieties of people who
inhabit it. After remaining some time at Paris, I went thro' Switzerland;
and am now prosecuting a journey which has already comprised the southern part of France, the most attractive objects of Italy, a part of Sicily,
thence from Malta to this country. I am as yet undecided whether I shall go
on as far as Asia Minor, but I hope on my return to Paris to see a portion of
Germany. Of the interesting spot in which I now am, you have read &
spoken so often that you cannot be indifferent to its fate. You would be
afflicted at the melancholy picture of fallen greatness of so venerable a
nation. Of the monuments of its former glory enough remain to guide our
researches & to justify all that history has transmitted of its grandeur. Yet
the most brilliant remains of art stand among a people unable to appreciate
them, & the works which attest their freedom are now witness [to] the
despotism of their barbarous tyrants [*the words* "trampled under foot by"
have been struck out after "are now"]. Such has indeed been the brutal violence of the conquerors of Greece [*the words* "of the country" *have been struck
out after* "conquerors of"] that the mind can find little enjoyment beyond
the pleasure of seeing the objects so dear to our infancy, & the melancholy
sympathy with its misfortunes. I have been delighted with what I have as
yet seen: Patras, Delphos, Livadia, Thebes & Athens are the only places of
note which I have seen, but I shall shortly visit the most interesting parts
of the Peloponnesus. A soil rich to profusion standing uncultivated for
want of inhabitants, a people whose character has become debased by oppression [*the words* "sunk under its" *have been struck out after* "character has"],
a host of inferior tyrants whose despotism has almost become intolerable for
human nature, is the scene which has succeeded the art, the glory the
freedom of ancient Greece. Yet the time does not seem very distant when
this country will be relieved from its [*the words* "rise against its" *have been
struck out*] oppressors; & again be distinguished.

I shall leave it with much regret. How soon I shall return to my country
is as yet uncertain. It is a moment to which I look forward with pleasure;
and to which every sentiment that can animate the heart renders dear to
me. But as I shall leave Europe for ever I hope previously to visit England
our mother in laws & language & birth & character. I shall then go home
carrying with me a firmer attachment to our institutions which I have

learnt to appreciate & to my friends whom absence has rendered endeared to me. What will then become of me I know not. I am as you remember a lawyer by profession only for altho' armed with a sort of letter of marque to kill & destroy, I am sadly arrears to my professional studies. These however I can easily acquit myself of, but I have not as yet an idea where I shall plant myself. Among the thousand prospects which have amused my speculative moments I have been suspended between two plans. The first, perhaps congenial to the feelings of my heart & most soothing to the indolence of my temper is to retire like yourself into some quiet corner, & looking calmly on a world which has lost its attractions pass some twenty or perhaps thirty years of tranquillity, & then die. The other to which the habits of my life seem to impel me, is that of devoting myself wholly to the world & politics, & building a sort of name as a statesman. This object is recommended rather by my sense of duty than my feelings for I become every day more indifferent to what is called glory or the opinions of other men.

You yourself were once a projector,[3] & I shall be very much interested to know what you are doing. It is unfair my dear Watts not to have from you a line to apprize me of your welfare & your occupation. The course of time must have now made you a lawyer. Yet you were more anxious to be a man of leisure than a very occupied Attorney. Perhaps you may have become a legislator, tho' I suspect you had scarcely zeal enough to be very active at a horse race or a barbecue. Perhaps you have been unfortunate. Are you married & how many little ones? Yet you once I remember boldly resisted the enemy, & tho' wounded made an honorable retreat. But *"omnes eodem ruimus"* singeth the Poet.[4] What has become of Lewis Mosely & Watkins & all the rest of you "damned Whigs" as our little army used to call you in spite of their leaders.[5] Remember me very affectionately to all who are within your reach. From this remote corner of the world I can offer you nothing political that will be new. My only object being to reproach you for your neglect & to assure you of the esteem with which I am

Yr. friend
Nicholas Biddle

3. One who undertakes a plan or an action.
4. "We all rush to the same place." Is this line a misquotation of Horace's *Odes* 2.3.25 (*omnes eodem cogimur*)?
5. At Princeton in Biddle's day there were two rival debating and literary societies, the Cliosophic and the Whig. Shortly after his arrival, Biddle became a member and soon a leader of the first of these.

IV

Trieste July 25th 1806

Dear brother [William]

This letter is the first which I have had an opportunity of sending to you since I left Malta. The interval has been passed in a country so insulated from the rest of the world that it was impossible to find any direct or safe communication with America. I have therefore now to inform you of my having finished the excursion into Greece mentioned in my last letters. In leaving Italy I feel that I have ventured beyond the permission or the expectation of the family as well as my own original intentions. Yet the transgression was at least very seductive, & as I could not ask either your consent or advice, I must leave it to the affections of you all to excuse an error which has been harmless and is now past.

Greece has given me more satisfaction than any thing I have seen since I left America. Tired of the noisy quarrels which agitate the greater part of Europe, I was glad to find a retired corner undisturbed by the sound of foreign cannon, and forgetting for a moment the events of the day, bury myself among the ruins & the recollections of former times. No scholar can be insensible to the pleasure of witnessing the scenes which have been hallowed by the arts the virtues & the arms of a great people; nor can we retire without amusement and perhaps instruction from an intercourse with two nations foreign to all our habits and modes of thinking, & different at once from ourselves and from each other. You will perceive by this outline what parts of Greece I have visited. I mention the ancient names since there is no modern accurate map of that country. From Zante to Cyllene through to Patras. From there to Aegium, and across the gulph to Delphos. Then to Livadia, Chaeronea & Thermopylae; and downwards thro' Leuctra & Plataea to Thebes. Thence directly to Athens. An excursion to Aegina & another through Attica by Marathon Pentelicus & Sunium. From Athens to Eleusis Megara & Corinth & Sicyon. Thence thro' Nemea & Mycenae to Argos & Nauplia. Thence to Tripolitza the modern capital near Mantinea & Tegea. Thence down to Sparta. From there following the course of the Eurotas up to Belmina and Megalopolis. Thence thro' Arcadia to Olympia, Elis & Patras. Beyond Thermopylae as I learnt from travellers there is nothing to reward the fatigue & perhaps danger of a journey. I would have visited some of the islands. But the weather was becoming extremely hot, & to have left the continent would have carried me too far as I should have incurred the risk of waiting a long time before I could return. I therefore confined myself to the most interesting points; & have perfectly gratified my curiosity.

The situation of that country is afflicting beyond description. The descendants of a free nation who inherit their talents without their fortunes & who may one day rival the brightest glory of their ancestors now live under the most frightful despotism which not confining itself to the property or even the lives penetrates the feelings [&] the hearts of these wretched slaves. The soil is covered by a host of little tyrants, who openly purchasing their power, repay themselves by the most unlimited extortions & whose inferior agents domesticate as it were the visage of oppression in the bosom of the family. I thought I had seen as much as nature could bear under the despotism of civilization; but it has since been my melancholy good fortune to witness the proverbial terrors of eastern tyranny. Independently on any of the acts of cruelty to which they are every day liable the general relation between the Greeks and Turks is that of master and slave. The Turks pay no taxes; the whole burden falls upon the Greeks—all the offices are in the hands of Turks. The Turks always go armed; all kinds of weapons are forbidden to the Greeks. A Turk takes without restraint from the peasants whatever he may want, & occasionally as a favor pays for it. Such in short is the alarm which their very name inspires, that it is the practice of the country to pacify children in the cradle by saying there is a Turk coming. These enormities have ripened the animosities of the people into every thing but rebellion. The higher classes are more alive to these misfortunes from the sad remembrance of what Greece once was; & even the meanest among them who has forgotten that he is a Grecian, feels that he is a man. Within some years past their hopes of deliverance have become more strong; & the few Turks who now govern them tread on the treacherous ashes, the smothered embers of sedition & revenge. But divided among themselves, jealous of each other without arms & without a leader, they dare not express their indignation but wait for foreign assistance. How easily they might free themselves may be imagined from the great superiority of their number over that of the Turks & from the example of a small town which resisted for 18 years the Turkish arms & yielded at last thro' treachery. The probability is not I think very remote of an invasion of that country. The extension of the French power along the western shore of the Adriatic lays open all Greece to their arms, & the possession of it will be of infinite importance, as the direct road to Egypt & thence to India. The conquest would be easy & much stronger motives than the rescue of Chris-

tianity from subjection to its enemies conspire to incite an honorable crusade in favor of human nature. The misfortunes of Greece are the more to
be regretted, from its capacity to be happy, since there are few countries
possessing so many advantages. A fine climate an unclouded sky the thin
and subtle aid of genius, forms a robust as well as a lively acute people.
The soil is rich & yields profusely to the hand of industry; but we must
again deplore the effects of the unhappy servitude which impedes the progress of population, which drives from Greece all who can escape beyond the
limits of its oppression, & which has reduced to barrenness so large a portion of its territory, for want of inhabitants. What a melancholy contrast
between the flourishing ages of Greece when Arcadia alone counted a hundred thousand slaves, & its present depression when all Peloponnesus can
boast only about [four hundred] fifty thousand souls.[1] The scenery, the
general face of the country is extremely picturesque, an equal disposition of
mountains [and] plains, the first by its narrow passes so well protecting the
fertility of the second; the towns beautifully situated, the scattered villages
uncommonly rural; & a number of ports which even the progress of navigation has respected, are among the objects which interest an observer of
nature. These remarks apply particularly to Boeotia & Attica, two of the
handsomest provinces of ancient Greece. Those whose researches penetrate
beyond the surface of the country will not be less pleased on examining the
two nations who inhabit it. The Greeks are naturally quick sprightly & full
of genius; but having little education to direct & refine these qualities, they
have degenerated into cunning. In comparison with their masters a Greek
constantly obliged to exercise his talents is much more acute than a Turk
who has generally no employment & who receives without any exertion on
his part, the fruits of the labor of his inferiors. Yet the character of the men
of Greece bears the plain & sensible mark of servitude. Like other slaves,
they are vile & abject in their submission, haughty & cruel when they can
be so with impunity. Unable to act, they scarcely dare to think freely; and
every thing, even down to their music and the miserable nasal noise of a
slave afraid to speak out aloud, tells us that they have a master. They are
accused of carrying the same spirit of low cunning into their dealings with
others. I am unwilling however to adopt hastily this national reflection,
since I do not myself remember to have seen any thing more than is common among the people of the south of Europe. With regard however to
Greek character it is an interesting fact that we still trace nearly the same

1. In his second journal Biddle lists the figure as 450,000. Hence my correction.

varieties which formerly distinguished the people from each other. Such is the power of local situation, & perhaps the inveteracy of institutions when once fixed, in forming the disposition of men. The scale of refinement is diminished, but the proportions are still the same, nor was there perhaps formerly more difference than there is now between the rude & vicious habits of the Thebans, & the soft & affable habits of the Athenians. There is among them very little education. In the larger towns there are schools for the ancient Greek, but there are few who arrive at any tolerable acquaintance with it; & even the best informed have learnt that Greece was once great & free, rather from the admiration of strangers than their own studies. Yet it would be ungrateful to deny that I have seen some very amiable Greeks & experienced occasionally a real and honorable hospitality. Nor is it less true that Greece has felt sensibly that amazing impulse which within thirty years past has purified the knowledge & improved the conditions of Europe. Since that period they have made such rapid advances, that half a century of freedom would nearly redeem them. At present they may be considered as half barbarous. They are connected with civilization; but in dress, in manners, in society they approach very near the level of the Mahometan nations. With regard to their religion it might have been rendered very serviceable. But the [glimmering?] lights of the church have not conducted them beyond the outskirts of Christianity. Their piety confines their reading to some melancholy book of dogmas and rituals; their zeal is bewildered among the mazes of ceremonies; and what is worse the beneficent influence of the climate is overturned by a system of fasting during more than half the year just sufficient to preserve them from the grave whose honors it pretends to earn for them. Their commerce too being chiefly if not wholly conducted by themselves invites few strangers from abroad; & the Greeks who carry their produce to other nations are not very sollicitous to adopt their improvements. The state of their society corresponds with the rest of their character. The females (for their treatment is the fairest criterion) enjoy a liberty something superior to that of the Turkish women, but which does not approach the freedom of European manners. They are in general confined to the nursery, & their education is about adequate to their employment. When they venture into the street which is rarely, they are always covered with a mask or a veil, & avoid with alarm the presence of a stranger. In the families accustomed to receive foreigners they may be occasionally seen & even spoken to; but in common they do not appear. There is nothing like our intercourse between the sexes, no danse, no theatre, no social meeting; & the only thing like society is a grave assemblage from which females are excluded, & the whole employment is to smoke a pipe.

The history of their language & literature is short & unsatisfactory. The modern Greek is the lineal descendant of that language, so long the object of the real or affected admiration of scholars, and bears a very striking resemblance to it. As soon as I had overcome the difficulties of pronunciation I was astonished at the similarity between the Greek of the schools & the current language of the country. The ancient Greek has only suffered what every thing traditionary will suffer in its passage from a civilized nation to its barbarous posterity; the embellishments, the beauties are gradually forgotten as the refinement which created them ceases, till at last nothing remains but the substance adorned with the shapeless ornaments which a rude people loves to offer to the object of its affections. Thus the foundation of the Hellenic is perfectly preserved in the Romaeic, the names by which the Greeks distinguish the ancient from the modern idiom. The seeds of the two languages are the same; but unaided by education, unpruned by care, the latter has run wild & lost its purity by encroaching upon its neighbors. It will be unnecessary to specify minute differences since we may judge of the change by learning that the modern grammar rejects the dual number, the middle voice, the two aorists, & that multitude of nice necessary distinctions of time & person, the natural exuberance of a subtle metaphysical people. The language of a simple nation will always partake of its simplicity, & the modern Greeks without perplexing themselves with subtleties accommodate their divisions of time to their own purposes and go no farther. The Romaeic is however a sonorous & forcible language & were there more scholars who would purify & chasten it, would be equal if not superior to any in Europe. All the rich phraseology, the boasted abundance of the Hellenic would be at their disposal; and they could naturalise & arrange the multitude of foreign idioms from Italy & the East which commerce has introduced. Unfortunately however letters are but little cultivated. The Greeks of Constantinople are considered as the most learned of their nation; but from Greece itself almost all the scholars emigrate to the cities of Italy and Germany where they are employed as teachers. The Physicians, who are generally speaking the most informed men of Greece, are mostly from Cephalonia and a knowledge of the ancient language makes no part of their erudition. There is one Greek press at Constantinople, a Greek newspaper at Corfu, but the Greek books are commonly printed at Venice or Vienna, so that a Greek must leave his country before he can present to it the fruits of his talents. The consequence of all this is that there are very few original works in the language. The lives of the saints & little books of devotion with some few translations of popular stories from the French & Italian form the substance of a Grecian library. Yet a better period seems approaching, the twilight which precedes the rising of freedom. There is some activity among the men of letters. Of the two principal scholars of Athens, one has written an esteemed work on the later history of his country; the other gave me a pastoral poem published by one of his acquaintances & has himself translated a part of the travels of Anacharsis. The pastoral I think no length of quarantine should induce me to read, tho' I perceive among the very first lines tempting mention of butter & milk, and as the Poet no less mellifluously than justly sings "καὶ τόσα καλὰ ἄλλα."[2] Yet even a Pastoral may be counted as it indicates some attention to poetry & in conjunction with other late efforts evinces that Grecian literature is advancing.

I have paid much attention to their mode of pronunciation. On that subject the Greeks have certainly a right to dictate, as it seems a very unreasonable presumption on the part of Europeans to pretend to teach a nation how to pronounce the language of its ancestors, & I have never heard any good argument to support it. I must reserve until I see you a full explanation of the difference between the two modes, since writing is so imperfect a conveyance of sounds. So much however do they differ, that they are mutually unintelligible. We pronounce Greeks words as if they were English; a manifest error since no two nations ever did give exactly the same sounds to the same combinations of letters. The ancient Greeks had of course a mode peculiar to themselves, which we can search for no where so naturally as among their posterity whose pronunciation is evidently justified by ancient and existing monuments. In generally they observe strictly the accents, but pay no attention to metre, about which they are careless since all their poetry is rhyme. You can scarcely imagine the revolution it makes when Beta is changed into our V; Delta into TH; Epsilon and Eta the reverse of our manner, and Upsilon into our F, with a number of others. Away go our imaginary elegancies, the harmonious accommodation of sound to sentiment; no more rattling of stones, no roaring of salt water; the majestic dignity, the stately train of the Hexameters is nearly overturned; and even Ζευς himself, like other great men more es-

2. "And so many other fine things."

teemed abroad than at home, grand & musical as he may seem to strangers,
among his own countrymen dwindles into plain Zefs, a degradation which
I heard at first with a most classical horror.

A traveller is disappointed and mortified at the very few and imperfect
remains which Greece can offer to curiosity. Such has been the fury of the
successive conquerors of this country, that if we except Athens, there are
few places which retain more than enough to indicate their position, and to
verify in the midst of their humility, the history of their greatness. Their
very calamities contribute however to the interest they inspire. The ruins of
a majestic temple, of some monument raised to heroism, standing among
the servitude & degeneracy on which they seem to [ponder?], recall and
contrast the memory of a nations glory with the presence of its misfortunes.
These sentiments may now be felt more acutely since the ruins of Greece
have lately suffered from a new & unexpected enemy. Since the days of
Attila & the conquest of the Turks the monuments of Greece have comparatively sustained little real injury. The Turks had no motive to persecute
the relics of a religion which could no longer rival their own, and as they
attracted the curiosity & the wealth of strangers they were still in some
degree respected. The fragments of the arts, a beautiful head or a limb
which accident had dislocated, even an occasional statue was purchased by
men of taste & taken away. But the objects fixed to the soil were as yet
untouched. Men attached to the arts loved to see the products of the [past?]
on the spot where they had grown, & some of which derived their only
interest from being placed there by antiquity & having been unhurt thro' a
series of ages. Men of feeling admired without coveting them; they felt that
there was a sanctity around them, that like insurance, they were protected
by their weakness, that they were to be seen & not stolen; and even men of
decency were afraid to plunder what those they called barbarous had spared.
There appeared at last a person who had no such scruples. A man named
Elgin, a Scotsman & a lord, was sometime since the British minister at
Constantinople. He availed himself of the interest of his situation to procure permission to take from Greece whatever he chose that had no proprietor. Armed with that order & the resources of a large fortune, & stimulated by another man, a sort of chaplain, who with a zeal becoming the
priesthood seems to have thought every thing Pagan a fair object of plunder
he began the work of destruction. For him the temples had no sanctity.
Without taste without judgment without selection all that could be bought
or stolen was put into boxes & sent to England. The Deities of the country
seemed offended & shipwrecked his vessel. Had he been on board we might

have balanced the losses and been consoled. Yet nearly all was recovered; and I believe he is now about to add the only thing remaining to complete his disgrace, & sell his plunder. If as a man of taste he had presented to his country the fruits of his journey, the generosity of the action would perhaps excuse his conduct. But to use his influence as a public agent, to take from a wretched country not only what was ornamental but really useful to it, to dig up the tomb of Agamemnon, and then go home to sell what he had thus acquired, is something beyond the reach of common meanness. In comparison with this, there is something high & honorable in the emotion of the man who destroyed the temples of Ephesus. Had he stolen the fragments he too might have *made money*; but he was actuated by a much nobler principle, & some indignant historian of Grecian misery may one day do him justice by declaring that Herostratus burnt for glory, Elgin robbed for gold.

The Turks of Greece being the masters, are in fact the gentlemen of the country. They are much more affable & civilized than in any other part of Turkey & indeed one motive for my not leaving Greece was that I saw more of them more of their real character than I could have done at Constantinople itself. Accustomed to see strangers who they know come only to see the antiquities they are extremely civil, & in the present situation of their politics, are particularly well disposed towards Englishmen. Their very tyranny is sometimes serviceable to strangers, who like all the rest of the world, lose much of their horror for despotism when once they can get it on their side, so seducing so comfortable is the exercise of arbitrary power. I have never yet seen a man to whom I would trust it for five minutes. Thus travelling in Greece with a Turk you are secured from all embarrassment. If you enter a village where you are unrecommended, he will immediately find a house for you. If you want any thing he gives orders for it, and if they are not immediately obeyed, makes no ceremony in enforcing the execution of them with a pistol or a sabre. You obtain at last what you want, without any trouble to yourself, but what must be the feelings of the miserable Greeks? When such is the practice it is scarcely necessary to ask the form of their government. Yet it is not uninteresting. Greece is governed in some degree feudally. The country in general releives of the immediate Pasha of the District, but some places, such as Athens, the Mainots, & a few of the islands depend immediately on some Lord at Constantinople & are exempted from the Pasha's jurisdiction. There are three Pashas in Greece; one for the Morea one for Negropont & the neighborhood; & one at Yanina in ancient Epirus. These men have absolute power over the property

& the life of every thing within their territory; in their system of justice there is neither ceremony nor appeal; and I had a very good opportunity of observing its exercise. Whilst at Levadia the Pasha of Negropont just appointed past thro' on his way to his Govt. Being a Pasha of three tails & going to occupy his post he had the right to be supported by the towns on his route. He came carrying fire & desolation before him. After quartering upon the people a numerous and hungry tribe of followers, he demanded a contribution three times greater than any former tyrant had ever asked. The principal Greeks in vain represented the misery of their city, & their incapacity to raise the amount of what he wished. He declared if they did not bring the money immediately, he would set fire to the town, & reminded them that their own heads were perfectly at his disposal. The money very soon appeared. In the midst of all this, two English gentlemen and myself paid him a visit, & he showed us as much politeness & distinction as he did cruelty to his subjects. This very man had already taken off abundance of heads at Smyrna & elsewhere for some delay in producing what he demanded.

The govenment of these Pashas is subdivided into districts which are provided with three Turkish officers who purchase immediately of the Grand Seignior. The Voivode, or as it ought to be written to conform to pronunciation, the Vyvuda is the governor military and civil; the Ian (i-an) is the financial officer a sort of committee of ways & means of extortion; the Cadi is the judicial officer. In controversies between Turks or Greeks & Turks, the law is the Koran which contains it is supposed a solution of all difficulties. The Greeks are naturally anxious to evade a foreign jurisdiction & bring their causes before their own Bishop. He acts as a Kind of Justice of the Peace, governed by the Theodosian code the system of church law; but his authority is merely that of an arbitrator & an appeal may be made from his decision to that of the Cadi. This last has authority in criminal & civil cases, but as is natural to suppose the judgment of criminals is a good deal influenced by the Vyvuda. Neither of them however can deprive a man of life unless they can procure from the Mufti or Archbishop a passage from the Koran which declares the offence punishable with death. This way of getting behind the Prophet is also practiced by suitors in civil cases who procure passages for themselves under the Mufti's hand & seal & come before the Cadi who is obliged to save the veracity of Mahomet from the snares of contradiction. The only share which the Greeks have in the govt is that in the towns there are several of the most respectable & the richest men who under the name of Cujabashes form a council for the Vyvuda, who asks their advice & makes use [of] them as screws to press the people. With regard to this system it should be understood that very little of the oppression comes immediately from Constantinople. The Haratch or Poll tax, the only one paid to the G[rand] Seignior, is the very last of the grievances of the people who are plundered by the swarm of small despots. Indeed the court seems to make it a point of policy to let the Pashas & Vyvudas go on quietly until they are ripe & full, then under some pretext, cut off their heads & confiscate their property. The treasury gains, but the Greeks are not the better for it since it lets loose upon them a new & famished master.

I have thus my dear William mentioned superficially some of the objects which I thought might interest you. For myself, falling as it were suddenly among a people so new, a world of foreign ideas presented themselves to my observation. Nor has it been the least of my gratifications, to have so brilliant a light reflected on all my ancient reading. To have been on the spot elucidates the text of history more than all the criticism of the most ingenious commentators.

I have now seen Italy & Greece. It is but right that I should stop somewhere, & I am not unwilling to make the columns of Sunium my goal. Henceforward all my steps will be towards home. I have now gratified the ardent wishes the fervid curiosity to see other men & to mingle with the world which might once have rendered my life unhappy. I begin to feel that it will soon be my turn to cease to be only an observer; that the age at which society has its claims upon me will shortly arrive; and that I have many duties unperformed to my country & my family. I am not insensible how far I have wandered beyond our original expectation nor how widely I am separated from those who are most dear to me, & to whose happiness I am so closely connected. These ideas have sometimes filled me with melancholy sensations, when I have felt with Cicero that *"amicitiae consuetudines vicinitates, ludi denique & dies festi, quid haberent voluptatis, carendo magis intellexi quam fruendo."*[3] Of these objects the recollection mellowed by distance & solitude & saddened by the terrible uncertainty of their situation, have often been painful, and I look forward with you to the period when I shall return to the bosom of my family. You are far above the idle expectations of improvement from travelling. Yet I think no traveller can look upon the

---

3. "What pleasures there are in friends, companions, neighbors, dependents, and in the games and festival days—all these I have come to understand more by lacking them than by enjoying them" (Cicero's *post Reditum ad Quirites* 1.3).

general lot of mankind without being contented with his own; no man can
examine the world, without confirming & increasing his affections to the
early objects of them; no American can compare the institutions of his
country with those of Europe without being grateful for its happiness without exulting in its destiny without adoring its freedom.

I occasionally speculate on what is to become of me on my return. My
profession is of course fixed. Of the practical part I must confess my self
sadly ignorant, tho' it will be easy to recover what I have lost. But there is
a higher service connected with it which is to me much more attractive. To
govern man by means of eloquence seems to be the fairest object of ambition among a free people, & is particularly inviting in America. Towards
this my early habits & studies have directed me. It has since been recommended by many motives; nor have the scenes which I have just witnessed;
the Roman forum, the tribunals of Athens, nations once saved & enlightened by oratory, contributed little to confirm my attachment. If at this
moment I feel any ambition, any wish to gain the applause of others, it is
by becoming not an Attorney, not a Lawyer, not a Pleader but an Orator.
To you I need not explain the majesty of the name. Yet I sometimes retire
before its difficulties when I consider how few have been able to overcome
them, & the labors thro' which its pursuit will conduct one. It is not the
miserable groan the debasing sentiment of despair, but the honorable humility of ignorance and weakness. I have never seen, hor have later times
produced any thing like an orator: of its labors what shall we think when
he who best knew them declared that no man can be an orator *"nisi
erit omnium rerum magnarum atque artium scientiam consecutus."*[4] It would demand unwearied study. The judgment is to be matured by slow & tedious
investigation, and fancy must pluck a flower from every science to illustrate
and adorn. In more tranquil moments the woods tempt me with their
humble quiet independence. I shall leave it to fortune & yourself to dispose
of me.

I expect with anxiety on my reaching Paris to find in my letters Papa's
directions. He was kind enough to promise me a visit to England where my
own inclinations also lead me strongly; I hope he will not recede from it.

I have been so long without letters from home that I know very little of
the position of our most interesting domestic concerns; and can only hope
that you are all well & happy. Enclosed is a letter for my old & worthy

4. "Unless he will have pursued the knowledge of all great subjects and arts" (Cicero's *de
Oratore* 16.6).

college friend Watts. Where he now is I really do not know but some of his acquaintance for instance Crawford can perhaps tell you. His former address was Liberty, Virginia. There is also a memorandum for our sweet cousin.[5]

This letter which I look back upon with affright, & which seems more like a dissertation than a letter is written *to you*. Do not let it escape beyond the bounds of the family since it is in no condition to travel. Believe me with the warmest affection for you all

Yr. Dear brother

Nicholas Biddle

William S. Biddle Esquire

5. Is this a reference to Biddle's cousin Ann, the wife of General James Wilkinson, governor of Louisiana and confidante of Aaron Burr in the filibustering expedition in the summer of 1806, which led to Burr's trial for treason?

Index

238

INDEX

Library of Hadrian, 150
Long Walls, 118, 152–53
Lyceum, 49, 113, 123, 152–53, 218
Lykavettos, 137, 143
Lysicrates' choregic monument (Capuchin convent), 111, 151
Minerva, temple of. See Parthenon
Minerva Polias, temple of. See Erechtheion
Mouseion Hill, 113, 115, 123, 137, 144
Neptune Erechtheus, temple of. See Erechtheion
Nike temple, 154–55
Nymphs, Hill of, 137
Odeion of Herodes Atticus, 114, 142
Odeion of Pericles, 141
Olympieion (temple of Olympian Zeus), 112, 115, 137, 144, 153
Painted Stoa, 49, 150
Pan, cave of, 115, 140, 154
Panaghia Spiliotissa, 141
Panathenaia, 139
Pandroseion, 140
Parthenon, 113, 115, 139, 154–55
Pelasgi, 140
Pelasgian Wall, 154
Phaleron, 118
Philopappos, monument of, 113, 115, 144
Piraeus, 113, 118–19, 152–53
Pnyx, 112, 115, 123, 137, 143
Praxiteles, 152–53
Propylaia, 114, 154
Prytaneion, 113, 218
schools (modern), 155
stadium, 116, 152
Stoa of Attalos, 150
Stoa of Eumenes, 142
Temple of Victory. See Nike Temple
Themistoclean Wall, 117, 153
Themistocles' tomb, 118
Theseus, temple of. See Hephaisteion
Thirty Tyrants, 143
Thrasyboulos, monument of, 152
Thrasyllos's choregic monument, 141
Tripod Street, 151
Turkish government, 148–49
Wall of Theseus. See Pelasgian Wall
Winds, temple (tower) of, 151
Attila, 219, 230
Austerlitz, 13

Baiai, 51–52
Bainbridge, William, 17, 74
Ball, Alexander, 66, 68, 70, 75, 79, 81, 204
baratrairs, 163
Barbary states, 15–16. See also piracy
Barnes, Joseph, 51, 56, 59, 66
Barron, Samuel, 17, 72, 77
Barthélemy, 82, 108, 113, 120, 140, 150, 152–53, 166, 179, 183, 186, 200
Barton, Benjamin Smith, 70, 80
Beninzello (Athenian schoolmaster), 155
Bergman (Russian captain), 204
Biddle, James, 17, 65, 69, 194
Biddle, Nicholas
 anticlericalism, 10–11, 55–56, 58–60, 76. See also fasts; Greeks, character of
 architectural Hellenism, 11–12
 career, 179–80, 223, 234
 cosmopolitanism, 9, 90
 duties in Paris, 4
 early education, 2
 English travelers, 169–70, 186–87. See also Mackenzie; Palmer; Walpole; Williams
 family background, 1
 instruction in Greek, 55, 166
 itinerary, 4, 224
 journal-keeping habits, 4, 38–43
 literary pursuits, 5, 43
 military titles, 3, 65
 neoclassicist, 1, 6–7, 11, 29, 44
 oratorical interests, 2, 179–80
 Pennsylvania Academy of the Fine Arts, 10
 political views, 2, 5–6, 10, 138
 Port Folio, 3, 5, 10
 portraiture, 8–9, 26
 pursuit of fame, 6–8, 179–80
 relation to Romanticism, 31
 Second Bank of the U. S., 5–6, 11, 44
 travel writer, 28–31, 43
 Tuesday Club, 3
 U. S. Bank of Pennsylvania, 6
 value of Greek travel, 49–51, 193–94, 211, 217–19, 221–24, 233–34
Biddle, William, 3
Blake, Joshua, 70, 74–75
Blodgett, Samuel, 68, 76
Boudinitza (Mendenitza), 105–6
Brasidas, 183
Broadbent, John, 59
Brown, Thomas, 65